Playing through Pain

DANIEL SAILOFSKY

Playing through Pain
The Violent Consequences
of Capitalist Sport

The University of North Carolina Press *Chapel Hill*

© 2025 Daniel Sailofsky
All rights reserved
Set in Arno Pro by Westchester Publishing Services
Manufactured in the United States of America

Library of Congress Cataloging-in-Publication Data
Names: Sailofsky, Daniel, author.
Title: Playing through pain : the violent consequences of capitalist sport / Daniel Sailofsky.
Description: Chapel Hill : The University of North Carolina Press, [2025] | Includes bibliographical references and index.
Identifiers: LCCN 2024045120 | ISBN 9781469685861 (cloth) | ISBN 9781469685878 (paperback) | ISBN 9781469685885 (epub) | ISBN 9781469685892 (pdf)
Subjects: LCSH: Violence in sports. | Sports—Sociological aspects. | Sports—Economic aspects. | Capitalism. | BISAC: SOCIAL SCIENCE / Violence in Society | POLITICAL SCIENCE / Political Ideologies / Capitalism
Classification: LCC GV706.7 .S35 2025 | DDC 306.4/83—dc23/eng/20241031
LC record available at https://lccn.loc.gov/2024045120

Cover design by Christopher Tobias, Tobias Outerwear for Books.

For product safety concerns under the European Union's General Product Safety Regulation (EU GPSR), please contact gpsr@mare-nostrum.co.uk or write to The University of North Carolina Press and Mare Nostrum Group B.V., Mauritskade 21D, 1091 GC Amsterdam, The Netherlands.

Contents

Introduction 1

CHAPTER ONE
The Point Is to Change It: A Marxist Theoretical Framework 12

CHAPTER TWO
In-Game Violence: Concussions, Injury, and the Consequences 37

CHAPTER THREE
Outside the Lines: Violence against Athletes
outside of the Field of Play 63

CHAPTER FOUR
(In)Action Speaks Louder than Words: How Sport Organizations
Respond to Athlete-Perpetrated Violence against Women 81

CHAPTER FIVE
Labor and Violence: American College Sports and
Minor League Baseball Exploitation 105

CHAPTER SIX
Crowd Violence: Winning at All Costs and Imagined
Communities under Capitalism 134

CHAPTER SEVEN
Mega-Events and Mega-Harm: Structural and Environmental
Violence, Sportswashing, and Celebration Capitalism 154

CHAPTER EIGHT
The Way Forward: Reimagining Sport Now and for the Future 184

Acknowledgments 199

Notes 201

Index 239

Playing through Pain

Introduction

On February 7, 2021, in Tampa's Raymond James Stadium, the Tampa Bay Buccaneers defeated the Kansas City Chiefs 31–9, and first-ballot Hall of Fame quarterback Tom Brady captured his record-setting seventh Super Bowl championship. The Buccaneers' defense and pass rush dominated young superstar Patrick Mahomes and the Chiefs, pressuring the all-world quarterback from the first whistle to the last.

This was also the first time a team played and won the Super Bowl in their home stadium, adding a bit of extra poetic narrative to an event already (and always) dripping with dramatization, pageantry, and spectacle.[1] While the Brady-Mahomes matchup made for great headlines, the game was one of the lowest rated Super Bowls in recent years, drawing "only" 91 million American viewers; maybe this had something to do with the global pandemic still raging at the time of the game, which by that point had killed more than 2.3 million people worldwide and about 1.1 million in the United States. Only 24,835 people were physically in attendance, again due to COVID restrictions. CBS, broadcaster of the game, charged $5.5 million for each 30-second commercial advertising time slot.

Two years later, with the devastation wrought by the pandemic mercifully slowing, the 2023 Super Bowl returned to its former capitalist and consumption glory, with the Kansas City Chiefs and Philadelphia Eagles drawing a record 115 million American TV viewers for the game and Rihanna drawing almost 119 million American viewers for her halftime show. Glendale, Arizona, hosted the game for the fourth time, with almost 67,827 in attendance at State Farm Stadium.[2] Around the world, Super Bowl parties were hosted in basements, bars, and restaurants throughout the world, and the various purveyors of chicken wings, pizza, and beer rejoiced. The sport mega-event money machine continued to pay out, with the lucrative addition of newly legalized sports betting in several US states and in Canada.

The Chiefs managed to finish the job this time, coming from behind to win a back-and-forth battle. Mahomes capped off an MVP season with a Super Bowl MVP and his second Super Bowl Championship. Other heartwarming narratives framed this game as the "Andy Reid game"—Reid coached Philadelphia for thirteen years before moving to Kansas City in 2013—or the

"Kelce Bowl"—brothers Jason and Travis Kelce were offensive starters for the Eagles and Chiefs, respectively. The game also featured two Black starting quarterbacks (Mahomes and Jalen Hurts) for the first time in Super Bowl history, another talking point used to illustrate "just how far the NFL has come on race."

I hope you enjoyed this generic, media-style sports talk, because this is the last of it here. This is not a book about record-breaking revenues and superstar athlete performances. It is a book about the darker side of sports.

When I say, "the darker side," I don't mean the individual stories of corruption, cheating, doping, and gambling, or individual acts of criminality by athletes, coaches, management, or owners, though these one-off tales may make for interesting newsclips. They've been discussed ad nauseam in sports journalism and other work and seek to dehumanize athletes and individualize social problems that have much deeper roots.[3] The problem is bigger than that. It's not about a few bad apples; I'm coming for the whole orchard.

In this book, I'm inviting you on a tougher but hopefully more rewarding journey to understand where all the violence, harm, and injustice in sports comes from. In short, we're going to think about events like the Super Bowl quite a bit differently.

We might talk about narratives like the "Kelce Bowl," but only to show the ideological roots of these "feel-good" narratives and to examine how they are weaponized by sport organizations and leagues to justify and elide responsibility for the violence, harms, and inequities they produce. The 2023 Super Bowl narratives of performative justice included a celebration of two Black starting quarterbacks by a league that blackballed Black quarterback Colin Kaepernick for his protest against police brutality and systemic racial injustice, inviting Native American leaders to perform a land acknowledgment while the fans of one of the teams perform the "Tomahawk Chop" celebration most games; and touting an all-women US air force "flyover" as a heartwarming moment in what can only be described as a meme about "progressive" American militarism come to life.

Rather than just seeing the 2023 Super Bowl's commemoration of former NFL player-turned-soldier-turned-antiwar-activist Pat Tillman as a solemn salute to a fallen hero, we will interrogate the historical links between militarism and sports and between masculinity and sports. Tillman is still often celebrated by the NFL for "making the ultimate sacrifice" and forgoing his promising NFL career to serve in the US military during the Iraq war. What they fail to mention, every time he is brought up, is that Tillman was killed by fellow American soldiers in a case of friendly fire, just as he began speaking out more boldly about the horrific nature of America's intervention in Iraq and American imperialism more generally, even calling the war and occupation of Iraq "illegal as hell."[4]

Instead of fawning over billionaire oligarchs like Elon Musk and Rupert Murdoch in their luxury boxes—2023 Super Bowl announcer Kevin Burkhardt's exact words were, "Well, you've got some brilliant minds in that photo"[5]—we'll examine how ruling-class interests have historically used sport, and how they still use it today, both as a vehicle for personal wealth creation and as an ideological tool to legitimize "meritocracy" and winner-take-all capitalism, or to "sportswash" their nefarious business activities using the positive veneer of sports.

Rather than debating the merits of Tom Brady versus Joe Montana or whether Patrick Mahomes is on track to be the greatest NFL player of all time, we will examine the hundreds of recorded and unrecorded concussions every NFL season,[6] along with other injuries that follow athletes around for the rest of their lives. We'll look at how football, hockey, rugby, boxing, MMA, and other sports are linked to debilitating brain injury, dementia, and CTE, and how leagues like the NFL and NHL have tried to deny, deflect, and avoid bearing any of the responsibility for the harm these sports cause.

There will also be no glorification of coaches and management who "do whatever it takes to win" or "push their athletes to the limit." We will instead examine the psychological, emotional, mental, and sexual abuse and trauma that arise in sport cultures where coaches are given ultimate authority and control as long as they are winning. We also won't simply parrot NFL talking points about the "need" for events like the Super Bowl to lift people's spirits up amid COVID-19 restrictions, but instead use this case and others like it to understand the coercive conditions that force many athletes (and temporary workers in stadiums and other seasonal sport work) to work in unsafe working conditions for the benefit of owners, sport stakeholders, and the larger society. These conditions include physically unsafe athletic environments and contexts where athletes are forced to work under abusive trainers and medical staff, violent coaches, and exploitative management and ownership.

Instead of talking about the incredible speed, power, and athleticism of athletes like Tyreek Hill and Antonio Brown, we will look at why and how the Chiefs and Buccaneers justified employing these two men in 2021, after they had both just recently been arrested for acts of violence against women (Hill was a repeat offender). We will also try to understand why so many sports organizations make the same choices with other violent athletes, and how these organizations get away with promoting violence, aggression, and dominance on the field while in the same breath announcing that they care about women and other victims of violence.

We will talk about the huge sums of money produced by major sport spectacles, but not just to uncritically tout the "positive economic impacts" of sports or blindly celebrate GDP growth. Instead, we will use this to demonstrate how little of this money actually goes to the athletic workers at the very heart of producing the spectacle, especially for the exploited collegiate football players who eventually become Super Bowl participants. We will not glorify the players who "made it out" of their low-income neighborhood to a (usually very short) NFL career. Instead, we will frame this story differently, seeing it as evidence of the structurally coercive conditions that force young people to "choose" football and other violent sports, forgoing other pursuits for the one-in-a-million chance to make it big in professional sports and give themselves and their families the upward social mobility that is otherwise not available to them under cutthroat capitalism.

We will examine the extreme fandom and outsized importance of events like the Premier League and other professional leagues, to highlight how these levels of fandom are ultimately responsible for the spectator violence and harassment we see in the stands, in parking lots, outside sports venues, and even in youth sport settings. Rather than simply chalking fan violence and spectator abuse up to personal failings, "working-class culture," alcohol use, or fans' overidentification with their favorite teams, we will focus on alienation and the role of sports in providing the emotional fulfillment and community that people so often lack under capitalism, and on how this alienation produces the emotional volatility that leads to violence among fans.

Finally, we will analyze the real impacts and interrogate the narratives and stories told about mega-events like the Super Bowl, Olympics, or World Cup, assessing whether these events truly provide the type of material benefits to cities—and to working people who populate these cities—that they claim to. We will look at the population displacement, environmental devastation, and over-policing that these events bring to working people in the countries and cities that host mega-events, as well as the way these events are used to enrich ruling-class elites, build goodwill for politicians, and justify forced gentrification, evictions, and the building of militarized security apparatuses that are used against marginalized people. We will look at how privately owned sports teams still manage to convince governments to publicly fund stadium builds and renovations—in 2023, the Tennessee Titans secured a record $1.26 billion of public financing to build their new stadium[7]—and how elite capitalist sport continues to harm both people and the planet.

These are the sorts of sport stories we will discuss in the following pages. While the Super Bowl is perhaps the most obvious case to illustrate nearly all the different types of violence and harm that emanate from and are justified by sport, it is far from the only event—and American football is far from the only sport—where these harms occur. Under our contemporary global capitalist system, sport systems and organizations across nearly all sports and geographic contexts have become spaces where violence and harm are in some combination encouraged, tolerated, and expected.

Sports, Violence, and Harm

Now that you know what this book is about generally, it's important to clarify some of our key concepts.

First, sport. While scholars have spent thousands of pages discussing what counts as "sport" or "organized sport," I will keep this definition simple: Sport is any physical competition with an agreed set of rules, at least one referee, and a formal governing structure. Pickup basketball doesn't count here, but organized youth basketball or college basketball does. Going running on Saturday morning doesn't, but competing in a formally organized and timed 10K race does. The sports that you will read about in the following pages include all levels of organized sport, and are not just limited to professional leagues (e.g., NFL, English Premier League, NBA, La Liga) and international and national competitions (e.g., the Olympics, World Championships, National Championships).

There is obviously variation in the levels of harm in different sport contexts, and often these variations are based in how "elite" the competition level is, and whether material financial rewards are on the line. The more money involved, generally, the more violence and harm we see. This is also why more words are devoted to more obviously "elite" sport contexts like professional leagues, national teams, and international competitions. But I include all of these levels of sport because unfortunately, so many of the causes and mechanisms through which dangerous, violent, and harmful behavior arise happen at all levels, and occur in surprisingly similar ways.

The next definitional question concerns violence and harm. As you've probably gathered by now, both these terms include far more than just *physical* violence and harm, and beyond this, more than just *interpersonal* violence and harm.

The definition of violence provided by the World Health Organization (WHO) is a good starting point: "The intentional use of physical force or power, threatened or actual, against oneself, another person, or against a group or community, that either results in or has a high likelihood of resulting in injury, death, psychological harm, maldevelopment, or deprivation."[8] While this is the not the exact definition I use in my work, the end of this definition is instructive in terms of the breadth of outcomes that qualify behavior as violent. Violence, as I use the term in this book, includes behaviors that result in or are likely to result in "injury, death, psychological harm, maldevelopment, or deprivation."[9] It is not just about physical bruises or emotional scars, but includes more structural harms related to lack of opportunity and resources. This speaks to the zemiological, social-harms-based perspective[10] that I use in this book, which "encompasses the study of harm in its multiple forms."[11]

Zemiology arose as an area of study to counter criminologists' tendency to use strictly legalistic definitions of crime, as this narrowly legal perspective ignores the role that powerful actors have in influencing what is and isn't considered legal, as well as the many harms that can emanate from behavior that is technically legal. As critical criminologist Raymond Michalowski explains, this kind of legalistic approach can especially advantage powerful corporate actors under capitalism (an expanded definition and breakdown of capitalism will come in chapter 2), as "the social injuries and harms resulting from the corporate pursuit of profit, capital accumulation and power are not subjects for criminological inquiry."[12]

Defining violence does not only depend on the range of harms it can encompass, but also on what types of behavior (that produce this harm) are included. This is where my definition strays a bit from the WHO definition, as I consider violence to include both acts *committed* by individuals and larger entities, as well as acts of *omission* by individuals and entities. This means that violence can be accomplished through explicitly *doing* something to someone, and can be accomplished by *not doing* something, when the inaction in question causes the adverse outcomes mentioned above. I'm also less concerned with the intentionality of the behavior or inaction, at least in terms of organizational actors' *self-perceived* intentions to commit harm. Rather, in assessments of wrongdoing, I am more concerned with whether the behavior causes harm, and whether this harm is and was foreseeable to those either acting or neglecting to act in the way that they did.

To put it in more concrete terms, if an individual punches, emotionally abuses, or sexually assaults someone, these are all acts of violence, but it is also an act of violence when an organization displaces people from their homes or a company purposefully or knowingly drops toxic chemicals in a river. These are all violent acts of commission with harmful consequences, committed by both individuals and larger organizations. At the same time, if a coach or doctor does not adequately protect an athlete from physical or emotional harm, an organization refuses to remove abusive coaches from their programs, a government allows sport organizations to destroy a forest or pollute a city, or that same organization refuses to pay its employees the wages they need to live comfortable lives, these are also acts of violence. It doesn't matter if there is no strict law or guideline mandating the removal of a coach, or if a government or sport organization is not breaking any law as they allow for a forest to burn or an employee to suffer. Violence does not require illegality to be harmful and worthy of inquiry.

To put it as succinctly as possible (or TLDR, as the kids say), inaction can still be violence, if it leads to harm. And harmful inaction or action is still violence even if it's legal.

The Theoretical Framework

Reading these first few pages, and especially given how violence and harm have just been defined, you may have already guessed the political orientation of this book. If you have, I'm glad. As I explain in chapter 1, there is no bias-free, ideology-free analysis, and I don't plan on hiding my biases or the worldview that shapes this book.

In this book, I will focus on the ways that the structure of elite capitalist sport produces all manner of physical, mental, labor-related, political, and environmental harms for athletes, sport industry workers, the wider population, and the planet. To understand how this violence and harm manifests, I will use a Marxist theoretical framework that situates athletes and all of those involved in elite capitalist sport within the racial capitalist structure that impacts all that they do. Chapter 1 explains exactly what this Marxist framework entails.

The Context

While this is a book about sport and harm under global capitalism, I will not cover every sport and every part of the world. A lot of my examples come from hockey and football, because these are sports I have spent more time studying. My examples also come from Canada and the United States, because they are the countries I have studied and know the most about. In the case of Canada, it's where I grew up. The United States is also—from both a dollars and cents perspective and an ideological one—the center of global capitalism and of elite capitalist sport. What happens there, whether we like it or not, still has far-reaching consequences.

This does not mean that the United States and Canada are the most important countries, or that the sports I will focus on here are the most important sports. The examples I use are to illustrate phenomena that are present throughout the elite sports world—unfortunately, the harm suffered by athletes and communities that I describe are not unique to these countries or sports. I simply don't have the space or the expertise to dive deep into each example; sadly, there are just too many.

What I hope you can draw from this book is that the problems are bigger than any particular individual or team. They are not a product of just one country's laws or one sport organization's governing, nor are they due to "human nature" or individual people's biological or psychological makeup. They reflect the way our economic and incentive systems are structured. The harm and violence we see in and around sport are both a reflection of the wider world we live in and part of what continues to create and mold this same world. It is a cycle that produces harm, but it can and must be stopped.

Let's Get Structural

As I hope I've made clear, this is a book about sport organizations, leagues, and sport culture, and the way that the larger capitalist system that structures all of our elite sport systems produces the conditions for violence and harm to run rampant. This does not, however, mean that individual stories or the agency and free will of individuals will be ignored. It just means that instead of jumping right away to individual, biological, and even psychological explanations for violent behavior, exploitation, or other types of harm, we will first turn to the structural, to the macro, to the bigger picture.

Many people, when they think of violence, think about individual demeanor, psychological or mental health conditions, or what might have happened to a person that day or recently that led to them act out. These factors are undoubtedly important, and thinking this way is intuitive. The hegemony of neoliberal thinking and the individual personal responsibility discourse of capitalism (more on this in chapter 2) has trained us to think of ourselves only as individual people (or really, individual consumers) who operate in our own personal vacuums, unaffected by our material conditions and larger capitalist imperatives, and responding only to our own "natural" desires.

The façade of freedom under capitalism requires this kind of in-a-vacuum thinking.

These individual factors—as well as our human agency and ability to resist social structural and ideological imperatives[13]—are still important, and we can't lose sight of them. Whether we're talking about someone's likelihood of acting violently, of getting into a good university, or of being convicted of a felony, individual and psychological factors still matter. It matters how disagreements were handled in our home environment growing up, whether we work hard in school or at work, and whether we've developed good self-control over our own behavior. But these factors don't provide complete explanations of the vital role of social structures (e.g., capitalism, the criminal legal system), institutions (e.g., schools, media), and larger culture have in influencing our behavior, and coercing or nudging us into particular actions and inaction.

Anyone who follows professional sports knows the cliché that "sports are a business," but rarely do we stop to consider what that means not just for player transactions, ticket sales, and TV contracts, but for how and why sports remain such a harmful institution for so many. Even though we have seen more critical conversation around social issues in sports—and declining rates of participation for violent sports like football in the States and hockey in Canada—it is less common for these conversations to veer into critiques of sport institutions or the political economy that underlies them. It is especially rare for many to consider how not just individual actors, but the capitalist organization of sport more generally—and the ideology that capitalism promotes and requires—acts as the structural scaffolding for the harm we see in sport.

This is by design. It benefits ruling classes for us to see capitalism, *not* as an ideology and as just one of many ways to organize society, but instead as the "natural" and therefore an "apolitical" state of affairs. In a world where capitalism has for so long been our dominant mode of production and the primary influence on how we organize society, it is difficult to even notice how this economic system impacts our sport systems and any of our other institutions. Capitalism and its contemporary expression in neoliberalism are so entrenched that they have ceased to even exist as ideologies in the collective imagination. The "totalizing logic"[14] of these ideologies not only creates the conditions for harm and violence to happen (in sports and in society more broadly), but also blinds us to alternatives.

The dissolution and failures of past national socialist experiments also add to our collective inability to see and think beyond capitalism, and thus hinder us from considering its impacts or how sport (or anything else) might look under a different system. While there were undoubtedly failures and mistakes in the various socialist nations of the twentieth century, these failures are often exaggerated and were in many ways either directly caused or greatly influenced by the actions and decisions of capitalist countries that had a vested interest in seeing them fail. These sabotaging countries are also the same ones that constantly repeat and exaggerate the failures of past socialist societies, while ignoring the successes of these states (in areas as diverse as science and technology, education and literacy, health, poverty reduction, and sports), and ignoring or hiding their own failures.

And yet, especially in the West, much of this nuance is glossed over and outright ignored, with the blanket statement that any noncapitalist country has led, and will always lead, to disaster. Ignoring the many positive social developments and improvements that occurred under socialist governments and societies, this type of statement also implicitly ignores the many disasters and cruel conditions that still afflict so many in capitalist countries and in a capitalist world. This includes both conditions for the working class in richer, Western countries, but even more so for those in more periphery countries, whose oppressive working and living conditions subsidize the quality of life for workers in the core, richer capitalist countries.[15]

This kind of nuanced discussion of the merits of capitalism is mostly nonexistent in Western discourse (outside of academia and some select spaces), and especially so in sport. As such, for so many, thinking of sport without capitalism would be like thinking about a world without gravity or water: both an intellectual and an imaginary impossibility (*How can I even imagine that?*) and a waste of time (*What's the point of imagining that?*), because there is no world without gravity or water.

But a different system *is* possible, and violence and harm in sports are not just things we need to accept. As critical sport scholar and University of Connecticut professor Chen Chen explains, for too long capitalism has been a "ghost" in the study of sport, where "it is taken as the natural, neutral context wherein sport industry, organization, and management processes are located in the past, present, and future."[16]

In this book, I hope to change that, and make the impacts of capitalism on violence and harm in sport as transparent as possible, while mapping out new possibilities for our sport future. I aim to explain how capitalism structures the decisions and behavior of athletes, coaches, management, and even fans and consumers, how elite sport and capitalism provide vital ideological support for one another, and how the win-at-all-costs imperatives of sport produce harm in so many ways for so many people.

Our contemporary sport systems have problems, and the first step to fixing any problem is diagnosing its root cause. Though sport is only one part of society, and for many it might seem like a trivial one, it remains "one of the most dominant and popular cultural forms in much of the world today," and because of this, a cultural space where "audiences and participants latently learn, create knowledge, and form beliefs about crime and deviance through sport that can then manifest in other areas of daily life."[17] Only with an understanding of how capitalism influences sport can we begin the vital work advocating and fighting for the significant and long-lasting changes necessary to improve the lives of all those who participate in or are in other ways involved in sports, with the loftier goal of harm reduction and revolutionary change in society more broadly.

As Karl Marx famously said, "the philosophers have hitherto only interpreted the world in various ways. The point, however, is to change it."[18] This is a tall task, and one that will require above all, the collective efforts of many. This book is just one tiny piece of this puzzle, but every piece counts.

CHAPTER ONE

The Point Is to Change It
A Marxist Theoretical Framework

There is no such thing as ideology-free, unbiased, or completely atheoretical work, and this book is no different. Even this sentence itself is not free of ideology or epistemology, as the simple idea that all knowledge is biased or based on a particular worldview is evidence of a more interpretivist or standpoint epistemology and framework. I've already given away my hand and some of my bias, and in the following pages I'll tell you exactly what theoretical perspective will guide the rest of this book.

While many may shudder, cringe, or let their eyes glaze over when the words "theory," "epistemology," or "theoretical framework" come up (I still often do myself), these terms don't need to provoke such a reaction. A theory is an explanation; Newton's laws of motion explain how matter moves across space, and Edwin Sutherland's criminological differential association theory explains how people come to different understandings of the acceptability of crime, based on the people they associate with, and then are more or less likely to commit crime. Though these two examples are describing different phenomena in vastly different fields (physics and criminology), their goals are similar—to explain how we move from point A to point B. In the case of Newton's physics example, we're speaking about the literal movement from a physical point A to another physical point B, while for Sutherland, point A is a person not committing crime, while point B is that same person committing it.

This is, of course, an oversimplification of theory, but it is nevertheless a starting point to ask other questions related to our theoretical framework and our epistemology. How do we define and observe our point A's and point B's? Who makes these definitions? What does it mean for something to be observable? Do we have a theory first, and then the data, or does the data inform the theory? What is the purpose of understanding specific point A to point B movements? Is it about understanding things for understanding's sake, or is there a wider goal related to social good, to emancipation, to liberation?

Whether one chooses to explicitly answer these questions or disclose their own theoretical and ideological leanings is up to them, but for transparency's sake, I feel it best to be as clear as possible. This book will use an explicitly Marxist theoretical framework to analyze violence and harm in elite sport. Elite sport is our point A, violence and harm our point B, and a Marxist understanding of society, power, and labor is the way we are going to get from one to the other.

A Marxist Theoretical Framework: Base and Superstructure

Hundreds of thousands of words and pages have been written on Marxism, Marxist epistemology, and Marxist theories of knowledge. It is not the purpose of this chapter or of this book to legislate on these great debates or summarize differing positions.

Instead, I want us to be on the same page about the basics. To understand how elite sport causes harm both in sport and outside of it, we must understand where sport is situated as a cultural institution (or *superstructure*) in modern society. Marxist scholars have often conceived of society using the metaphor of a building, with a *base* or *foundation* from which the rest of society—the institutions and organizations that constitute the superstructure—rises up. The "foundation" of this building (and thus of society) is its *economic mode of production*, which is made up of its *material forces of production* and its *relations of production*. As Marx writes in *Capital: A Critique of Political Economy*, "In the social production of their existence, men inevitably enter into definite relations, which are independent of their will, namely *relations of production* appropriate to a given stage in the development of their material forces of production. The totality of these relations of production constitutes the economic structure of society, the real foundation, on which arises a legal and political superstructure and to which correspond definite forms of social consciousness."[1] Material forces of production are the tangible and intangible objects and things that are used to produce the means of survival and subsistence for the human population. These are also often referred to as the *means of production*. From a basic logical perspective, the importance of the means of production should be clear. We all need certain means of survival to keep living and to keep reproducing, and how we go about acquiring and using these means of survival should thus play a pretty important role in terms of how our society is organized.

These means of production include instruments of labor and subjects of labor. Put simply, *instruments of labor* are machinery, devices, tools, and whole factories or production centers that are used to build, shape, break down, and mold raw materials into the products needed for survival. These raw materials—natural resources, minerals, food, seeds—are the *subjects of labor*.

Individual people and whole companies use the instruments of labor on the subjects of labor to produce goods and services. In the past, shovels and animals (instruments of labor) helped turned seeds (subjects of labor) into food (labor product) to be eaten or sold. Now, to go along with turning seeds into food, factories and machines (instruments) turn oil and gas (subjects) into energy (commodity), or lithium into batteries, or ingredients into meals, also to be used or sold. What kind of means of production are available at a given period of historical development helps determine what mode of production exists at that time.

The second part of any economic mode of production is its *relations of production*, which describe the relationship between those who own the means of production and those who do not. It is also based on who uses these means of production and for what purpose. If everyone in a particular territory jointly owns and controls the means of production, this would likely be evidence of some form of communal society. Throughout history, societies like this have existed (often referred to as primitive communist societies by Marxists), but over the last 500 or so years, they have mostly disappeared. If land is owned by a king, lord, or leader of some sort, but used and worked on by those living on this land to sustain themselves (while giving some percentage of what they produce to the owner), this would be evidence of a feudalist mode of production. If most people do not own the means of production, and are forced to sell their labor for a wage, now we are moving to capitalist relations of production.

Although I am speaking about the means and relations of production as if they are separate entities entirely, this is only for purposes of explanation. The level of development of a particular society (and thus its means of production) is intimately linked to its relations of production. Capitalism as it exists now, or even as it existed 250 years ago, would not have been possible with the means of production of 500 years ago, and surely not with the means of production that had been developed before that. It's impossible to imagine contemporary global capitalism with the communication and transportation methods of the 1500s. For Marxists, the means of production and relations of production co-constitute each other, such that certain means of production are necessary for certain relations of production, and vice versa.

Once we have our mode of production, or our "foundation" in Marx's analogy, the rest of society—its superstructure—is built from this foundation. By "the rest of society," I mean its legal, education, criminal justice, and religious systems, its media and community organizations, and even its art, leisure, and cultural institutions. For any particular society, the economic base will determine the features of that society's superstructure—what that society's larger institutions and organizations look like, how they operate, and for whom. However, it is important to stress that Marxists, and even Marx and Engels specifically, did not strictly conceive of the relationship between base and superstructure as unidirectional, with the superstructure flowing only from the base, and never in the opposite direction.[2] The base and superstructure often work in a reciprocal manner, with the superstructure reinforcing the legitimacy of the mode of production and/or serving ruling-class interests. It is important to note, however, that in cases of revolutionary change, ruling elites might still defend older social institutions or forms of organization that are incompatible with the new mode of production. For example, in eighteenth-century France, the Church continued to defend feudal property and the aristocracy, even after capitalism had overtaken feudalism as the dominant mode of production. In this case, ruling-class interests fought tooth and nail *against* the change to society's mode of production, attempting (in vain, ultimately) to maintain feudalism-era superstructure. However, once capitalism took hold as the dominant mode of production, elites began and continue to defend and maintain organizations, institutions, and cultural forms that preserve capitalist interests. This is especially important to consider with regard to sport, as a cultural formation that is both a product of a capitalist base and a reinforcer of that base.

Capitalism, Marxist Economics, and the Labor Theory of Value

For the past 300 or so years, most of the world has lived under a capitalist mode of production. The institutions and forms of organization that constitute the superstructure—our political, legal, and education systems as well as our media, art, cultural events, and yes, our sports systems—are all a product of this economic system and this mode of production. From a Marxist standpoint, capitalism (as the current dominant mode of production) shapes all of the systems of power and culture that make up capitalist society, from the overarching legal and political systems to the media and culture that we listen to and watch.

Marxist definitions of capitalism describe it as a mode of production based on private ownership of the means of production—where capitalists own and control the factories, facilities, banks, raw materials, companies, and so on, and these means of production produce commodities to be sold *for profit* on the "open" market. The presence of markets alone, or of products made for exchange, or even just of private ownership of the means of production, is not enough to constitute capitalism. Those who own and control the means of production must use these means of production (and most importantly, workers' labor) to produce commodities *for profit*. To any of the finance or libertarian bros reading this, *no, we have not had capitalism for thousands of years, and no, it is not just "in our nature."*

Commodities, from a Marxist perspective, are any product or service that can be exchanged. Technically, a commodity can be exchanged in kind (bartered or traded, exchanged for another good), but the vast majority of the time, it is exchanged for money. While money may have long ago been tied to specific precious metals (like gold) or other materials (like cowrie shells, a form of currency originating in West Africa) with perceived value in and of themselves, it is now more than ever just a universal equivalent of exchange, a token to represent value. Most money today is represented only by numbers on a screen, moved around virtually.

Under capitalism, commodities are the thing that is sold for money, and money is how each person can pay for the means to satisfy their needs (shelter, food, water, clothes, emotional fulfillment). It is extremely rare to find people who live a subsistence-based life, where they produce all or even most of their means of subsistence without needing to use money. Though some communities like this still exist, they become rarer by the year.

Capitalism has extended its tentacles into every corner of the globe, and capitalists—those who own the means of production—have ownership of the commodities produced using these means of production. They sell these commodities to pay for their means of subsistence, to reinvest in their own companies or assets, and increasingly, to pay for all manner of luxuries. So what about workers, who, in the transfer from feudalism to capitalism, saw capture and enclosure of public lands and were violently pushed off their own personal lands? These workers, who do not own the means of production, have nothing to sell on the open market other than their own *labor power*. Importantly, it is not their labor that they sell, but their *labor power*—their ability to perform labor. Without access to the means of production, workers have no choice but to sell their labor power to capitalists in exchange for a wage, which they then use to purchase the necessary commodities to sustain their lives. Under capitalism, we all must sell commodities, and for the vast majority of workers, the only commodity they can sell is their labor power.

According to Marx's labor theory of value, all value created in the economy is created through workers' labor. Commodities that are produced by workers are *valued* based on the "socially necessary labor time" required to produce them, and their eventual prices reflect this valuation. Socially necessary labor time is generally understood as the amount of labor required by average workers with the average tools, knowledge, and skills of their era to produce whatever it is they are producing. The amount of socially necessary labor time to produce a shirt, for example, is substantially lower now than it was 100 years ago, which was substantially lower than it was 100 years before that. As socially necessary labor time decreases, generally the value of commodities will as well, reflected in lower real prices (that is, adjusted for inflation).

While liberal economists might point to supply and demand or the fancier sounding "marginal utility theory" to explain prices—saying, in short, that the price of anything is simply based on whatever people are willing to pay for it, given supply and demand—Marxists would dispute this. Of course, supply and demand have some fluctuating effect on prices, and will determine why a product might cost slightly more one day and slightly less another. But these fluctuations will happen around a specific value, determined by the socially necessary labor time it takes to produce the commodity in question. Another way of thinking about this is to think about the price of a commodity when supply and demand are at or very near equilibrium—in other words, when supply and demand are equal, what determines price? Why does a car cost more than a notebook? If simply supply and demand were at play, the value of products should be equal at equilibrium, but we know that they are not. There is more at play, and this "more" is workers' labor.

Given that is it labor that produces value, and that capitalists produce for profit, the exploitation of labor is what produces profit. For a crude example of what this exploitation looks like, consider garment workers. Let's say these workers each produce ten shirts in eight hours, and that each of the shirts will be sold for $22 on the open market by the capitalist who employs them. Assume they are paid $12.50 an hour for their work, the going minimum wage of wherever they work. This means that over their eight hours of work, each garment worker has produced $220 (10 shirts × $22 per shirt) of value and yet, is being paid only $90 (8 hours × $12.50 per hour). The difference between the value workers produce and the amount they are paid is the *surplus value* extracted by the capitalist.

There are, of course, other costs borne by the capitalist associated with the production of these shirts, including the raw cotton or other material, the machinery and physical factory space necessary to make them, the marketing budget to sell them, the shipping costs to get them to customers, and so on.

These costs are accounted for in the value of any commodity sold for exchange, and they are considered the *constant capital* within a commodity. If each shirt contains $5 worth of raw material, machinery use and space, marketing budget, and shipping costs, that means that there is $50 worth of constant capital in the ten shirts. Over the workers' eight hours of work, they've therefore each produced $170 of new value, because each ten shirts can be sold for $220 total. The workers, however, have only been paid $100; the capitalist has exploited $70 of surplus value from each worker.

Again, it is only from the surplus value generated through the exploitation of workers' labor power that capitalists derive their profits. No matter what the capitalist pays the workers in wages, the *constant* capital that must be invested to produce these ten shirts will not change—they still need the raw material, the machinery, marketing, and such. Capitalists may, of course, try to increase the productivity of their machinery, buy better materials for less, or raise prices—but these changes will only create a fleeting advantage, soon replicated by other competitors. Advantages in tech or machinery may create a temporary advantage in the market, allowing the capitalist to lower prices and undercut competitors while still maintaining profits, but this advantage doesn't last. As soon as other capitalists acquire the same tech or machinery, this advantage disappears. And even when capitalists increase the productivity of machinery or introduce technological change in labor processes, this does not mean that they stop exploiting worker labor. It is through the exploitation of the labor power of workers, also called *variable* capital—due to the varying level of input and output that can be derived from workers, in contrast to the unchangeable nature of *constant* capital—that capitalists derive their profit. By paying workers less than the value they produce, capitalists increase their rate of surplus value and thus their rate of profit.

Let's think about this in sports. In 2023, Steph Curry finished his fourteenth season as an employee of the NBA's Golden State Warriors, having earned almost $303 million in salary in his career to that point. This averages to just over $21.5 million per season. When we think about the plight of the modern worker, Curry is not the person who first comes to mind. But he is still a worker, Curry may have other parts of his life where he is not a worker—he might own a company or rental properties, for example—but in his relationship with the value produced by the sport spectacle that he takes part in, he is a worker. Curry sells his labor power for a wage, and like all workers under capitalism, the capitalists who pay him this wage are extracting surplus value from his labor.

When Joe Lacob, the owner of the Golden State Warriors bought the team in 2010, after Curry's first season, he bought it for $450 million. Fourteen years later, the team is valued at $5 billion.³ This means that over Curry's tenure with the team, their value has increased by over $4.5 billion. This increase in team value is also only one part of the equation: according to Statista, between 2009 and 2021 the Warriors averaged $262 million in revenue each season.⁴ If we project another $262 million for the last two years—which is likely low, given that the Warriors won the 2022 Championship and were consistently in the $400 million territory in the late 2010s—then during Curry's tenure the team made $3.676 billion in revenue.

Of course, no matter how great you think Steph Curry is, he is not solely responsible for this value creation. He shares this accomplishment with the other workers—players, coaches, scouts, managers, stadium workers, cleaners—who earn a wage from the Warriors. While they do earn wages of various sizes—and NBA players earn 50 percent of total team and league revenue, due to collectively bargaining for this share in labor disputes with ownership—they do not earn all of the team's revenue, and they would see *none* of the profits from an eventual sale of the team. Warriors' shareholders and Joe Lacob would share those profits, though they themselves are not responsible for the labor that produced these profits.

Again, it should be clear that this is a simplification of value creation in the NBA and by the Warriors. The team has all sorts of costs that go beyond the salaries paid to players and other workers; the NBA also has revenue sharing, where teams put revenues into a communal pot for the financial stability and health of the league; you can even argue ownership and shareholders make key decisions that impact revenue and team value, including which players (workers) to employ. My point here is not to delve into sports economics and calculate how much each member of the Warriors has contributed to the last fourteen seasons of the franchise. Rather, it is to demonstrate that the surplus value is created by workers, but split up by ownership. Regardless of whether one calculates that Steph Curry is responsible for 30 percent of the value produced by the Warriors, or 10 percent, or 5 percent, he and his fellow workers are responsible for all of this value, shared in some breakdown between them. Under capitalism, however, they earn their wage, and nothing more.

This basic understanding of surplus value and the labor theory of value should lead one to thinking about capitalism's most basic internal contradiction: it is in the best interests of capitalists to pay their workers (like Curry) the lowest wages they possibly can, to extract as much surplus value as possible; whereas the workers (Curry, his teammates, and all the workers on the different teams professional sports) have goals that are diametrically opposed, as they hope to sell their labor power for as high a wage as possible. Both parties may want their industry (professional basketball) to thrive so that the overall pie expands, but the question then becomes how big a slice each side gets. And I would respond to that with another, far more rhetorical question: Who is really responsible for the growth of that pie? The superstar athletes who excite fans with their skills, expertise, and physical efforts and sacrifice, honed over years of practice? Or the guy who writes the checks?

Grow, Profit, or Die

Beyond the contradictions between capitalists and workers, Marxist theorizing around labor and profit also stresses the importance of growth and accumulation for capitalists. Under the rules of capitalist competition, there can be no stagnation. Even if an individual capitalist or two wanted to slow down, reduce the rate of exploitation, and produce less profit, they generally are not able to. Any loss of productivity or stagnation means being outcompeted in the market and losing your share of that market. Throughout this book, you'll see examples of exactly this; teams or managers claiming that while they'd love to engage in a less ruthless version of sport, or put more emphasis on athlete or societal well-being than winning and profit, they're hampered by profit imperatives.

These imperatives force a logic of constant growth and the constant search for any small edge against opposition. Some individual sport leagues have built-in mechanisms to promote more parity and equity between teams—think salary caps, amateur player drafts, and revenue sharing—but the leagues as a whole and individual teams still operate as cutthroat capitalist firms. Leagues aim to capture as many sport fan eyes and dollars as they can across the globe, while individual teams look to gain any edge over their opposition in their quest for wins, fans, and profits. Though at considerably lower stakes, this endless search for new markets, new strategies, and new ways of extracting value mirrors the same kind of searches undergone at the global capitalist level. Over the last 300 years, we've seen empires, states, and now more often multinational companies do everything they can to enter new markets to both extract labor and sell products. Under capitalism, they have little choice but to do so.

Marxist Epistemology: How Do We Know What We Know

While I don't have the time, desire, or frankly the expertise to map out the history of philosophical thought, or to dive into the debates within Marxism about its epistemology, some more detail on this epistemology—specifically dialectical and historical materialism—is necessary to understand how we come to the conclusions we arrive at.[5]

Dialectical materialism is the Marxist philosophy for how knowledge is produced. The "materialism" part of this philosophy refers to the study of the material, real, tangible world. Marxist philosophy bases itself first and foremost in observation and "sense-perception" of the physical world, rather than starting from ideas. Marx writes in *A Contribution to the Critique of Political Economy*, "It is not the consciousness of men that determines their existence, but, on the contrary, their social existence that determines their consciousness."[6] Marxist epistemology requires that we take experiential knowledge of the particular and use this to abstract to general knowledge, laws, and patterns. Once these patterns are developed, we move back to the particular to continue to test and retest our knowledge.

While this may seem obvious for many, and especially those who haven't studied philosophy—*of course we base our knowledge on the "real" world*—many philosophies are instead based in idealism. Berkeley, Kant, Hume, and even Hegel, whose work in dialectics ultimately paved the way for the dialectical materialism of Marx and Engels, were all idealists.

Idealism in this case does not mean optimism or a sunny disposition, as it's colloquially understood. Rather, idealism (explained by Berkeley) is the notion that human consciousness and the human mind determine our "reality," and that what we observe as other people and things are merely our perceptions of them—the qualities of people and things only exist insofar as someone is there to experience them. Hume took this one step further, explaining that since we can only know our own perceptions, we cannot even say whether there even is a material reality. However, his position was more agnostic, leaving the possibility that a material reality did and does exist, even if we cannot be certain of it.

While Kant believed that an objective material world did exist independently of our perception, he also wrote that we cannot truly know anything concrete about it, because again, we know only our perceptions. This once again reflects the idealist position, where thought comes before matter. Hegel also believed that there was an objective reality independent of our senses and minds, and rejected Kant's argument about the limitations of perception. But for Hegel, that reality was essentially based in the "mind" of God or the supernatural.

Conversely, materialism posits that reality has a true existence outside of the sense perception of people, and that this should be the starting point for all analysis of the social world. Splitting from Hegel, Marx explained that material reality can be grasped by human beings, and perception is not a barrier. At the same time, Marxist materialism is not based solely on personal materialist experiential knowledge—if I have never personally seen an elephant, that obviously doesn't mean they don't exist—but involves taking our or others' experiential knowledge of the particular, tangible thing being observed and deriving knowledge of the general.

This brings us to the "dialectical" part of dialectical materialism. Dialectics, in its most basic definition, refers to the use of dialogue and conversation to produce ideas or knowledge. While the back-and-forth nature of conversation is a good anchoring analogy for what dialectics are in Marxist terms, it is not as simple as this.

The first "law" of dialectics is the unity and struggle of opposites. Each field of study, process, or individual thing is said to contain a thesis (idea) and antithesis (opposing idea), which struggle against each other and from which, through testing and argumentation, we develop a new synthesis. This synthesis then becomes the new thesis, and process restarts.

Dialectics is used to understand change within society, and describes the process by which change can and does occurs. Marxist understanding of change is based on the notion that all matter is constantly changing, and this change is based on the contradictions that exist within different things and ideas. It is these *contradictions* within a particular sphere of life or thing that propels it into motion, and eventually results in change. Vladimir Lenin's explanation provides some key examples of these sort of "contradictions," which can also be thought of as opposites: "In mathematics: + and—, differential and integral. In mechanics: action and reaction. In physics: positive and negative electricity. In chemistry: the combination and dissociation of atoms. In social science: the class struggle."[7]

This dialectical method also must remain firmly rooted in perceptual experience, which then forms into general knowledge or theory, often called abstractions. Mao Zedong wrote in *On Practice* that we "start from perceptual knowledge and actively develop it into rational knowledge; then start from rational knowledge and actively guide revolutionary practice to change both the subjective and objective world."[8] Only after perception, once the particular thing observed can be analyzed within its context and over time, can we derive more general knowledge and theory about it. "Rational knowledge depends upon perceptual knowledge and perceptual knowledge remains to be developed into rational knowledge—this is the dialectical-materialist theory of knowledge."[9] Even though most knowledge is still based on indirect experience—we know what happened in history or somewhere else in the world without having experienced it ourselves—our indirect experience with it is still based on someone else's direct experience. Thinking back to our elephants, if many elephants have been observed and shown to display high levels of intelligence, we can abstract that elephants in general are intelligent. But we will still go back to individual elephants to keep testing, to confirm our new synthesis, or to add more depth to it. The act of testing and retesting is fundamental to Marxist methods.

The dialectical method can also help explain why people are more comfortable performing any task after having completed it already; we learn from our successes and our failures, building new knowledge about the task. It is also quite easy to understand for anyone who's done any sort of experimentation, whether it be a scientist in a chemistry lab, a farmer trying out a new fertilizing method, or a baseball player testing out a new batting stance. The "dialogue" and "struggle" happening between opposing viewpoints or data points is part of the dialectical method, and in many ways is closely related to what is generally understood as the "scientific method" in contemporary research and academic circles.

The struggle between opposites then leads to the second law of dialectics, the transformation from quantity to quality. Examples abound of this kind of change. Water increases in temperature (quantitative change), all the while still remaining water. However, at a certain point (in this case, 100 degrees Celsius), the change of temperature in the water creates a *qualitative* change, into steam, from a liquid to a gas. From a class society perspective, we can think about the change from feudalism to capitalism. As the characteristics of feudal society became less prominent—workers moved from the countryside to crowded cities, individual proprietors and the merchant class grew in power compared to the landed aristocracy—eventually, society reached a breaking point, marking a qualitative leap from feudalism to capitalism.

Closely related is the third law of dialectics, the negation of the negation (or negation and affirmation). This describes the process by which the old state of the object or thing is negated, and transformed into something new, from which it then sets the stage for its own later negation. In Marx's arguments for the transformation of societies and their modes of production, capitalism negates feudalism (while still keeping some remnants of the feudal mode), and then this negation will create the conditions for socialism, and hence capitalism's (the first negation) negation by socialism. Capitalists' expropriation and stripping of the means of production from workers, centralization of these means of production, creation of global world markets, advancement of technologies, and methodical transformation of labor from individual to cooperative production (with the profits then taken solely by capitalists) creates the conditions for socialist society. As Marx writes in the first volume of *Capital*, "centralisation of the means of production and socialisation of labor at last reach a point where they become incompatible with their capitalist integument."[10] Workers must, of course, still engage in organizing and revolutionary efforts though, as dialectical materialism does not mean that development or change is predestined to occur without active involvement of workers. It is not a completely determinist philosophy.

As perhaps has already been made clear, *historical* materialism is an application of dialectical materialism, used to explain the development of society throughout history. More specifically, it is used to explain the principal contradiction of societal development—the contradiction and conflict between capitalists (the bourgeoisie) and workers (the proletariat). It bears repeating that for Marxists, it is not the ideas of great thinkers that set change in motion, but the material realities of life, and the ever-changing nature of our material world. More specifically, the mode of production and changes to this mode of production drive changes elsewhere in society (though again, this relationship is *not* unidirectional). Human activity in production—producing the means of survival and subsistence—is the ultimate "practice determining of all other activities."[11] Engels wrote: "Men make their own history, but in a given, conditioning milieu, upon the basis of actual relations already extant, among which, the economic relations, no matter how much they are influenced by relations of a political and ideological order, are ultimately decisive, constituting a red thread which runs through all the other relations and enabling us to understand them."[12]

Dialectical materialism is also not a purely empiricist philosophy, while also not being idealistic. It is important that we don't fall into mechanical thinking, something that Marxist epistemology tries to avoid.[13] By this, I mean that we cannot lose sight of the role of the individual, and of the ever-changing nature of society and social relations. The world is not static, and because something happened in a particular way in the past does not mean it will necessarily happen that way again. As Engels wrote, "the materialist method is converted into its direct opposite if instead of being used as a *guiding* thread in historical research, it is made to serve as a ready-cut pattern on which to tailor historical facts."[14] Social life is not predetermined by the economic relations or production, as each context is different, and humans have agency to impact the events that unfold.

Beyond Just Class

Even though class and economic relations of production take a leading role, our dialectical materialist understanding of sport and society must be holistic, seeing each issue and social relationship in its entirety, from all sides. It must extend beyond just class, which for Marxists (and, I would argue, everyone) should be only the "conceptual entry point into social analysis."[15] Inequalities along racial, class, gender, and sexuality lines are vital for a holistic understanding of the way sport systems, sport culture, and capitalist imperatives of profit interact with individuals. Some may protest that this is not orthodox Marxist analysis; I would argue that contemporary Marxist analyses must be attuned to the way inequalities manifest through other axes of identity, even if at their base, their root is capitalist relations of production. As Stephen Resnick and Richard Wolff wrote years ago in their discussion of economic determinism and Marxist epistemology, "Marxist theory must necessarily investigate precisely how all the other social aspects—the other (nonclass) economic aspects, along with the political, the cultural, etc.—interact so as to overdetermine the various forms of the class process so central to Marxism."[16]

From a dialectical perspective, it should be the goal of Marxists to understand the "ensemble of social relations"[17] that inform the class relationships that we care so much about. In short, the only way to understand class relationships and the extraction of surplus value from labor, is through an analysis of the "social totality" and through all other social aspects. We begin with class, but also seek to end our analysis with a synthesized, superior understanding *of* class, due to our analysis of this "ensemble of social relations." In doing so, we engage in dialectical analysis that leaves an improved definition of class as the starting point for future analysis.[18]

It is important to stress that though this book draws upon Marxist understandings of social relations, it draws on critical and cultural theory as well, and specifically, many of the tenets of the burgeoning field of critical criminology in sport. Derek Silva and Liam Kennedy write in their introduction to *Power Played*, an excellent edited collection on this very subject, "Critical theory moves beyond superstructural analyses of sport's role in class conflict to concentrate on the ways in which subjugation to sporting practice enables systems of exploitation, oppression, discrimination, and harm that feed class conflict."[19] We *must* take from more general critical theory when it's necessary, examining harm and oppression along race, gender, sexuality, and other identity lines, while still keeping an eye toward upending the profit imperatives and private ownership of the means of production that are at the root of this harm. It is also vital to understand how oppression along other identity lines and systems of power influence and elide class conflict.

The Goal

Why we seek to understand these social relations and the harm and violence they cause is also shaped by the Marxist orientation of this book. It is the final piece of our theoretical puzzle, and perhaps the most important.

If there was a March Madness style bracket or a World Cup of famous Karl Marx quotes, the final would likely come down to: "The history of all hitherto existing society is the history of class struggles" and "The philosophers have hitherto only interpreted the world in various ways, the point, however, is to change it." Notable about these quotes, beyond the fact that "hitherto" was a fashionable word in the mid-1800s, is that they act as one-line summaries of two vital parts of Marxist political theory: historical materialism on one side, and the ultimate goal, purpose, and orientation of Marxist epistemology on the other.

Marxist theory is fundamentally *not* about pontificating, speaking, and writing about society, social relations, harm, violence, or anything in the abstract, from the sidelines, or from the ivory tower (yes, I'm aware of the irony of making this point in a book). The purpose of any writing or work must be to improve society, to change it, with an eye toward revolutionary social change. We do not diagnose the issues inherent to capitalism in order to take advantage of these issues materially,[20] or to just ignore them.

While capitalism is our current mode of production and locks us into our current stage of development, we believe a better, more equitable, safer, and more fulfilling world is possible, through revolutionary change to this mode of production. Only with socialism, where the means of production and control of the economy is placed in the hands of the workers, and where this production is aimed at fulfilling the needs of all, rather than the profits of some, can we reach our next stage of human development. This is also why I use a Marxist theoretical framework in this book. My goals here are specific—to understand how harm and violence manifest and continue to exist in sport, with the express purpose of driving social change toward socialism to eradicate this harm and violence.[21]

We are not objective observers, floating above society to analyze and critique it. Marxist or not, I have yet to meet anyone or read any work that truly does this. Science and knowledge always have a bias to them, whether that bias is stated explicitly (as I've done here) or whether it is hidden behind false claims of objectivity. Feminist standpoint theorists know this just as Marxists do. The white, male, heterosexual, often-wealthy or land-owning perspective was for so long considered the *objective* viewpoint, without ever considering how this perspective really only represented a select few, *and* without acknowledging how it was used to maintain the power of this select few and the legitimacy of the status quo.

In sport and especially professional sport, fans, athletes, and even some scholars[22] often engage with sport as if it is apolitical. Fans, media, and some athletes decry those advocating for better pay and labor conditions or LGBTQ+ inclusion, or get angry at those who do use their platform as athletes to advocate for racial or gender equality, saying that they are "bringing politics into sport." This incorrect understanding of sport as apolitical wrongly assumes that the inequalities of society more generally do not impact sport, and that sport cannot or does not act as a vehicle for reproducing inequalities, exacerbating harm, or justifying the very conditions (both material and ideological) that produce inequalities in the first place.

The idea that sport is *inherently political*—especially in terms of inequalities by class, race, gender, sexuality, and ability status—has become more mainstream, but even this literature often fails to take adequately into account the most important overlooked aspect and factor in sport: the ubiquity of capitalism. Chen Chen, a critical and decolonial sport scholar at the University of Connecticut, writes in "Naming the Ghost of Capitalism in Sport Management" that sport journalism and sport scholarship often take it for granted that sport is played and organized under capitalism, which impacts all the facets that we then study. According to Chen, it is vital that we actually "name" capitalism, because only through "the action of naming "capitalism" ... can [we] single it out as a structure of both material and discursive significance (albeit interwoven with other formations) within our purview, making it identifiable and hence, analyzable."[23]

Harkening back to Francis Fukuyama's infamous suggestion that the dissolution of the Soviet Union marked "the end of history"—given the alleged clear superiority of liberal capitalist "democracies"[24] to all other systems—sport research often proceeds as if there is no alternative to capitalist sport, and as if capitalist sport is simply the "normal," apolitical state of affairs. Assuming capitalism as the default and unchangeable scaffolding of society shapes what kind of research is done, as well as who this research serves—those who own and have management stakes in sports leagues and teams, or those who are exploited and harmed by sport.[25] Instead, what is needed are analyses that center the workers and those exploited and suffering due to sport systems under capitalism. Again, this does not mean only focusing on labor or class; as Chen notes, class conflicts are "always conditioned by formations of race, gender, sexuality and nationalistic ideologies, etc."[26] It does, however, mean dispelling the notion of a capitalism as status quo and the unquestioned "best system" for sport and for society, and ensuring that our research and work seeks change *outside* of these capitalist parameters.

In a capitalist status quo predicated on inequality—between capitalists and workers in individual states, capitalists and workers worldwide, and even between individual states and between the workers in these individual states[27]—there is no atheoretical or apolitical position. If you stand by and watch as the powerful hurt the powerless, refusing to "take a side" and simply observing the way the powerful "succeed" in their harm, you have chosen a side already. As South African anti-apartheid and human rights advocate Desmond Tutu famously said, "If you are neutral in situations of injustice, you have chosen the side of the oppressor. If an elephant has its foot on the tail of a mouse, and you say that you are neutral, the mouse will not appreciate your neutrality."[28]

This is the orientation that guides Marxists in our analysis, and it is the orientation that guides this book. It is an especially important orientation when studying sports, given the tendency of writers, journalists, and even sport scholars to be uncritical of sport's institutions, structures, and overall impact on society. As Richard Gruneau wrote in *Class, Sports and Social Development*, one of the earliest explicitly Marxist books on sport, we cannot allow our analyses of sports to become "little more than a handmaiden of the status quo."[29] Marxist theory is necessary not only because of what it allows us to understand about the social relations, violence, and harm in sport, but also because, as Lenin writes, "there can be no revolution without revolutionary theory."[30]

Sport, Capitalism, and Social Development

I am not, of course, the first to write about sport and capitalism, and not the first to do so from an explicitly Marxist lens. Almost fifty years ago French sociologist and philosopher Jean-Marie Brohm's *Sport: A Prison of Measured Time* outlined some of the common arguments still made by Marxists regarding sport and other leisure pursuits. Taking an explicitly Marxist view, Brohm talked about sport's mutilation of worker bodies, as well as the use of sport as a means of pacification and control by state and private entities. For Brohm, sport had only a regressive, negative impact on society and on the working class; he considered it the new "opiate of the people," similar to how Marx described religion in 1843.[31] This understanding of sport situates it as part of the ruling class's "bread and circuses," a means of escape for workers that distracts them from their own oppression, and from participating in the progressive politics that could result in substantial social change.[32]

According to Brohm and other Marxist scholars, it's also important to understand that while working-class people could historically participate in this circus, they were never able to own or control it. Canadian sociologist Richard Gruneau found, in his historical overview of Canadian sport, that organized sport was played originally by the ruling classes as a sign of social status. This was an example of what Norwegian American economist Thorstein Veblen called "conspicuous consumption": the act of consciously wasting goods or time as a sign of social status, to show that one did not have to work.[33] By the late 1800s and early 1900s, however, sport took on a slightly different purpose. Instead of being only the realm of the elite, the ruling classes promoted sport to workers as a means to advance health and "civility," to maintain order in newly industrializing and growing cities, and to prepare workers for eventual war or military service.[34]

As sport began to professionalize (read: athletes could actually make money) in the late 1910s and early 1920s, spots on professional clubs were again reserved for upper- and middle-class white men. Even when sport participation was eventually opened up to the working class, this opening up of *participation* was paired with further professionalization of sport clubs, ridding them of any grassroots and worker control and ensuring that only those with independent wealth and capital could hold *ownership* stakes in teams and leagues.[35] By the 1930s, league ownership moved from a completely "free" market of individual teams run in an entrepreneurial way to a cartel-style ownership structure, where owners worked together to keep athlete wages down and limit competition between teams for attracting talent. This cartel structure still exists today in North American sports, with teams competing with one another for talent and on the field, but also working together to ensure wage suppression and the financial success of leagues as a whole. While these structures did allow professional athletes to make wages from their sports, it did not grant them any ownership stake in their organizations or any control of the sport industry more broadly, even as they were the burgeoning industry's primary value-creators.

During this period, the same was happening with workers more generally. To combat worker militancy, capitalist and ruling elites gave working-class some crumbs, but not the full loaf, and surely not the bakery; Canadian Pacific Railway even offered its workers sports opportunities and sports club access as a way to appease them, instead of delivering the wage increases and better working conditions these workers demanded.[36] These benefits were meant to distract from labor demands, and instill values related to discipline, obedience, and hierarchy in workers.[37] Even state-run sports programming, while ostensibly (and sometimes earnestly) about well-being and social outcomes for people, also help to reproduce capitalist workers.

Many of Brohm's initial arguments about sport, society, and class were picked up and added to by other sport scholars, though several were also contested. For example, British and Canadian sport scholars John Hargreaves and Richard Gruneau have a more balanced view of the agency athletes have within sport systems.[38] Both note that although sport *can* be a place of mutilated bodies and ideological repression, it can also be a place of resistance and liberation, a view that is also echoed by non-Marxist sport scholars like Allen Guttman. Gruneau stresses the importance of a dialectical approach to sport, considering all parts and all sides of its institutions and culture, to understand not only the structural imperatives that shape athlete experiences and behavior, but also the agency athletes have for creativity and transformation within these systems.

Sport sociologists Norbert Elias and Eric Dunning take an even more positive outlook, discussing sport as part of the broader "civilizing process" in human historical development, whereby violence is reoriented from interpersonal violence, group conflict, and war to codified, controlled sport contexts.[39] However, many scholars refute this notion of sport as "civilizer," as even today many sports remain incredibly physically violent, while also producing structural, political, and environmental harm for athletes and the general population. Though proponents of the "civilizing effect of sports" thesis might point to sport's position as a space for violent urges to be subdued in a less harmful way, Grace Gallacher writes in *Power Played* that "to accept claims about the civilizing process and its legitimate space for violence is to ignore the systemic harms that also result from sports, as well as any alternative explanation for why they are often so brutal."[40] It is also not clear if instrumental violence actually has any real violence-quelling effects—research has mostly found that punching bags and sport violence rarely actually decrease anger[41]—though this is more an empirical than a theoretical point.

More importantly, ideas around sport as a "civilizer" have historically been used to assimilate and erase Indigenous people and cultures in settler-colonial societies like Canada, the United States, Australia, and New Zealand. The Catholic Church and Canadian government infamously used ice hockey in residential schools to try to assimilate Indigenous youth, and cricket was introduced and used by British colonial authorities to try to "civilize" and imbue the people of India with upper- and middle-class British values. As Australian sport historian Malcolm Maclean writes, the introduction of formalized sports was often used by colonizers to erase and replace Indigenous culture with Christianity, through control of bodily practice. "A vital part of the erasure of Indigenous peoples was the control of their bodies, partly achieved through the extinguishment of distinctive body cultures—of forms of movement, physicality, play, and dance—and their replacement by rational body cultures as seen in regularized work, regularized leisure (that is, sport) and controls on body movement and display, including dress such as those derived from Christian modesty."[42]

Critics of the "civilizing process" theory of sport and especially of elite sport also note the harm, violence, and exclusion that still occur for so many groups marginalized in sport, as well as the "competitive ethos that (make athletes) resort to dishonorable behavior to gain the upper hand."[43] Brohm made these initial criticisms as well, discussing sport's glorification of capitalism and hypercompetitive capitalist values. Writing around the same time, German sociologist Bero Rigauer also described the "true" function of sport as "reinforcing the ethic of hard work, achievement and group loyalty which is necessary for the reproduction of a capitalist industrialist society."[44] Similarly, Rigauer explained that many of the methods and processes used to make workers generally more efficient and controllable—Taylorization (breaking down large processes into specific, repetitive tasks), rationalization, and bureaucratization[45]—are also seen in elite sport practices, where athletes are kept to strict performance and living regimens, often practice individual skills in isolation, and keep decision-making responsibilities at a minimum. Though there are, of course, detractors to this perspective, the view of sport as helping reproduce capitalist relations of production and capitalist values has received frequent support in sport literature, even today.

Social Reproduction, Alienation, Meritocracy, and Hegemony

One of the more explicit ways that sport reproduces capitalist relations is through *social reproduction*, a term introduced by Marxist feminist scholars to describe the variety of different and often hidden forms of labor required to reproduce the commodity of labor power.[46] In short, social reproductive labor is all the work that is done to ensure that youth can grow into valuable workers, and that adult workers can continue working. Feminist American sociologists Barbara Laslett and Johanna Brenner explain: "Social reproduction can thus be seen to include various kinds of work—mental, manual, and emotional—aimed at providing the historically and socially, as well as biologically, defined *care* necessary to maintain existing life and to reproduce the next generation."[47]

While feminist scholars have rightly focused on historically ignored and marginalized women's domestic labor in child-rearing, care, and education as forms of socially reproductive labor, Canadian sport sociologist and critical sport scholar Nathan Kalman-Lamb has expanded on this concept in recent years, explicitly calling for a recognition of athletic labor as a form of social reproductive labor.[48] This expansion relies on the fact that the athletic labor of athletes is what produces sport spectacle, which is then what provides emotional and spiritual fulfillment and meaning for *workers* under capitalism.

This is especially important today, given the *alienation* so many workers feel under capitalism. Marx uses the term "alienation" to describe the mental and physical state of workers who are physically and socially detached from their labor. As wage laborers, workers under capitalism are themselves turned into commodities, and they do not get to keep, or many times even *see*, the products of their labor. Workers do not generally earn the profits produced by their work, nor do they usually have a say over their workplace, work conditions, what or how much they produce, or for what purpose. As Marx explains, workers become "physically exhausted and mentally debased," as work is "only a means for satisfying other needs."[49] They are alienated from their labor, their own humanity and sense of creativity and fulfillment, and even from other workers. Sport thus acts as more than just a distraction, but as a way to create meaning and community with other people, fulfilling workers' emotional needs so that they can continue to work productively.

Another one of sport's most powerful *ideological* claims is that it is a "meritocracy," where class, race, gender, sexuality, and other considerations don't matter, and only one's performance determines an athlete's success. Here, there are two deceitful arguments actually being made—one empirical, and the other more philosophical.

On the empirical side, sport is simply not a meritocracy. Race, gender, sexuality, and especially class and wealth have a huge impact on athletic opportunity, as countless research and athlete experiences have shown. Just like capitalism's claims to pure meritocracy are based on a utopian premise that has never been true[50]—that each person has an equal chance to succeed regardless of the material advantages or disadvantages they have, and that only one's skill and effort matter—sport is based on the same false premise.

The second deceit is more philosophical, in that sport's self-promotion as a meritocracy is also meant to promote the *legitimacy* of meritocracy as a way to organize society more generally. Part of the value of having sport viewed as a meritocracy is to justify the use of "merit," "ability," or "productivity" as the right measures for how we distribute resources in society. *Even if* sport were a perfectly rational meritocracy (it's not), is a society where the most talented (or those judged to be the most talented) get huge material rewards while those less talented get much less or even nothing the best way to organize society? I would argue no, but this is why this is a philosophical or normative argument rather than an empirical one.[51]

Regardless of whether you personally think meritocracy is a good way to organize resource allocation, sport's glorification of meritocracy lends ideological support to this type of system, and to capitalism and neoliberalism more generally.[52] As sociologist Jo Littler writes, the neoliberal vision "finds legitimate vast inequalities of wealth and poverty as long as the potential to travel through them for those savvy enough is maintained."[53] By claiming that anyone can "travel through" the sport or civil society ranks through hard work and talent, sport is glorified as meritocratic, and meritocracy is exalted as equitable.

Sport thus contributes to capitalism and neoliberalism's *hegemony* throughout the world. Hegemony is a concept initially theorized by Italian Marxist philosopher and activist Antonio Gramsci to describe how ruling classes and political and economic elites maintain their power *without* needing to use physical violence or coercion. Instead of using physical force, hegemony allows for "political leadership based on the consent of the led, a consent which is secured by the diffusion and popularization of the world view of the ruling class."[54] This does not mean that Gramsci presumed cultural hegemony to be *more* important than the mode of production in determining behavior and social development, but rather that the capitalist mode of production is legitimized through hegemony.

Gramsci's addition of hegemony into the Marxist canon also forces us to contend with the fact that the relationship between the economic base and the superstructure is not strictly unidirectional, with the economic mode of production (capitalism) and superstructure (law, religion, media, sport, politics, and so on) reciprocally influencing one another. With an understanding of hegemony, it becomes clear that even if the economic base is ultimately most responsible for how the superstructure develops and operates, and it is the economic base that in the first instance produces this superstructure, there is still a reciprocal relationship between the two. Sport (part of the superstructure) can influence the economic base, and legitimize it.

Gramsci specifically divided Marx's superstructure into two "floors"—"civil society" and "political society." Civil society consists of schools, religious institutions, clubs, media, and likely sports ("likely" because Gramsci never wrote explicitly about sports); and political society is made up of courts, police, government, and the military, the more "official" arms of the state. While political society may have "direct dominion" over the affairs of individuals, and can use physical force and coercion, the institutions that make up civil society also have an important role in maintaining the hegemony of capitalist ideas. If "civil society" (using Gramsci's definition) can convince workers to "consent" to the capitalist system, then the institutions of "political society" can lie back and avoid using force.[55]

A huge part of why capitalism and neoliberalism predominate worldwide is the economic and military dominance of the United States and (to a much lesser extent) its allies post-World War II, but this material dominance is also sustained through capitalism's cultural hegemony. As Gruneau explains in *Class, Sports and Social Development*, even under capitalism, those with more resources and power do not have *all* of the resources and power, and they must therefore still create narratives and meanings that solidify their positions.[56] While Gruneau and Hargreaves also stress that this kind of cultural dominance can be and is still contested and resisted by athletes and workers within the sport sphere, hegemony plays an important role in solidifying the position of individual capitalists and owners, the elite sport system, and capitalism more generally.

Sport's own dominant narratives—that the goal of sport is winning and domination, and that the way to achieve this is through being a tough, devoted, loyal athlete willing to do anything to win—both maintain sport as a place of harm and violence *and* help legitimize the same principles that underlie capitalist relations of production. Capitalist society generally, like elite sports, demands a dog-eat-dog mentality and the ability to work *through* harm and suffering rather than an attempt to alleviate it for the masses. Hargreaves and Brohm also explain how sport's hegemony can produce nationalistic or tribal passions among sport consumers, focusing their attention on ritualistic and trivial ceremonies (sporting contests) that elide class relations and pull attention away from class struggle.[57] But Hargreaves is a bit more tepid in this assessment, as he considers sport to be a more autonomous cultural form rather than simply a mirror of capitalist relations of production.[58]

More recent sport literature has extended the values prescribed by sport to include "healthism"—the idea that a population's health is a matter of personal responsibility, with poor health and disease framed as personal moral failings.[59] Healthism both drives consumer demand for trainers, coaches, and personal fitness products, and promotes an aesthetic ideal for what is "healthy." Beyond this, healthism reinforces neoliberal ideas around personal responsibility for physical and other kinds of health and well-being.

Finally, hegemonic masculinity, another vital concept in sport studies that describes the "culturally exalted masculinity"[60] in any particular space and time, is also based on the notion of hegemony. Sport's hegemonic masculinity has for decades been that of the tough, violent, domineering, and misogynistic man who is devoted to his sport, to his team, and to his teammates. While at times athletes are physically forced into behaving like this "ideal" man (through hazing rituals or demands from coaches, for example), for the most part this coercion is cultural and ideological. Athletes (both male and female) act in ways that fulfill the hegemonically masculine image, but they don't do this freely in any meaningful way, because the sport's culture and ideology coerce them into this behavior.[61]

Conclusion

Armed with an understanding of Marxist views on economics, labor and the labor of theory of value, dialectical materialism, the emancipatory goals of Marxist thought and practice, and concepts like social reproduction, alienation, and hegemony, our tool kit for the rest of this book is nearly complete. While there are still some Marxist and critical concepts, terms, and explanations that will be explored in the coming pages, these should help guide you in the early going.

In professional and elite sport, capitalist imperatives of competition profit—for athletes to win and outcompete their opposition, and for ownership and management to extract as much value as possible from athletic laborers—are at the root of the harm and violence you will read about it in the coming pages. That does not mean that each story is the same, or that the harm is *only* due to capitalist profit imperatives. These imperatives and the dominance and internalization of capitalist ethos more generally operate in different ways, have met varying levels of resistance from athletes and sport consumers, and manifest in different kinds of harm.

Sport is only one sphere of culture in society, but it is an important one—not just because of the millions of participants worldwide and the harm that they are far too often subjected to, but because of sport's ability to reinforce capitalist ethos and logics. When you ask the average person about the impact of sport on society, many would say that it is overall a positive one. There remains overarching belief in sport as a universal good, with it encouraging healthy and active lifestyles, showing people the value of hard work, teamwork, and responsibility, and on the elite side of things, producing jobs and economic development as well as a path of upward mobility for aspiring athletes. Some of these benefits can and do arise through sport. But this does not excuse the harm and violence we see. It also does not mean that elite sport, as it is currently organized, is the *only* way to achieve these benefits. And for some of these potential "benefits," further interrogation might show us that they are not really benefits at all.

If we do not dig deeper into the harms of sport produced by capitalist imperatives of profit and competition, as well as the way sport can reinforce capitalist ethos, these harms can be multiplied, and violence and competition given more justification. The base (capitalism) influences the violent, harmful, and unequal practices of the superstructure (sport), and the sport superstructure reinforces the validity of the base. It's a vicious cycle of capitalism creating harm and then legitimizing this harm.

Though this book is Marxist in its orientation, there will still be mention and discussion of reforms and incremental improvement. We must always balance the need for harm reduction *right now* with the need for revolution as soon as possible. But our eyes must be set on the kind of revolutionary societal change that will lead to long-lasting, sustainable improvements to the way sport (along with the rest of our culture, leisure, and art) is organized and run. Let's get into it.

CHAPTER TWO

In-Game Violence
Concussions, Injury, and the Consequences

"He was on the road and almost killed himself, not on purpose. Driving on a road he drove all the time and he just said, 'Mary, I blacked out. I don't remember what happened. But I woke up and I was headed straight towards the lake. And I was six inches from hitting a fence, and I hit my brakes and closed my eyes and I stopped.' He said, 'I don't remember anything.' And he told me he was shaking."

These are not the words of a Vietnam or Iraq War veteran, nor those of a Vietnamese or Iraqi person who lived through these wars. They're not those of a victim of a terrorist attack or repeated domestic violence. These are the words of Mary Brooks, telling me about her father's deteriorating mental and physical health in his final years. Her father was five-time All Star Dallas Cowboys defensive end George Andrie.

Andrie played youth, high school, collegiate, and professional football. He died when seventy-eight years old of complications related to chronic traumatic encephalopathy (CTE) in 2018. CTE is described by the Boston University CTE Center as "a progressive degenerative disease of the brain found in people with a history of repetitive head impacts (RHI) often incurred during contact sport play ... and other activities that involve repeated blows to the head." Symptoms "include memory loss, confusion, impaired judgment, impulse control problems, aggression, depression, anxiety, suicidality, parkinsonism, and, eventually, progressive dementia."[1] Compared to so many other NFL players (and other athletes) suffering from the disease, Andrie lived a long life. Many don't make it past fifty.

Though Andrie lived longer than many of his former colleagues in the NFL, his life after his playing career was far from easy. Beyond the aches and pains and usual search for meaning and purpose that many former athletes face once their career ends, Andrie suffered from a variety of brain-related ailments starting in his fifties. Memory loss, blackouts, auditory hallucinations, suicidal thoughts, early-onset Alzheimer's; his symptoms varied, along with his moods. According to Brooks, her father admitted himself to a psychiatric hospital for the first time in 2004, fearing the harm he might cause. He was hospitalized several more times before his death.

If you've been paying any attention to the NFL beyond game day coverage and fantasy football, you know that Andrie's story is far from unique. By now, many can list some of the sport's most famous CTE victims: Junior Seau, Aaron Hernandez, Mike Webster, Terry Long, Vincent Jackson. These men suffered and died young. Several took their own lives.

Though the NFL would love nothing more than for its fans and the general public to focus solely on draft analysis, viral trash-talking clips, and game plan breakdowns, the link between football and CTE has entered the cultural mainstream. Thanks to the persistent and tireless work of neurologists, public health experts, athletes, family members, journalists, and critical sport scholars,[2] even the NFL and its bottomless bank account and army of lawyers and PR spinners can't refute the evidence (though they've tried).

The 345 *confirmed* cases of CTE (in data published as of February 2023) in former professional football players are only a small fraction of the true total.[3] CTE can only be diagnosed postmortem, and only if the family of the deceased agrees to a brain autopsy, which not all do. It's been fifteen years since Dr. Bennett Omalu first diagnosed CTE in football players[4]—and we're already at 345-plus *pro* players. These numbers don't account for the many former NFL players who died before this initial discovery, those whose brains will not be donated for examination, those living with the disease right now, and those still playing football right now. There are also more than one million high school football players in the United States every year[5] and over 70,000 playing at the collegiate level. You can get CTE without playing the game professionally.

CTE is caused by repeated blows to the head, which can include both concussive and sub-concussive blows at any level of the sport. As Hana Walker-Brown explains in "A Delicate Game: Brain Injury, Sport and Sacrifice," CTE "is a progressive neurodegenerative syndrome ... caused by single, episodic, or repetitive blunt force impacts to the head and a consequent transfer of acceleration-deceleration forces to the brain."[6] For those with CTE, their tau proteins—which play an important role in Alzheimer's and other forms of dementia—form "clumps that spread throughout the brain, killing cells."[7]

Dr. Craig Lindsley explains in the American Chemical Society's neuroscience journal, "CTE initiates focally, deep in the sulci in the cerebral cortex and spreads slowly over decades to eventually spread tau pathology across multiple brain regions."[8] The eventual effects of CTE may take time, but more frequent and more forceful blows to the head are more likely to have a harsh impact, and anyone who coaches, reports on, or watches the game will tell you that football players have only gotten bigger, stronger, and faster over the years, making collisions that much more violent. This is also true in hockey, rugby, boxing, and most other sports.[9]

To give you an idea of how many football players are likely suffering or will likely suffer from CTE, consider that in a 2017 study published in the *Journal of the American Medical Association*, researchers found CTE in 177 of the 202 former football players of all levels who were examined. Of the 111 NFL players' brains studied, 110 had the disease. The 202 former players who were studied obviously represent a biased sample, given that their loved ones decided to donate their brains to Boston University, but this is still 88 percent of studied former players, and 99 percent of NFL players, with confirmed CTE diagnoses. Similarly, a more recent 2022 systematic review of neurodegenerative disorder and sport participation published in *Neurological Sciences* found a higher frequency of neurodegenerative and neurocognitive disorders in former collegiate and pro football players, and a "significantly higher risk of CTE."[10] Another study of living former NFL players, published in the *British Journal of Sports Medicine* (*BJSM*) in 2023, found that these athletes were more likely to suffer from dementia and Alzheimer's than the general population in every age group studied.[11] They are also more likely to be diagnosed with these diseases earlier.

The only other sports that come close to these levels are boxing and other combat sports, and perhaps rugby;[12] another 2023 study in the *BJSM* found that of the 176 living boxers and mixed martial arts (MMA) fighters in their sample, 41 percent already had the characteristics to fulfill diagnostic criteria for traumatic encephalopathy syndrome, a precursor to CTE. The likelihood of fulfilling these criteria also increased with age, and was higher for those who started fighting younger, were knocked out more frequently, and had more total fights.

Beyond the statistics and likely underestimation, it's even more important to remember that these men—and their families and friends—are not just numbers. Personally, though I've been a statistics nerd since I can remember, it was the individual stories of the families of those suffering from CTE that were the tipping point for me to stop watching football entirely.

It's one thing to know that "a former NFL player has been diagnosed with CTE," and quite another to read about "Iron" Mike Webster, the first of Dr. Bennett Omalu's CTE patients, who was "occasionally catatonic, in a fetal position for days" before dying at age fifty. Or Terry Long, who died at forty-five with a brain described as that of a "90-year-old with advanced Alzheimer's." Or Vincent Jackson, a twelve-year veteran and four-time NFL Man of the Year award recipient, who died alone in his hotel room in February 2021, at thirty-eight. Again, these are just the stories we know about.

Brain injury may be only *one* of the many types of physical harm that athletes suffer from, but it is perhaps the most telling; if athletes are willing or are forced to sacrifice their brains for their sport, what wouldn't they do? Though (American) football is the biggest team-sport culprit, it is not alone. Ice hockey[13] and rugby[14] players also suffer from CTE and other concussion-related disorders. There's also a growing problem of under-diagnosed concussions in women's soccer, part of a larger trend of misdiagnosed and underdiagnosed injury in women's sports generally, owing to the sport research community's extremely disproportionate focus on men.[15] Of all collegiate athletes in the United States, women's soccer players are the most likely to suffer concussions.[16] Several sliding-sport athletes have also taken their own lives, after repeated concussions and post-concussive symptoms.[17]

I focus mostly on football and hockey in this chapter because they are some of the most popular collision sports, because their CTE and concussions issues are so stark, and frankly, because they are the sports that I know. Entire books have been written about the multitude of physical injuries and harms that athletes across a range of sports are subjected to. Here, we'll use examples from these two sports, and from a few others, to illustrate why this occurs across the sport spectrum.

We continue to subject young athletes to head injury and to all of its associated harms because, in short, violence sells, and professional and elite sports are just another form of business under capitalism. But why does violence sell, and why do athletes continue to sacrifice their health? And how do professional sport structures avoid blame for this harm? Let's dive in.

Can't Stop the Gravy Train: Profits and Head Injury

Revenue reigns supreme in professional and elite sport, and especially for the NFL. When Dr. Omalu uncovered his first case of CTE in 2005, league revenue from the thirty-two teams in the league was in the neighborhood of $5–6 *billion*, according to Statista. In the years following this initial diagnosis and subsequent research on the pervasiveness of head trauma, CTE, and early death among players, that number has dwindled year over year, and revenue is now much lower.

Just kidding.

The NFL's 2023 revenues were the highest ever recorded, $12.83 billion.[18] Since 2005 the NFL has made over $190 billion in revenue, and every team's valuation has skyrocketed.

The NFL, like all professional sport leagues, is first and foremost a business. And under capitalism, where profit extraction and growth are the only important orders of the day, the NFL is a damn good one. When I interviewed NFL front-office workers and journalists for research on NFL player violence against women, they admitted as much. *"All the NFL is at the end of the day is a business." "Winning is the bottom line we are all judged on in professional sports." "The only thing that the NFL cares about is wins and money."* These kinds of things were said openly, with no specific prompt or question about the nature of the NFL.

As long as the sport continues to produce revenue, NFL ownership and the many stakeholders who profit off the game—management, coaches, sponsors, television networks, merchandisers, fantasy sports and gambling companies, and yes, *some* players—will continue to do whatever they can to ensure the gravy train keeps rolling, no matter how many bodies are sacrificed along the way.

Boxing and combat sports are perhaps the purest encapsulation of this phenomenon. These sports do not exist without violence and harm to participants, and the profits raked in by promoters, managers, executives, and venues come directly at the expense of the health of athletes. With these combat sports specifically, athletes' labor relationship with the larger sport structures and governing bodies is more like that of individual contractors, so more training, more wins, and more fights are the only way athletes can earn a living. For just one example of this, the UFC (Ultimate Fighting Championship) produced over $5 billion in revenue in 2022, of which just 15.5 percent went to the athletes producing the spectacle and taking on all the physical risk.[19] In most professional men's team sports leagues where the players have unions (the NFL and NFLPA, NHL and NHLPA, etc.), revenue is split between ownership and the athletes at about a 50/50 rate, depending on the league. While this is still not enough (athletes and other workers should receive *all* revenue, with constant capital expenditures being pulled from this total), this is evidence of both the value of unions, and just how much capitalists in sport will take (in the case of the UFC) if they're able to.

It's Not Just "Human Nature": Commodity Fetishism, Social Reproduction, and Why People Need Violence in Their Sports

As hard as this might be to believe, physical violence in sport does not sell because humans are bloodthirsty creatures who crave pain and suffering. Ascribing characteristics like violence to "human nature" is a proposition that has been debunked and denounced by scholars' time and time again.[20] The competitiveness, domination, and desire to control and "beat" the opposition that we see so often in capitalist society are in reality the very product of a society that incentivizes and in many cases *demands* this sort of orientation. The discursive positioning of these competitive and dominance-based ethos as "simply human nature" benefits those capitalists (as well as other purveyors of "hustle culture") who are advantaged by this status quo, and thus it directly benefits them to try to make this understanding of "human nature" or "common sense" stick.

While business bros and libertarian zealots may have internalized Thomas Hobbes's depiction (which was based on zero empirical evidence) that if humans were left to their own devices, our lives would be "solitary, poor, nasty, brutish and short," research from a variety of fields has shown this not to be the case. Whether it is communities coming together to aid in natural disaster relief[21] or in support of those struggling with illness or injury,[22] tons of empirical work demonstrates that as human beings, we are more naturally predisposed to cooperation, working together, and mutual solidarity. Pro-capitalist bastardizations of Darwin's work on evolution have focused on "survival of the fittest" as proof of the dog-eat-dog nature of human life, when in reality even Darwin (and many scholars after him) focused on cooperation and collaboration as the hallmarks of human evolutionary success.[23]

Even within sports, it is often the teamwork and cooperation between athletes and coaches that draw so many fans to the sport. Yet it is undeniable that violence, given sport in its current iterations, sells. Whether it is football, hockey, rugby, boxing, MMA, or even noncollision sports like basketball and baseball, fans cheer and lose themselves in a big hit or a fight.

The lack of care or attention paid to athlete injury and harm speaks to the commodification and dehumanization of athletes, and to the general commodification of labor under capitalist society more generally. Labor has become so alienated from the products it produces that fans seem to lose sight of the harm that the laboring bodies (athletes) may be enduring. This is a clear example of commodity fetishism—Marx's term for the way capitalism produces relationships between products of exchange (such as sport's commodity spectacle exchanged for the money spent by sport fans) rather than relationships between people (the athletes and the fans), *fetishizing* the exchange of commodities and the commodity form itself.

The fact that this sort of commodity fetishism occurs in sport is somewhat surprising, given that the labor involved here is so hypervisible, especially compared to other labor relationships. Consider how much easier it is to ignore or forget about the various disconnected groups of workers that help produce a piece of clothing or car that we buy, compared to the visibility of the athletes who are right in front of you, producing the commodity spectacle we just paid for. They are often even hobbling or grimacing in pain on the field, court, or ice, as we sit there and watch.

But maybe it's not actually that we ignore this pain, but instead that we notice it, enjoy it, and to some extent, need it. Some critical sport scholars have pointed out that the enjoyment of and attraction to sport violence and to the harms suffered by athletes are not simply accepted by or incidental for sport fans but are actually a *feature* of why we love the sport. It is not just that sport violence is exciting to watch, but that athletes caring enough about their sport to put their own physical well-being in harm's way and risk serious injury *justifies* fans' *own* involvement and investment in the sport.

As explained by Nathan Kalman-Lamb—a critical sport sociologist who has written extensively about injury and harm in professional and elite sports—violence in sport is "logically consistent with the fact that professional (sports) must have high stakes in order to entice fans to invest meaning and finances into the game."[24] If athletes were not willing to play through injury, the fiction of the elevated importance of the sport—the life-and-death stakes that many athletes (and fans) ascribe to the results of what is at its core an entertainment product—crumbles.

The *centrality* of athlete harm to the value of the product (the athletic commodity spectacle) is also what separates athletic labor from other types of labor. As Kalman-Lamb explains:[25]

> The garment worker, incidentally, gets hurt. But the capitalist doesn't care if they get hurt. Sure, they're willing to get them killed, hurt them, that's all true.... But actually, them getting hurt doesn't *benefit* the capitalist specifically. That's not where the value is coming from. But in the context of athletic labor, we're trying to produce a fiction or a fantasy for the fan, that we are talking about something that has almost militaristic life or death stakes, because that is what *engenders* the investment in the entire enterprise. That is what gives value to the commodity spectacle. And so it is necessary for the players to play through pain, to experience harm; it's necessary to celebrate the harm, because that actually builds value for the product being sold [my emphasis added].

Under capitalism, injury, harm, and death occur to hundreds of thousands of workers every year. However, the point here is that this harm is not usually what provides value.[26] A piece of clothing is not more valuable because workers were hurt in making it. The workers might be hurt, and capitalists (and consumers) usually don't care that it happens, but it's not necessary. In sport, the harm and sacrifice are the point.

The Youth Movement: Early Involvement in Violent Sport

To ensure that fans remain invested in sport leagues and that they continue to grow, professional sport leagues and teams also have a vested interest in the youth levels of the sport. Like any enterprise under capitalism, standing still means stagnation, and growth must be sought at all costs. In the case of the NFL, the youth of today are the beer drinking, fantasy football playing, sports gambling adults that sustain professional sports, and this means the NFL must ensure that children develop their love for the game.[27] While football is already part of the very fabric of many communities in the United States, especially in the South and Midwest, one of the best ways to grow interest and commitment to football is by actually having children play the game.

This has a double value for professional leagues like the NFL, as promotion of the game at youth levels both produces future fans and improves the quality of the future players (by starting them younger) who will populate the league. The same is important in boxing; as Macintosh Ross, a kinesiology professor who has written about boxing and athlete abuse, explains:

> To get to the point where you could be a world champion of boxing or an Olympic champion of boxing, you pretty much have to start as a child. So, unless we change the expectations at the very top, nothing's going to change at the very bottom. So, it'll always be a sport that draws children in way too young, that aren't able to make decisions about their brain health, that that maybe their parents can't make proper decisions or aren't making the best decisions about their brain health. . . . The argument for the promoters, of course, will be that the quality of boxer will go down dramatically. That's true, but the vast majority of people will be better off for it.

Promoting tackle football or boxing to children is the first step for those wishing to continue growing these sports, and it is perhaps the most dangerous. Dr. Chris Nowinski, formerly a collegiate football player and professional wrestler, and now neuroscientist who has become one of the leading voices on concussion in sport, has said that if there was one thing he could change about football instantly, it would be not allowing children to play tackle football until high school. While there may still be a commonly held belief among sport coaches, fans and parents that introducing contact in sports like hockey is actually *safer* for young athletes, because it teaches them proper hitting technique and the proper way to "take a hit," research has shown that this "experience" with collisions and body checking does not make athletes safer in the short or long term.[28]

Brains are still in their early stages of development before adolescence, and subjecting these brains to repeated head trauma at such ages is especially dangerous. Ross makes a similar point to Dr. Nowinski, advocating that children should not be allowed to box, both because of the inability to properly consent to injury risk, and because of the damage that repeated head injury does to developing brains. Taking an even sharper stance, Dr. Omalu has repeatedly said that when parents enroll their children in football, before the children are able to properly understand the risks of the sport, this is a form of child abuse.[29]

This does not mean that these children are being *forced* to play football or to box—at least not in the way we generally think about force, coercion, and consent. In many cases, children really want to play these sports. Children also might really want to drive a car, or eat candy for breakfast, lunch, and dinner. I think it's pretty obvious why we don't let them do these things—children are not mature enough and don't have the necessary information to make these kinds of decisions in a responsible way. Dr. Omalu and many others are arguing that parents *do* have the information about the harms of football or boxing, and that not acting on this information is a dereliction of their duties.

In the case of football, the sport also has an important cultural hold on significant parts of the United States. Combine parents' lack of knowledge and inaction with the cultural hegemony (the elevated importance and entrenched position atop the cultural hierarchy) that football maintains over many communities and the NFL's targeted attempts at cultivating youth fandom,[30] and it's no surprise that so many kids want to play and that so few parents are willing to say no. Allison Guiliotis reports that the NFL explicitly told her marketing firm that they wanted to "get to kids as early as possible," using fantasy football aimed at youth, cartoon TV shows, "sponsored education materials" at preschools and elementary schools, and targeted workshops with parenting bloggers.[31]

In these workshops, parents were even incentivized with merchandise, dinner, and restaurant coupons, which might be an even stronger draw for lower-income families that are already more likely to enroll their children in the sport. The NFL also deploys "everyday" people to champion their sport, running advertisement campaigns built around feel-good stories, with parents and athletes talking about what the sport has meant to them, how it may have lifted them into university and social mobility, or how it's brought their family together. The focus on these anecdotal cases obfuscates from the harm done by the sport. This kind of messaging also relies on neoliberal logic built around personal, educated choice (to play or not play football), often using the false presentation that all sport and all parts of life are dangerous, and therefore football is not any more so than any other activity.

Beyond its modern-day marketing, football has long held an outsized role in the American cultural zeitgeist, beginning from its roots as the quintessential "man's game" at the turn of the twentieth century. Sport has long been theorized as one of the primary ways men can "prove" and demonstrate their manhood and masculinity,[32] especially in violent sports like football, rugby, boxing, and hockey.

As explained in chapter 1, these masculine values promoted by organized capitalist sport also serve to justify capitalist relations of production. Young boys playing football, rugby, or hockey are taught to use violence, yes, but instrumentally. They are to use this violence to dominate, to win and beat their opponents at any cost, but also to play a specific role within their team and to obey their coach's commands. In its earliest iterations, sport, like the military, was thought of as a way to teach discipline and obedience to authority. It was even explicitly thought of as a way to prepare young working-class men both physically and mentally for military work and obedience. An article in the *United States Service Magazine* in 1910 declared that "training for sport is training for war."[33]

Football is still mythologized to teach boys how to become men,[34] and perhaps in a certain sense it does. Football teaches boys to be competitive, violent, obedient-to-authority cogs in a larger violent machine, willing to sacrifice their well-being for their "bosses." The primary goal is domination of the opponent; the only cooperation is between members of your own team, or in-group. From this perspective it is much easier to see the "close and abiding relationship between masculinism and capitalism—practiced, modelled, and animated through the culture of sport"[35] that writers like Varda Burstyn, Jean-Marie Brohm, and many others have written about.

Even if you do believe that football is a net positive for society at large, due to the values it teaches, it is far from the only sport or activity that can provide benefits like socialization and physical health, or learning accountability, teamwork, and the value of hard work. Other, less violent team sports like basketball, volleyball, handball, and dance (among many others) teach many of the same lessons about teamwork while promoting physical health, and youth can learn all of these skills through a variety of activities beyond sport altogether, through artistic or other cultural pursuits. It would be ridiculous to claim that *only* football teaches important skills and lessons. Violent sport, in general, is far from the only way to teach youth whatever values we hold most dear in a particular society.

Violence and Fighting in Hockey

Moving away from football and boxing, elite hockey has many of the same injury issues, including some related to CTE. Like with football, violence is intimately connected to the sport's history and mythology. Canadian hockey masculinity, which has been studied at length by sport scholars Kirsti Allain, Cheryl MacDonald, and others[36] is based on a mythologized heterosexual, white-settler masculinity that privileges toughness, playing through pain, self-sacrifice, and group loyalty to one's team and to the larger hockey in-group (which has historically been white, male, and heterosexual). This form of masculinity is not unique to Canada either, as hockey culture more generally shares many of these same characteristics.

Ignoring (for now; don't worry, we'll get to it in chapter 5) the effects that hockey culture has on rampant misogynistic treatment and sexual violence against women by male hockey players,[37] the privileging of this type of masculinity, combined with capitalist profit imperatives in sports, sets the stage perfectly for an environment where physical injury and harm is ever-present. From a young age, violence is taught in hockey as instrumental and necessary to the ultimate goal of winning.[38] Athletes receive positive reinforcement for playing through pain, and they are shunned and ostracized if they are not willing to "sacrifice" for their teams.[39] If hockey players want to progress in their sport, it is imperative that they internalize the warrior mentality that is present from the lowest levels of the sport—to "rub some dirt in it" and "play through it." They are expected to play through broken bones, torn ligaments, and chronic pain, and to continue to take and deliver body checks and to block shots coming in at over 80 miles per hour.

Fighting is also still legal in most professional and semiprofessional leagues in North America and has been a major part of the culture of the sport since its inception. Hockey is the only sport that allows players to bare knuckle box;[40] for some players, fighting is their primary role on the team, and the main reason they're employed. Unsurprisingly, we've seen several early deaths and postmortem CTE diagnoses of former NHL fighters, though not as many as in the NFL.

While some might again point to "human nature," or the "natural violence" inherent to players who fight, many enforcers have described their role as nightmarish. Georges Laracque, who finished his thirteen-year, 695-game NHL career with 53 goals and 131 fights (about one fight every five games), explained the anxiety and stress of a career as a fighter, in a CNN article in 2011:[41] "It's the night before, the day of the game, before it starts. It's the shivers that it gives you, the worry in the head and the brain. It's when you go to a movie and you can't watch it because you're thinking the next game about having to fight Derek Boogaard or someone like that. Or you don't feel well, but something happens and you have to go out there.... It's that pressure that's nonstop that you live with." The expectation that hockey players fight through pain, injury, and fear is exponentially higher for enforcers. While skilled players who are employed for their ability to score goals, create chances, or defend can try to keep themselves out of harm's way (though they are still expected to play through injury), for fighters, once again, the violence is the point. It is fairly common during preseason games in the NHL and at lower-tier leagues to hear announcers explain that a young, scrappy player is trying to "earn his spot" on the team by fighting. Add in the fact that many elite hockey players have little education or other skills to fall back on if their hockey career doesn't work out, and enforcers have little real choice in fighting and risking severe concussion and future brain-related issues.

At the highest levels of hockey, there is some hope that things are changing, though it's taken major tragedy (and other factors unrelated to player protection) to get to this point. In the summer of 2011, the sudden, early deaths of NHL enforcers Wade Belak (age 35), Derek Boogaard (28), and Rick Rypien (27) over just a four-month span prompted more mainstream coverage of the risks of fighting. It brought to light the experiences of enforcers, as described by Laracque above, and produced increased conversation about the harms of fighting.

And fighting has decreased in the NHL in recent years; there were 734 fights in the 2008–2009 season,[42] 320 in 2021–2022, and 311 in 2023–2024. The anti-fighting chorus that long existed on the fringes of hockey has also become much more mainstream in the last ten to fifteen years, with sport scholars and physicians calling for an outright ban on fighting.[43]

Some of the reduction in fighting is due to a better understanding of its harms and (somewhat relatedly) to less appetite from fans. Teams have also perhaps realized, thanks to some research on the matter, that fighting might not sell like they thought it did.[44] This is an especially interesting development given that NHL fans seem no less entertained by the controlled violence of the sport and its brutal body contact. Moreover, when players do fight, crowds do seem to still (anecdotally) react with excitement. In the 2023–2024 season, New York Rangers forward Matt Rempe became a cult hero and fan favorite for fighting three times in the first five games of his Rangers career,[45] demonstrating that there may still be some bloodthirst among NHL fans.

It is equally important to keep in mind that a lot of this reduction in fighting can also be linked to improvements in player evaluation and performance analytics in hockey.[46] As teams and scouts have used more advanced methods of player evaluation, they've learned that pure enforcers (who do little else but fight) do not provide a lot of value for teams in terms of improving their chances of winning.[47] Elite teams have realized that they are better off filling the roster spot that they used to use on an enforcer with another skilled player. In short, protecting players from injury and harm is not necessarily the motivation for reducing fighting. Since at the highest levels of pro hockey, wins drive revenue and keep management employed, reductions in fighting often come down to pure cost/benefit calculations.

This also becomes clear when we consider the still-common presence of fighting in lower-level pro hockey leagues. According to HockeyFights.com,[48] in the 2021–2022 season, the NHL had 320 total fights in 1,312 total games—about one fight for every four games. In the same year, the East Coast Hockey League (ECHL) had 437 fights in 972 games, or about one every *two* games.

Even Canadian junior hockey—a feeder system consisting of the Quebec Major Junior Hockey League (QMJHL), the Ontario Hockey League (OHL), and the Western Hockey League (WHL)—whose rosters are made up of unpaid sixteen- to nineteen-year-olds, still mostly allows fighting. While the QMJHL took the important and much-needed decision to ban fighting starting in 2023–2024, there were 255 fights in the OHL (one every 2.66 games) and 319 fights in the WHL (one every 2.34 games) in the 2023–2024 season.

Move to significantly lower-level leagues like the Southern Professional Hockey League (SPHL) and Ligue Nord-Américain de Hockey (LNAH) and the number of fights balloons upward. In these leagues, fighting is often the main draw the teams are selling. In the 2023–2024 SPHL season, there were 175 fights in 224 games, or one every 1.28 games. In the LNAH, there were 118 fights in 84 games in 2021–2022, or *more than one (1.4) every game.*

The range for SPHL salaries is US$200–$800 per week over a twenty-five-week schedule (US$5,000–$20,000 per season); LNAH players are paid an average of CA$275–$600 per game, or CA$7,700–$16,800 for a twenty-eight-game season.[49] In lower-level professional and semiprofessional hockey, it is those making the least who take on the most risk of severe, long-term, and debilitating head injury. And in these leagues, as long as fighting continues to sell tickets, it is unlikely to stop.

The same is true in lower-level professional leagues outside of North America. British sport scholar Victoria Silverwood, who has studied the lesser-known British Hockey League (BHL), describes an environment where players are structurally coerced into fighting, incentivized with extra pay, food, and beer if they are willing to fight. These small "payments" are all based around maintaining profits for the organizations employing these players, with no care for the impacts this violence has down the line. Many of the players Silverwood has spoken to describe early-onset ALS or dementia, fentanyl and methadone addictions stemming from their time in professional hockey, and other substance issues, culminating in early deaths for some of these players and their former teammates.

Exponential Harm: Injury and Painkillers

Injury and expectations around playing through these injuries has also resulted in painkiller addiction and overuse for many collision sport athletes, including most prominently hockey and football players. As seen from Silverwood's work in the BHL, this kind of addiction is not limited to the upper echelons of professional sport.

In a 2020 investigation, Canadian journalist Rick Westhead documented how players are taught and forced to play through injury. This teaching and coercion are done both explicitly and implicitly, through the culture of the sport and the constant pressure to perform for fear of being replaced.[50] This pressure, both internal and external, pushes players toward using painkillers, with Toradol emerging as the most popular for players in the NHL and other sports. According to former NHL star Ryan Kesler, "every single player in that locker room is on a painkiller" of some sort. He aptly summed up why: "When it was really bad, I'd use Toradol. I never wanted to hurt the team, so I knew I had to play. And to play, you gotta take painkillers, because if you don't do that, you're going to be labeled as a guy that doesn't battle through injuries.... That mindset, it made me want to play every game. I'm focusing on the now, I'm going to take a pill, I'm not going to worry about what happens to me 15 years down the road."[51] This is the culture that exists in hockey, where injury is exacerbated by the short-term prevention methods players feel forced to use, so that by the time their career is finished, they might have destroyed their hips and knees or have brain injury, along with painkiller addiction or complications from painkiller overuse. In

Kesler's case, his Toradol use resulted in colitis and several ulcers, and finally Crohn's disease.

There is no comprehensive tracking of Toradol or other painkillers in the NHL or NFL. Though doctors recommend that Toradol should not be used for more than five days consecutively, and should be used only in extreme cases, some NHL players have reported using the drug before every regular season or playoff game, so fifty to one hundred times a year.

Kesler was known and celebrated for playing through pain, but now admits that players are not in a position—given hockey culture's privileging of toughness, the accountability players feel toward their teammates and coaches to keep playing, and the pressure they feel to not be replaced—to make the right decisions about their long-term health. Research by sport scholars on how rugby players,[52] boxers,[53] and other athletes[54] neutralize concussion and other injury concerns is also revealing here. Athletes feel they know and understand their own bodies better than any "outsiders," including medical experts. While there is some good reason not to blindly trust in the words of team-employed doctors, "players' decisions about risk and concussion are framed by an institutional structure and a set of cultural values which prioritise sporting over health-related values and which reward serious risk taking."[55] Athletes internalize messaging around toughness and risk, based on ideas passed down from one athlete to the next, without proper analysis of the harms suffered by their peers.

Similar decision making by players occurs in football, where there are few available roster spots and careers average only three years.[56] Supply and demand, fueled by the dream sold early and often to young football players, ensures that athletes are always at risk of replacement if they don't or can't perform. There is always another young, comparatively healthier college football player rising the ranks. It is no surprise that Chris Borland and Andrew Luck, two of the players most famous for leaving promising NFL careers early due to injury concerns, were white players who came from relatively more affluent backgrounds than many of their peers.

Players—especially many aspiring NFL players from poorer communities—know that they have to maximize their short careers to make as much money as possible, and don't feel they can afford to think about their future health. In some cases, they also don't know the risks. Former All-Star NFL cornerback Byron Jones had a message similar to Kesler's, tweeting in February 2023:[57] "Today I can't run or jump because of my injuries sustained playing this game. DO NOT take the pills they give you. DO NOT take the injections they give you. If you absolutely must, consult an outside doctor to learn the long-term implications.... It was an honor and privilege to play in the NFL but it came at a regrettable cost I did not foresee. In my opinion, no amount of professional success or financial gain is worth avoidable chronic pain and disabilities. Godspeed to the draft class of 2023."

Former NHL defenseman Kyle Quincy also suggested players take team doctor recommendations with a grain of salt, emphasizing that these doctors are employed by their teams, not by the athletes. He explained that beyond letting him play through major injuries, team doctors did not and generally do not tell players about the side effects and addictive potential of painkillers like Toradol. From a profit maximization perspective, this makes sense. Professional sport organizations pay their players to perform, not to sit out due to injury. Under the framework of capitalist sport, the goal is to extract as much value as possible out of athletes for as long as they are employed, or as long as they continue to provide this value for ownership, management, and other stakeholders.

How They Get Away with It: Denial, Deflection, and if All Else Fails, the Illusion of Choice

I could spend the rest of this book just documenting horror stories of athlete physical harm and cases of injury mismanagement, in sports as varied as rugby, gymnastics, figure skating, soccer, boxing, and basketball. In rugby, concussion is common and expected, and former players are beginning to be diagnosed with CTE;[58] like football, there are similar macho expectations of "playing through the pain" in the sport.[59] Elite gymnastics and figure skating are known for abusive coaching and overtraining, resulting in spinal and joint injuries.[60] Overuse leaves elite men's and women's tennis players with muscle and ligament strains and long-term damage.[61] Football players suffer from heat exhaustion at higher rates than any other athletes; players weighing over 300 pounds are still forced to practice twice a day in the blistering August sun.[62]

These problems arise because of the structures and profit imperatives of elite and professional sport under capitalism, not just because of a few bad-apple coaches or teams. Structural factors mean that athlete (worker) well-being is sacrificed for performance, athletes are treated as labor to be squeezed out and thrown away, and injury and harm help provide the stakes and importance that make fans feel so invested.

But how do sport organizations, leagues, and those in charge get away with all of this? If we know about the injury and harm that athletes suffer, how do they avoid blame and responsibility for changing these conditions?

In short: denial, deflection, and if all of that fails, good old-fashioned PR spin.

Denial and Deflection

The NFL and other sporting bodies have known about the disastrous effects of violence on brain injury for years, and in the case of football, since well before Omalu's initial diagnosis in 2005. The first football concussion crisis happened in 1906, when the Harvard football team reported 145 injuries in one season, many of them concussions.[63] Many US pacifists already thought the game was too violent, and these repeated injuries, and eighteen deaths in football games in 1905,[64] eventually led President Teddy Roosevelt to make several changes to the game to increase safety.

While these changes may have stopped the deaths, they did not stop brain injuries. In 1928, pathologist Harrison Martland published a report on "punch-drunk syndrome" in the prestigious *Journal of the American Medical Association* (*JAMA*). The focus of Martland's article was predominantly boxing, but another researcher at this time, Edward Carroll Jr., "noted that 'punch-drunk is said to occur among professional football players also' and urged officials to make it clear to laypeople and athletes that 'repeated minor head impacts' could expose them to 'remote and sinister effects.'"[65] Other research from the NCAA and academic journals in the 1940s and 1950s continued to link these kinds of "sinister effects" with head injury, and specifically with head injury from boxing and football.

Like tobacco or fossil fuel companies, the NFL knew about the harms of its product, but did all that it could to shield themselves from blame. The league tried so hard to deny and deflect their sport's breeding of concussion, brain injury, and early death that they made a movie about it. And I'm not talking about some small indie documentary from a radical filmmaker. In *Concussion*, Will Smith stars as Dr. Omalu, and though the film was not a huge box office success, it did bring wider recognition to concussion and brain injury problems that are part and parcel of playing football. Maybe just as importantly, it also brought attention to the lengths that sport leagues like the NFL will go to protect their reputation, brand, and their capital, even when all the evidence points against them.

Dr. Omalu was treated to the whole suite of vilifications that meet scientists who make discoveries that could threaten the business interests of powerful capitalists. His work on former NFL star Mike Webster's brain was immediately attacked; it was claimed to have "serious flaws" by three members of the NFL's Mild Traumatic Brain Injury (MTBI) committee.[66] None of these three were neuropathologists, and the head of the committee was a rheumatologist,[67] a specialty of medicine that works in the "diagnosis (detection) and treatment of diseases that affect the muscles, bones, joints, ligaments, and tendons," according to rheumatology.org. Nothing in there about brains.

Not only did the NFL 's MTBI committee refuse to believe the evidence of Webster's brain trauma at his death, but they also refused to acknowledge the harm the sport had caused him while he was alive. Webster had shown clear signs of brain injury and memory loss, and was evaluated by four separate doctors, who all confirmed that he had a closed-head injury due to multiple concussions. When Webster's lawyer, Bob Fitzsimmons, applied for disability from the NFL, Webster was awarded the lowest possible level: partial disability, and $3,000 a month. This came even after the NFL's own doctor evaluated Webster and found that he had a closed-head brain injury. Thankfully, Fitzsimmons filed and won an appeal with the US District Court, which reversed the decision of the NFL's pension board, the first time in history this had happened. Even after this ruling, the NFL continued to fight, claiming that Webster, "who had endured probably 25,000 violent collisions during his career and now was living on Pringles and Little Debbie pecan rolls, who was occasionally catatonic, in a fetal position for days," did not qualify for disability.[68]

The NFL demanded a retraction of Dr. Omalu's work, published in the prestigious academic journal *Neurosurgery*. Thankfully, the editorial board of *Neurosurgery* refused. A year later Omalu published a second article in the same journal, after examining the brain of Terry Long, another former player, who died at forty-five when he drank antifreeze after suffering years of symptoms similar to Webster's. Omalu described Long's brain as being like that of a "90-year-old with advanced Alzheimer's."[69]

The NFL responded by calling Omalu's work "speculative" and "preposterous." In a 2007 press conference, the head of the MTBI committee stated that "the only scientifically valid evidence of CTE in athletes is in boxers and in some steeplechase jockeys. It's never been scientifically, validly documented in any other athletes."[70] To the NFL, apparently two published articles in a top peer-reviewed neuroscience journal did not count as "scientifically valid." Omalu continued to be vilified and delegitimized by the NFL, with friends warning that he had perhaps bitten off more than he could chew by trying to go after the league. When Omalu originally published the research, he naively thought that the NFL would be receptive to it and would use the research to try to take care of the problem.

Now fifteen years later, over 345 former NFL players have been officially diagnosed with CTE, including Demariyus Thomas, a former All-Star wide receiver who died in 2021 at age *thirty-three*. Sadly, these numbers will only continue to go up, as CTE can only be diagnosed postmortem, and not all players' families agree to donate the players' brains to be studied. The NFL has reluctantly—but never explicitly—recognized the sport's impact on the brains of its players, settling a class-action lawsuit from players for approximately $700 million in 2017, and making minor rule changes over the last ten years.

It should also be noted that a 2024 *Washington Post* investigation of 15,000 documents and 200 interviews found that the NFL has used all sorts of legal workarounds and machinations to avoid paying players out of this settlement, including denying independent neurologists' diagnoses of dementia using their own extremely high threshold for diagnosis, stalling on approving medical evaluations, and even denying their *own* hired doctors' claims.[71] In one example, a player's dementia claim (based on an approved diagnosis from a doctor who had been observing the player for years) was denied because the player continued to drive and exercise, even though the doctor in question says that he actually *recommends* that his patients exercise for as long as they can, in part to offset or delay the impacts of their brain injuries. This athlete was trying to take care of himself after the harm inflicted on him by the NFL, and because he attempted to slow the progression of his illness the NFL refused payout for him. In another example, a player was diagnosed with dementia by his own doctor in 2016, after getting lost while driving so often that his family put a GPS tracker on his car. Two years later, he did not score low enough on the NFL's settlement test to qualify, even though he was diagnosed with dementia according to the standard medical definition.[72]

It should come as no surprise that since the 2017 settlement, the league has approved 900 dementia claims and denied 1,100 others. Fourteen of these men died before receiving their settlements, and were diagnosed with CTE postmortem. Importantly, this settlement also only covers players with a (NFL-approved) diagnosis of dementia, and does not cover other "behavioral and mood-related symptoms associated with CTE, such as depression and rage-control problems."[73]

In terms of rule changes, the NFL now penalizes targeting the head and helmet-to-helmet contact, but these rules generally only apply to "skill position players" like receivers, running backs, and quarterbacks. The battles in the proverbial "trenches" between offensive and defensive lineman are still full of blows to the brain and are rarely, if ever, penalized. Many unpenalized plays also still produce the type of head trauma that can result in CTE.

A 2020 study from the journal *BMJ Open Sport & Exercise Medicine* found that the new rules implemented by the league "have proven too weak to make the NFL game safer."[74] This same study did show that players missed more time due to head injuries, perhaps due to better understanding of the severity of these issues—but this is thanks to Dr. Omalu and other independent researchers, not the NFL. An increase in missed games from head injuries could also be due to players simply suffering more serious head injuries that require more time off.

The NFL unsurprisingly contends that their protocols on concussions are working, and they've found quite an ingenious way to make this claim. When the number of concussions in a particular year is down from the previous year, the league claims it's a sign that the game is less violent and causing less injury; when the number of concussions is up, the league claims this is "evidence" that the warrior culture around football is improving, because players and teams are more likely to admit to pain and diagnose it properly.[75] This is "heads I win, tails you lose" logic, but about changing the narratives on debilitating and deadly brain injury.

Even if the rate of concussions *has* come down in recent years, and assuming that these rates are a true reflection of what's happening on the field (quite the assumption, given both players' and teams' desire to "play through the pain" and not miss games), concussion totals in the NFL remain extremely high. The three-year average from 2015–2017 was 266 per season, with a high of 281 in 2017, followed by 214 in 2018 and 224 in 2019. Ignoring the COVID-shortened season in 2020 (which had four fewer preseason games), there were 187 concussions in 2021, 213 in 2022, and 219 in 2023.[76] This *is* small progress, but we shouldn't lose sight of the raw total—219 *recorded* concussions, in one year, for a professional sports league, is an absurd number. Dressing this up as "protecting players" and as some sort of grand improvement is insulting to the players, their families, and the many who have seen their loved ones' health deteriorate following their football careers. It is also important to stress that CTE does not come directly from concussions, but from repeated hits to the head, which even non-concussed football players suffer constantly.

While the NFL may be the deadliest case of a league and team sport shielding itself from blame for the injuries of its athletes, it is far from the only one. The NHL, the junior leagues that feed into it, and the variety of low-paid professional and semiprofessional leagues around North America are also known for their physical play. The culture around hockey takes warrior masculinity to a level unlike any other sport, other than perhaps football and rugby.

As explained above, hockey players are expected to play through all sorts of pain and injury, including head injuries. Take the NHL playoffs, which have two major traditions: (1) players grow out gnarly "playoff beards" in solidarity with their team (mostly harmless), and (2) fans, journalists, and former players fawn over players who announce, only once their team is eliminated, a list of horrible injuries they were playing through (definitely not harmless). In the 2022 playoffs, many celebrated the fact that the Colorado Avalanche's Andre Burakovsky had played the last *eight games* of the playoffs with a *broken* ankle. The NHL has created and still upholds a culture where athletes are expected to play through these kinds of injuries, to the detriment of their current and future health.

In the 2019 NHL playoffs, the league released a 1-minute playoff montage/advertisement that showed nothing but player after player blocking shots—that is, blocking hard rubber disks flying at 50 to 90 miles per hour—while grimacing and wincing in pain on the ice and the bench. The masochistic ad finished by celebrating the "sacrifices" that players are willing to make to take home the Stanley Cup, the NHL's ultimate prize.[77] The league eventually took the ad down after some backlash, but if they were willing to promote this image to the public, just imagine what is expected of players behind closed doors.

While head injuries in violent sports like American football, ice hockey, rugby, and combat sports like boxing and MMA likely come to mind first (and for good reason), injury from overuse and *expectations* of overuse and playing through pain occur in everything from individual sports like gymnastics, tennis, and track and field to team sports like volleyball, basketball, and soccer. They also happen in both men's and women's elite sport. Stories of former athletes unable to throw a ball, fathers who can't bend down to play with their kids, and mothers and other women who can no longer run without pain are so common that they don't even make the news.

Thankfully, the work and advocacy of sport scholars, (some) media, and athletes themselves have made the links between overtraining and these medical problems impossible to ignore. Sport organizations and their PR machines, however, have not decided to simply, as the kids say, "take the L" and admit that they're to blame. The impossible-to-deny link between overtraining, sky-high expectations, athlete warrior mentality, and debilitating injury has simply caused them to shift their blame-avoiding strategies—focusing instead on narratives of choice and agency.

The War on Science May Be Lost: On to the Narrative Battle

The "warrior" mentality that we see in the NHL, NFL, and other sports isn't just a matter of sport culture. Athletes do not pop painkillers, withstand cortisone shots, and play through wooziness just because they feel a sense of kinship with their teammates or coaches or because they want to seem tough. The win-at-all-costs nature of sport and the capitalist imperatives to win and dominate mean that athletes are constantly at risk of losing their spot, being replaced, having their reputation tarnished, and ruining their chance to earn money from their athletic labor. The idea that athletes have any real choice on whether to participate in the most violent and harmful aspects of their sport is a fantasy that leagues and sport organizations use to avoid taking responsibility for the harm athletes suffer.

Due to the work of people like Dr. Omalu, as well as other sports doctors, scientists, critical journalists, academics, and some former athletes and their family members, leagues have more trouble than they used to in hiding the connection between their sports and the major injuries their athletes suffer. This has moved the battleground from the realm of science and the dangers of sport to one of narratives around choice. The narrative terrain is well-trodden: *Sure, football may be dangerous, but the players choose to play. They know the risks. Gymnasts can just quit if they don't want to get hurt. No one is forcing them to play football. NHL players can just sit out if they're injured.*[78]

These narratives bring to the forefront ideas around consent and coercion in sport, and especially in violent sport. Sport scholar Kevin Young, who has written extensively about sport-related violence, explains that "much of what happens in sport, including sport-related violence, is rationalized on the basis that athletes are seen to consent to it."[79] Much of the violence we see in sport, especially in terms of injury and harm suffered *by* athletes, is justified by fans, coaches and even athletes by claiming that athletes understand the risks and potential rewards of their sport participation and consent to all of it.

This thinking throws context completely out the window. It assumes that all athletes (and all people) are in front of a buffet of great choices and are aware of the ingredients, side effects, and collateral damage of each one. For many athletes, both the assumption of choice and the assumption of knowledge about these choices are fantasies. Athletes are neither in front of a buffet—they are presented with only the option to play—nor do they know the ingredients of what is in front of them.

Football offers the best example of this. Football is not just promoted as a positive outlet for young boys to learn toughness, teamwork, and responsibility, but it is also framed as the main potential "way out" of precarious economic circumstances for many youth in poor, often-Black American communities. Retired NFL running back Thomas Jones, on the Associated Press Pro Football Podcast in 2022, talked about how he's not sure he would've played football knowing what he knows now about football's links with CTE and brain trauma, and doesn't think he would let his own children play the sport. But he also noted that football was his "only outlet, it was almost like a one-way ticket."[80] Looking back on it, Jones felt he had no choice but to play football, because it was his chance for some financial stability, either through a professional career or at least via a full-ride scholarship to university.

To give true and meaningful consent, the consent must be free, informed, and ongoing. For years, many athletes have *not* known the risks of playing their sport, as leagues and powerful structures within those sports have done whatever they can to obfuscate links between severe long-term injury and the sport, or downplay the risk entirely, as explained above. But I would argue that the "informed" part of consent is not even what's most at issue here. Many athletes do *now* understand the risks of their sport and participate anyway. Whether they are truly "free" to consent is another story entirely.

From a Marxist perspective, freedom is not understood from the classical liberal standpoint as simply "independence from the arbitrary will of another."[81] It is not just about *negative* liberty, or the ability to make choices without constraints; instead it's about *positive* liberty, which is based on having the social conditions necessary to achieve a goal. In the case of decision making, positive liberty means having the social conditions necessary to be able to make a choice.

For another example of negative and positive liberty, consider housing policy. A policy that no one can be discriminated against in the purchasing of property would be an example of negative liberty; there is a prohibition on personal infringement on someone's ability to purchase. An example of positive liberty in this same housing sphere would be a policy guaranteeing a minimum level of housing for each person, within certain minimum standards. Here, there is a guarantee of getting something, rather than a guarantee of not being blocked by another person or entity from getting that thing. If you do not have the money for a house, the negative liberty described above would mean very little to you, especially compared to a positive guarantee.

Marxist conceptions of freedom are based far more in the structural, and specifically in the structural constraints of capitalist society. Under capitalism, the only commodity that workers can sell is their labor power, and thus if this is our only means of survival, this is not real freedom.[82] In short, if our "choice" is between selling our labor power or being without food and shelter, then this is not really a choice at all. Negative liberty means very little, because it does not matter if, technically, there's no person stopping us from refusing to work, if in reality we are forced to work nonetheless. Put another way, if an athlete has to choose between getting hit in the head a bunch but having food on the table and a warm place to sleep at night, or avoiding the head trauma but going hungry and homeless, is that really a choice? To be clear, I am not arguing that all young men are left with only a binary choice between violent sports and starvation. However, it is important to understand that athletes' choices and the consent they give are only truly "free" if there are legitimate alternatives for life success and social mobility.

The lack of these alternatives and choices in contemporary capitalist society is what allows for structural coercion to occur in sports. Structural coercion involves "the ways in which the broader context acts upon individuals to compel them" to behave in a specific way.[83] It's a term closely linked to structural violence—the "social arrangements that put individuals and populations in harm's way."[84] These "social arrangements" or "broader context" refer to the political, economic, and social organization of the world we live in, and the constraints that people thus live under. Living under cutthroat capitalism—and the dearth of real opportunities that stem from it—is the primary constraint that exists for most people, and in the realm of sport, its impacts are incredibly far-reaching.[85]

The fact that many young men believe (and are often correct in believing) that their best way to make a better life for themselves and their families is through excelling in violent sport is an example of a structural constraint. The fact that the university is a path to upward social mobility but is unaffordable for most in the United States[86]—except if they excel at football or another sport—is another example. These facts, and the broader capitalist system that they stem from, coerce young athletes into "making choices" that are never really choices at all.

Structural coercion shifts our understanding of the "coercer" from a particular individual forcing someone to do something, to the entire social structure around them. Sure, there are individual coaches or parents who may force a child to play football, to keep practicing their gymnastics or figure skating routine even when their back and ankles ache, or to get back on the ice after getting crunched into the boards, but the structural coercion of capitalist society and capitalist sport on athletes can be just as powerful. You can have the kindest, most supportive coach in the world, and still be in a situation of structural coercion and structural violence.

The win-at-all-costs, next-(wo)man-up nature of capitalist sport means that players are expected to endure physical pain, blows to the brain, sprained joints, broken bones, heat exhaustion, and abusive coaches. If they don't want to play, they can watch themselves get replaced, and lose their chance to get a college offer or make the junior national team. If they're already in college, maybe they get a reputation as a "whiner," someone who "doesn't care about the team," or (worst of all) as "soft" or not tough.

Knowing that their status as athletes is so heavily impacted by coaches and management can paint athletes into a dark corner with very little agency. It is the reason University of Maryland football player Jordan MacNair died after continuing to practice to the point of heat exhaustion; he died arriving at the hospital with an internal body temperature of 41 degrees Celsius (105.8°F), hours after practice ended.[87] Or why NHL player Dan Carcillo—whose career eventually ended because of too many concussions—learned to "game" the NHL's concussion imPACT test by intentionally performing poorly on the baseline assessment in the summer, "so that you can pass it if you do happen to get injured (and) come back sooner."[88] Unfortunately, these are only a few examples of structural and status coercion leading to harm. As long as sport maintains capitalist imperatives of winning and revenue above athlete safety, the stories will continue to pile up.

When we say that athletes could just quit or refuse to play when they are injured, and that their not doing so implies consent to the pain and harm they may endure, we are ignoring all of the structural and status coercion that lies behind these "decisions." This is what organizations want us as viewers and consumers of sport to do, because it ignores *their* role in creating conditions that put athletes in no-win situations. This kind of thinking is also present in narratives around the "free" market and "agency" under capitalism more generally. As explained in chapter 1, sport values thus act to reinforce capitalist and neoliberal values based around "freedom" (which isn't really freedom at all), meritocracy, and personal responsibility

This discourse places ultimate responsibility on individuals for the choices they make, even when there are no good options to choose from. Under this perverse structure, if a person living in a neighborhood where there aren't any proper grocery stores buys unhealthy food, it's that individual's fault, not the fault of the city, state, or county for allowing for food deserts where no healthy food is available. It is the service worker's fault for getting COVID and infecting their family, not the fault of the state that doesn't provide adequate safety measures at work or paid leave for those who are unwell, so that the worker doesn't have to choose between missing work because they're sick or keeping the heat on at home. In contemporary capitalist sport, it is the athlete's fault for "consenting" to participate in dangerous sports and playing through debilitating injuries, not the fault of a larger sport culture that preaches toughness and playing through pain, of ownership and management that are ready to replace athletes the moment they are no longer "valuable," or of a broader social system that puts so many young people in situations where their only path to social mobility is through these violent sports. Capitalism structures the choices we make, and elite capitalist sport is no different; athletes are not *choosing* to play their sport in unsafe work conditions, at least not in any meaningful way.

CHAPTER THREE

Outside the Lines
Violence against Athletes outside of the Field of Play

It all started when I was 13 or 14 years old, at one of my first National Team training camps, in Texas, and it didn't end until I left the sport. It seemed whenever and wherever this man could find the chance, I was "treated." . . . For me, the scariest night of my life happened when I was 15 years old. I had flown all day and night with the team to get to Tokyo. He'd given me a sleeping pill for the flight, and the next thing I know, I was all alone with him in his hotel room getting a "treatment." I thought I was going to die that night.

Because the National Team training camps did not allow parents to be present, my mom and dad were unable to observe what Nassar was doing, and this has imposed a terrible and undeserved burden of guilt on my loving family. . . . People should know that sexual abuse of children is not just happening in Hollywood, in the media or in the halls of Congress. This is happening everywhere. Wherever there is a position of power, there seems to be potential for abuse. I had a dream to go to the Olympics, and the things that I had to endure to get there, were unnecessary and disgusting.

—McKayla Maroney, Victim Impact Statement, *Michigan v. Nassar*, December 22, 2020

US Olympic gymnast McKayla Maroney was just one of the over 150 athletes Dr. Larry Nassar sexually abused when he was team doctor for the Michigan State University (MSU) gymnastics team and for USA Gymnastics (USAG), the governing body for US Olympic gymnastics teams. Nassar worked with USAG as its head medical coordinator from 1996–2015.[1] The first allegation of inappropriate behavior came from a parent in 1997. Nassar was finally convicted of sexual abuse in 2017 and received a life sentence, after hundreds of girls and women came forward.

Nassar's behavior was despicable, and the fact that he *initially* engaged in this behavior does not fall at the feet of USAG or MSU. But those organizations' failure to respond to frequent complaints—covering up allegations and continuing to employ him for almost twenty years—does. The USAG and MSU kept Nassar around, or at the very least did not sufficiently investigate his behavior when complaints were made. According to the criteria they cared about—victories, medals, success—he was doing a great job. As former

US National Gymnastics team member Jennifer Sey explained:[2] "Gymnastics and the US Olympic Committee didn't want to scare off sponsors and they didn't want to risk the piles of Olympic medals. So they covered it up. And at a certain point they were so far in on the cover up that they were implicated. So they dug in deeper to protect themselves from criminal and civil liability." In his own statement at the trial, Nassar even said something similar, claiming, "I was a good doctor because my treatments worked."[3] Nassar was constantly massaging the women and girls (some as young as thirteen) under his care, often in their hotel rooms or other private areas. He massaged the genital areas of the young women in the gymnastics programs without gloves, and there were several reported cases of digital penetration. But Nassar was protected by the institutions in power, and as long as the teams kept winning, nothing was done about athlete complaints.[4]

These elite gymnasts also described a pressure-filled environment where they felt silenced and forced to receive ongoing "treatment" from Nassar to be able to practice, improve, and keep their prestigious spots on the team. From one of the affidavits in the Nassar trial: "Victim B stated that as a competitive gymnast, you would do anything to get yourself better and that the coaches were always pressuring them to get better. She said it was like you were always in trouble if you were hurt. At the time, she thought she had to submit to this treatment to get better and never told her parents because she had to get better. Victim B stated that she and all the gymnasts trusted Nassar and that he was like a god to the gymnasts."[5]

To Joan Ryan, who wrote *Little Girls in Pretty Boxes* about the abusive practices in gymnastics, the sport is uniquely suited for this type of abuse, gaslighting, and cover-up. "These girls are groomed from an incredibly young age to deny their own experience. Your knee hurts? You're being lazy. You're hungry? No, you're fat and greedy. They are trained to doubt their own feelings, and that's why this could happen to over 150 of them." The environment created and maintained by USAG (and many other sport organizations) has been conceptualized by some scholars as an example of *institutional violence*, which includes "norms of violence caused by the socio-organizational context of certain sport environments."[6]

Though Ryan is correct that gymnastics is rife with abuse, the conditions she describes exist in all manner of elite sports. Jerry Sandusky's sexual abuse of Penn State football players was swept under the rug for years, as the football team and its longtime head coach Joe Paterno, who knew about the allegations, were celebrated for their continued success on the field.[7] Kyle Beach[8] and Theo Fleury[9] were sexually abused by authority figures in their hockey careers. In 2023, tennis coaches in France[10] and the Netherlands[11] were arrested for sexual abuse of female and male players, and Sierra Leone's women's football team has come forward with allegations of inappropriate sexual behavior.[12] The QMJHL is investigating widespread hazing and bullying practices,[13] and Canadian gymnasts are speaking out about all manner of abusive coaching practices. Sexual, psychological, and emotional abuse are not limited to one particular sport, to one particular sex, or to one specific type of coach or authority figure.

In this chapter, we'll look at why this is the case, how this abuse persists, and what we can do about it.

Institutional Violence and Abusive Coaching: the Case of Canadian Gymnastics

Elite sport environments are too often sites of institutional violence. Whether it's national teams, professional sports organizations, or elite college and even youth clubs, elite sports include intense training regimens and performance expectations, initiation and hazing routines, high media interest and pressure, and often, decentralized training centers that separate young athletes from their families and other support systems.[14] The infamous Karolyi Ranch, an elite USAG training center in Texas, epitomizes and embodies the institutional violence of some elite sport environments. Remotely located in the forests of southeast Texas, the ranch is a 2,000-acre property still owned by Bela and Martha Karolyi, former USAG coaches brought in because of their success at molding champions by whatever means necessary. The ranch was designated as the US Women's National Team Training Center in 2001, and the USAG National Team Training Center (for both women and men) in 2011.[15] For years US gymnasts were brought here to train, and were disciplined and surveilled by coaches and trainers, with no parental or adult supervision beyond those working for USAG. The ranch only closed in 2018, after Nassar, who abused athletes at the facility and was known to treat them at night on their beds, was sentenced to 175 years in prison.

These kinds of environments create relationships of dependency between athletes and their coaches or organizations, where the athletes are *structurally unable* to demand better working conditions and where abusive behavior is normalized. In elite sport bubbles, abusive behavior that would not be acceptable in any other sphere of life—try to imagine bosses yelling at their employees the way coaches often yell at their players—is normalized to the point that athletes might not even realize it's wrong.[16] This normalization is exacerbated by the fact that sport environments exist as an almost "separate space," or what Erving Goffman might have called a "total institution," with seemingly different rules and norms than "regular life."[17]

We know that the sport space is one where instrumental violence on the field and off of it are seen as "part of the game."[18] This is the sort of "positive deviance" that sport scholars Robert Hughes and Jay Coakley wrote about as early as the 1990s,[19] explaining how adherence to the "sport ethic" creates an alternative set of social norms that takes behaviors that would be unacceptable in conventional society and turns them into accepted and even *expected* practice. Conversely, protecting oneself and looking out for one's personal well-being are framed as a form of negative deviance from this same sport ethic.

Recent investigations into Canadian gymnastics have revealed how these sorts of conditions manifest. In a W5 investigation by CTV News in November 2022,[20] Canadian gymnasts opened up about the toxic culture in elite gymnastics, and how this culture promotes physical, emotional, psychological, and sexual abuse and harm. This culture often starts with coaches and, in the case of gymnastics especially, the deification of these coaches. Coaches often begin working with athletes as young as five years old, demanding obedience and creating unhealthy relationships of attachment and dependency. Melanie Rocca Hunt, a Canadian gymnast and athlete who participated under the tutelage of club and Canadian national team coach David Brubaker, described an environment where it was understood that "whatever Dave says, I need to do," including not "being caught eating junk food" and trying "not to cry."[21]

Disordered eating is a common problem in a variety of sports, and especially in gymnastics and other "aesthetic" sports where thin, lean bodies are expected and idealized.[22] Though it's not discussed as often, disordered eating and the problems that arise from it happen to both men and women, and athletes in general are more likely than nonathletes to engage in disordered eating[23] at all levels. In national, professional, and collegiate environments, athletes in sports like track and field, swimming, football, and wrestling[24] can be subject to invasive body composition tests that determine their standing on their teams. These tests can be invasive and harmful in and of themselves, not to mention their psychological toll and their potential to trigger disordered eating in those already prone to it.[25]

To be able to enact and maintain this sort of control over athletes' bodies and decisions, coaches also often create a mythology around their own expertise. Rocca Hunt's father recalls Brubaker *himself* saying that "he had to brainwash these kids and make them believe he's like an almighty" so that the girls could perform dangerous skills and trust him. Vladimir Lashin, another coach in Canada's elite system, was also described as holding himself "like a god" at his gym.

Lashin was known for berating his athletes, especially if they refused to perform a particular skill or stretch for fear of injury, or if they tried to advocate for themselves and their well-being.[26] Beyond the constant verbal and emotional abuse, Amelia Cline and Cassidy Jones, two of Lashin's athletes, both had hard falls in practice that ended their careers prematurely. They severely injured themselves when they were forced by Lashin and his wife Svetlana to perform skills that they were unprepared for. Both athletes, teenagers at the time, remember telling their coaches they didn't want to do what they were being asked to do. When Jones broke her leg, she was left on the ground without attention or treatment "for 45 minutes to an hour,"[27] and was eventually hospitalized. Both women today still suffer the physical and psychological impacts of having been forced to do whatever their coaches demanded of them when they were children and adolescents.[28]

This sort of physical overtraining is a feature of many elite sports, and it has disastrous consequences. Beyond the fact that overtraining is a form of abuse in and of itself that can result in lifelong and debilitating physical injury, it has a compounding effect with psychological and emotional abuse.[29] Along with early sport specialization, overtraining also makes athletes more vulnerable to other forms of abuse from those in positions of authority.[30] Young elite athletes in sports like gymnastics, swimming, and tennis can be especially vulnerable to all of these forms of abuse, as they are often isolated from parents and left alone with coaches. Early specialization and overtraining are also happening earlier and earlier, and becoming the norm for youth sports, even at non-elite levels in North America[31]—a product of the continued commercialization of sport and the hypercompetitive nature of leisure and cultural pursuits.

The all-encompassing world of elite gymnastics—and the total control ceded to coaches *who produce medals*—can also result in sexual abuse.[32] Canadian national team gymnast Abby Spadafora, also coached by David Brubaker, said she felt like "a little soldier" who was constantly trying to please Brubaker, while "absolutely petrified of him." She described inappropriate expectations of her and her teammates when they were on the road competing, as they were expected to kiss their coaches whenever they walked into or out of a room, when they woke up, and when they went to sleep. Spadafora recalls being told that this was "part of European culture." She was eventually told by

Brubaker that he "wanted to touch her" while in a hotel room at an international competition, part of a pattern of inappropriate massaging and sexual abuse that Rocca Hunt and other gymnasts also described.[33]

According to Tracy Vaillancourt, a violence prevention researcher at the University of Ottawa, these sorts of behaviors are the culmination of a long-term grooming process. Coaches create relationships of dependence and initiate a "grooming process, this gradual indoctrination," where "the perpetrator is trying to acclimatize you to this, and once you get used to these little indiscretions, they go to the next step, and the next step, and you find yourself in a position that you don't even understand how you got there."[34] Isolating athletes from their families, controlling their bodies through overtraining and weight management, and creating a sense of fear and idolization are all typical techniques used by coaches, and they mirror how domestic abusers control their victims.[35]

Coaches—as well as many sport fans and media commentators—often euphemistically refer to the kinds of coaching practices described above as simply "tough" or "old school." They cry that the world has "gone soft" and that "masculinity is in crisis!"[36] Given the long-entrenched imperative of winning, and the similarly long-held belief that athletes succeed in "tough love" environments led by "tough" coaches, some coaches even frame winning and well-being as an "either/or" proposition.[37] They think it is not possible to both succeed on the field *and* foster a positive, inclusive environment for athletes; former Dutch elite gymnastics coach Gerrit Beltman confessed as much, saying that he "went too far because (he) thought it was the only way to instill a winning mentality" in his athletes.[38]

Beyond the fact that empathetic, supportive coaching should be the norm for strictly *moral* reasons, this view is flawed from a performance-based perspective. Though we have seen abusive and controlling coaches "succeed" (in terms of their on-field results), there are also many who have failed. When teams or athletes with abusive coaches succeed, it's not clear if this success is due to the coach or in spite of them. We also almost never have the counterfactual: Would the same athlete or team have won without this coach or with a different coach? Asking whether dealing with abusive coaching is *worth* the psychological harm assumes that abusive coaching works in the first place, which is very often not the case.

Research from both outside and inside sports has found that positive reinforcement is more effective for producing better performance by employees,[39] without even considering the other short- and long-term benefits this kind of coaching or mentorship has. Yet the ubiquity of abusive coaching, and the generally accepted view that abusive coaching leads to winning, can also result in abusive practices being subconsciously understood (by athletes and the public) not just as acceptable but as proof of good coaching.[40] Even when these practices are not effective, people assume they are, because their own reference points for the "great coaches" of the past also engaged in this kind of behavior. This kind of flawed, inductive logic (e.g., "Bob Knight won a lot of games, Bob Knight was abusive and yelled at his players constantly, therefore all abusive coaching is good coaching") still permeates elite sport circles and is bolstered by win-at-all-costs imperatives.

What Can They Do? Structural Constraints for Athletes Responding to Abuse

Even when athletes identify that the behavior of their coaches or other authority figures has crossed a line—seeing past the normalization of abuse, indoctrination into masculinized sport culture, and the adults, coaches, and teammates telling them that they are just being "soft"—they are very often unable to meaningfully demand change. This inability to act is often due to the same structural violence and coercion described in chapter 2. When athletes know that their spot on a team or advancement in their sport hinges on the decisions of their coaches and sport institutions, and it is these same authorities that are harming them, they are left in an unequal power relationship that does not functionally allow them to speak up. Athletes may technically be at liberty to report their abuse, but if a coach's word is the difference between making the national team or being drafted following your collegiate career, this is not really a choice. As recently summed up by Fatmata Kamara, a former under-twenty international soccer player for Sierra Leone who spoke out against abusive coaching practices in her federation: "If you speak up, you're never gonna play soccer anymore. This is the threat."[41]

Speaking out about abuse often also requires that athletes push through one of sporting culture's strongest institutional norms, that of sport spaces—gyms, arenas, locker rooms, even team group chats—as "sacred spaces" that demand secrecy and loyalty.[42] These physical and ethereal spaces, which for professional and other elite athletes are functionally *workplaces*, are discursively constructed by sport culture, coaches, and athletes as spaces where whatever happens should be kept only between members of the team.[43] These expectations of secrecy were cited by Canadian gymnasts as some of the main reasons Canadian gymnasts did not initially report the abuse they suffered. Spadafora explained, "What happens in the gym stays in the gym,"[44] a common refrain in many sports. Any show of disloyalty to the team is often considered an affront to the rest of the team and its coaches and can stunt an athlete's personal and professional development. The stability of the team, with an eye toward the ultimate goal of improvement and winning, is often put well ahead of athlete well-being. This is a bastardization of the collective solidarity and teamwork that many tout as vital lessons learned in sport, because the importance of the collectivity is weaponized to excuse harm and silence dissent in pursuit of sporting "success," rather than for the flourishing of the athletes themselves.

This culture exists even in less elite contexts. Before I became a full-time university professor, I worked part-time as an assistant basketball coach at several colleges in Canada. While Canadian college basketball is not at the level of the top schools in NCAA Division I in the United States, the quality is somewhere between Division II and some of the lower-end Division I teams, with the best Canadian schools at the level of Division I "mid-majors." For any Americans who don't believe me, just Google "Carleton Ravens NCAA games" and you'll see why many top NCAA schools stopped scheduling the Ravens for their fall exhibition games in the mid-2010s.

Though most Canadian collegiate basketball players will not play the game professionally,[45] the commitment expected of the athletes and the work that they put into their sports is similar to what we see south of the border, with athletes practicing five or six times a week, lifting weights, taking on full course loads, and traveling for games on the weekends. The pressure can also be very high on coaches, as there are only between 100 and 120 full-time basketball head coaching jobs (for men *and* women) in the whole country, and most assistant coaching jobs do not pay even close to a full-time salary.

I bring all of this up not to tout the quality of Canadian intercollegiate sports, or to flex my limited elite sport system experience, but because I saw abusive coaching practices firsthand, even at this level. When I was a twenty-three-year-old assistant women's basketball coach, our head coach was abusive to players, berating them, pitting them against one another, running them for mistakes, and stoking a sense of fear and confusion at all times. Players came to me after practices in tears, telling me that they were afraid to make the smallest mistakes in games and even practices, fearing the anger and vitriol that would follow.

Though this coach seemed at times to show genuine care for our players and might have thought that the abusive behavior was the "tough coaching" we so often idolize, this coach created an atmosphere of fear and discomfort that was palpable to anyone around the program. After our coach's first year at the helm (and my first as an assistant), six players quit, doing the only thing they really could do to get out of the situation. After the second—an awful season both on and off the court where this coach physically pushed a player during a practice, prompting an official complaint—the coach was fired, and I left to do my PhD.[46]

It is one of the biggest regrets of my life that I didn't do more for the athletes in those two years.

When I think back on this time, though, beyond the regret that I feel, I see a clear example of how much sport culture and the insular nature of and expectations of teams can warp our perceptions of right and wrong, of "tough love" and abuse. While the behavior I observed and let happen was not at the level of Nassar, Sandusky, Brubaker, or Lashin, it was clearly wrong. Sure, I was young, but looking back on it now, this much is obvious: Athletes who have worked their whole lives with the goal of playing in university shouldn't be quitting in droves, crying after games and practices, and attending therapy to be able to handle intercollegiate sports. But immersed in the elite sports bubble, and wanting to please the head coach that hired me and entrusted me with my first "big" coaching job, I either didn't see how bad it was, refused to see how bad it was, or didn't feel confident enough to step in. I drank the "we're a family, everything stays in-house" Kool-Aid and believed the "tough love" rhetoric. All of that, combined with my fear of losing my job and my "shot" in coaching, led me to become a bystander to athlete harm. While I still think about the mistakes I made, I now understand what the exact forces were that led me to make them.

The case of former NHL player Kyle Beach is another textbook example of the prioritization of winning, team "unity," and group secrecy,[47] this time at the highest level. Beach and another player were sexually abused and threatened by Chicago Blackhawks' team trainer Brad Aldrich in the spring of 2010. Though this was "an open secret" within the team, and players, coaches, and management knew what happened, no one intervened.[48] Hockey's culture of secrecy and "not upsetting the applecart" won out here, *especially* with the Blackhawks being in the middle of a playoff run that would end with them winning the Stanley Cup. When NHL players are expected to play through broken bones and torn ligaments in the playoffs, it is extremely difficult for anyone to speak out about abusive treatment, especially in a sports world that still does not treat mental and emotional harm the same way it does physical injury.

Professional hockey might be a uniquely difficult context for a player to speak out about the type of abuse Beach suffered, given how the hegemonically masculine culture of the sport would classify such a victim as a feminized, sexually dominated, and therefore weaker *other*. In other words, hockey's particular brand of masculinity is predicated on the physical and sexual dominance and objectification of women, and therefore being the victim of sexual assault would make it nearly impossible to demonstrate such a masculinity.

It is also important to consider how notions of hierarchy *within* sport and sport organizations, according to the value each athlete produces and other factors, impact both how athletes are treated and how management and the public respond to that treatment. Considering Beach's status as a career minor league player who had little effect on the Blackhawks' chances of winning that season, he had very little leverage to force any meaningful action from the team. He also had no real possibility of achieving safer working conditions by withholding his athletic labor or threatening to not play or move to another team. Without the vocal support of higher-profile teammates who could force the organization's hand, athletes like Beach have little structural power on their own to push for change or accountability.

When we think about professional athletes, our minds might immediately go to the most celebrated, famous, and high-earning ones who grace our screens: Lebron James, Lionel Messi, Serena Williams, Novak Djokovic, Patrick Mahomes, Caitlin Clark. But like actors or other entertainment professionals, the vast majority of professional athletes are those on the margins, in lower-level professional leagues or fighting to hang on to their spot at the highest level.[49] If we extend to elite athletes more generally, many of these athletes are teenagers and young adults. Athletic careers are also notoriously short,[50] leaving no time for professional athletes to waste and no money that can be left on the table. In these cases, teams and leagues hold the power, as they're the ones who determine whether athletes can continue to sustain themselves financially through sport.

Intersectional Constraints: Not All Athletes Can Respond Equally

Beyond an athlete's strict performance and production of value for management, intersectional identity differences can also impact the likelihood of fair and supportive treatment by coaches and managers, as well as the response of larger athletic governing bodies, leagues, organizations, and the public to this treatment. Research in employment, education, the criminal legal system, and sport have all shown that racial disparities persist in the treatment of Black people generally and Black athletes in North America and abroad.[51] This includes disparities in the ways that media and the public react when

Black people—and especially Black women—are the victims of abuse or violence.[52] These survivors are more likely to be blamed for the abuse that they've suffered, and less likely to receive support.[53]

In addition to their reluctance to come forward about general mistreatment, Black and other minoritized athletes are also still targets of racist abuse while providing their athletic labor. Whether it is the derogatory comments heard by Akim Aliu from his hockey coaches, teammates, and opposing players,[54] the ban on Caster Semenya and other Black track and field athletes from competitions due to pseudo-scientific biological restrictions that predominantly impact African and Global South athletes,[55] or the racist taunts and bananas thrown at Black footballers across Europe,[56] racist harm comes at Black athletes in a variety of ways.

The racist abuse many athletes suffer is not just the product of individual racists and their behaviors, but is also due to the extreme dehumanization and commodification of Black athletes and their athletic labor. While it is often fans who explicitly dehumanize athletes—thinking about them as pieces on a chessboard to be moved around, selected on their fantasy team, gambled on, or yelled at from the stands—these fans take their cues from larger sport structures (teams, leagues, sport culture). The nearly worldwide legalization of sports gambling and acceleration and normalization of sports gambling in North America over the past few years has ramped up this commodification. Toronto Raptors (NBA) player Chris Boucher, a Black athlete born in Saint Lucia, recently talked about how players receive all sorts of messages from fans regarding gambling. When Boucher didn't reach a particular statistical threshold in a recent game, one of these "fans" wrote to Boucher that he "chose the wrong slave today."[57] Under a racial capitalist system (which will be discussed in depth in chapter 6) that has always differentially valued and divided wealth, opportunity, and exploitation along racial lines, it is unsurprising that elite sport is a supportive and welcoming space for Black athletes *only* when they are producing value for ownership and fans.

Those of East Asian and South Asian, Middle Eastern, and Latin American origin also often suffer from racism, discrimination, and unfair treatment in a variety of sports, especially in European and North American sport contexts.[58] In some of my own research on youth experiences in sport, East Asian, South Asian, and Indigenous (Native) athletes described racist slurs and taunts from opposing players and fans, discrimination in team selection and player evaluation, and systemic barriers to sport.[59] Courtney Szto, a professor of kinesiology at Queen's University (Kingston, Canada), in her book *Changing on the Fly*, which looks at the experiences of South Asian Canadians in hockey, explains that minoritized groups are often still perceived as "outsiders" in Western sport.[60] This kind of outsider status—which can only be shed by displaying the "right" attitudes and conforming to the dominant, often white sport ethic of a particular sport—has been observed for a variety of minoritized groups in different American and European sport contexts, including for Muslims in England and Denmark and for African-origin athletes in France[61]. This "perpetual outsider" status can make some athletes especially reluctant to "rock the boat" or draw attention to themselves,[62] especially about abusive practices that many fans, coaches, and players have internalized as "just part of the game."

Difficulties in responding to abusive behavior can be further multiplied and amplified for athletes from disadvantaged economic backgrounds. If they don't have another source of income or savings to fall back on, or are expected to provide for family and friends, this can make an athlete think twice about risking angering coaches or management, or "becoming a distraction" by discussing their abuse.[63] These are similar conditions for structural coercion that we saw in chapter 2, and it is important not to lose sight of the impact that a generally unequal society and reduced opportunities for upward social mobility have on athletes' (and all people's) power within their workplace.

Finally, those whose sexuality and gender presentation does not conform to the hegemonic heterosexual and cis-gendered norms of sport may also be less willing to bring up their abuse. Some research has pointed to decreased overt homophobia and more inclusive practices in men's sports,[64] but in the spring of 2024 there were still only one or two "out" gay male athletes in the highest levels of professional sport, and only a few "out" male Olympians.[65] Men's sport's valorizing of hegemonic masculinity based in violence, dominance, toughness, and misogyny contributes to *all* athletes playing through injury and not reporting physical, sexual, and emotional abuse, but these impacts are perhaps most felt by gay athletes in men's sports.

Some gay or trans athletes in men's sports may feel that their sexuality or gender identity puts them at a disadvantage in terms of the "masculine capital"[66] needed to fit in and thrive in their sport, and they might feel forced to overcompensate. Research in the general population has shown that men do overcompensate by engaging in overtly hypermasculine behaviors when they feel their masculinity is "under threat,"[67] though research support for this phenomenon is not overwhelming. Research on heterosexual athletes has found that those who show "gender atypical" behaviors were more likely to engage in violent behaviors in sport and outside of it, in line with the overcompensation hypothesis.[68] Though this thesis also has not been tested for gay and trans athletes in men's sports—likely due in part to the fact that so few of these athletes are "out" in organized mainstream sport—logically this very well could be happening for these athletes too. Gay and trans athletes in men's sports may be especially reluctant to report abuse if the jeopardy of this minoritized sexual identity is multiplied by economic precarity or racial oppression.

On the other hand, gender- and sexuality-based overcompensation *has* been observed with gay athletes in women's sports, some of whom have felt that they need to overcompensate for their perceived masculinity by behaving and presenting in more stereotypically "feminine" ways.[69] Jonquel Jones, who was the 2021 Women's National Basketball Association (WNBA) MVP, has said that she believes she lost sponsors and marketing opportunities when she began to present in more overtly queer ways. After she came out publicly, Bahamas Telecommunications Co. dropped her as a sponsored athlete, even though her performance on the court stayed consistent and the only difference was that she was now "openly out and dressing differently."[70] These are the kinds of material considerations that queer athletes have to consider; they already do not fit into the neat heterosexual athlete box often required for sponsorship and staying power in sport,[71] and they might not want to "rock the boat" by discussing their abuse.

Public perceptions about Black and queer athletes in women's sports might be starting to change, though, as leagues like the WNBA have begun to embrace and market their Black and queer star players more publicly. Interestingly but perhaps not surprisingly, while acceptance of queer gender and sexuality presentation seems to be improving for athletes in women's sports, the same hasn't happened for athletes in men's sports. Some of this may be due to the lack of "out" men in professional sports, but it also speaks again to the ever-present celebration of competitiveness, dominance, and masculinity in sport, which remains intricately linked with capitalist relations of production and capitalist cultural hegemony.[72] It might be okay for women to trash talk, to be competitive and cutthroat, and for society to continue to valorize these characteristics, but it's not okay for men to reject these stereotypically masculine and capitalist values.

Some research has found that players' talent and value creation for team revenue are still what ultimately decides how players are treated by their organizations (beyond other identity characteristics).[73] This research has mostly been conducted only at the highest levels of professional sport, though. It does not account for players in more precarious professional athletic or nonprofessional elite contexts, which, it bears repeating, is where most athletes are situated. This research context also does not account for whether minoritized athletes *feel* that they will be supported when they come forward about their experiences of emotional or sexual abuse, even if statistically, the support they will or will not receive will be based on talent and productivity alone.

Because they lack the kind of structural power and leverage that more popular, more privileged, and higher-performing athletes get, the most that many abused athletes can hope for is a public outing of their abuser and of the organization that allowed for the abuse. This can be effective in certain cases, as public shaming can hurt a team's brand, reputation, and ability to recruit and retain other players, all of which can have material consequences on their revenue production. But for an athlete's public reporting of abuse to have any meaningful effect, there must be writers willing to write and amplify the athlete's story, lawyers who can win their legal battles, and a public and athlete community that care enough about the incident to withhold their consumer dollars (public) and labor (athletes) from harmful organizations. Journalists have gotten better at telling and amplifying these stories, and some athletes (including US gymnasts against USAG, and Kyle Beach against the Blackhawks) have won or received settlements in civil legal cases in recent years, but research has shown that the public is still willing to support organizations that do harmful things or employ harmful athletes.[74]

Suffering athletes also have to be willing to tell their story, risking re-traumatization, public ridicule, and ostracism from their fellow players. Perhaps more importantly—at least in terms of their careers—they risk being labeled a "problem" or "headache" in the whisper networks of scouts, management, and coaches, whose informal conversations and evaluations can be the difference between an athlete's next contract and being out of the sport altogether. And even if their story is told, and the public and players are publicly receptive to it, this does not ensure the player any form of compensation. They can go the legal route, and some athletes (like Beach) have, alleging and winning cases of negligence against organizations, and winning some payout. But these cases are far from a slam dunk, and in cases where the abuse or speaking out about the abuse hindered the athlete's career prospects, legal victories still do not enable athletes to wind back the clock and earn the money they could have earned from their athletic labor.

International Sport: Same Priorities, Same Problems

In a parliamentary committee on Safe Sport in Canada in March 2023, Canadian national team gymnast Ryan Sheehan described feeling "broken" from the sexual abuse he suffered at the hands of a team staff member and the subsequent failures of Gymnastics Canada to act meaningfully to protect and help him. Similar reports from other gymnasts and athletes in a variety of sports (boxing, soccer, fencing) have led to mobilization by athletes and sport scholars calling for a judicial inquiry[75] into abuse in Canadian sport. At the time of this writing, ninety-one academics and more than 1,000 Canadian athletes have signed on to a letter asking for this inquiry, "seeking immediate accountability and meaningful change from Sport Canada and the broader system it governs."[76]

To Macintosh Ross—who spearheaded the Scholars Against Abuse movement responsible for this letter and the call for a judicial inquiry—"Own the Podium," the Canadian Olympic Committee's slogan ahead of the Vancouver Olympic Games, is a microcosm of a lot of the problems we still see today. According to Ross, this slogan encapsulates Canadian sport's reverting back to the same practices that led to its first judicial inquiry in sport in 1989. Following sprinter Ben Johnson's failed drug test that caused him to lose his 100-meter gold medal at the 1988 Seoul Olympics, the Canadian government launched the Dubin Inquiry to assess why doping was taking place. Said Ross: "I teach sport policy, and we go from the Dubin Inquiry up to now, and we watch it revert back to exactly what it was. We're too obsessed with winning. This is not what sports are supposed to be. It's not healthy. It's destroying people. And we're right back where we started, as of 2010, when they brought in 'Own the Podium.' That's the exact mentality that led the judicial system to conclude that sports were morally bankrupt in Canada in the first place."

Ross was also quick to point out that Canada and other sport federations are responding to the larger international system of sport that places winning and competition at the forefront. As Roberts, Sojo, and Grant wrote in a systematic review of violence in sports, "a winner-take-all reward system may induce coaches and athletes to use whatever means necessary, including abusive methods, to achieve results."[77] This winner-take-all, win-at-all-costs reward system trickles down from national sport bodies, whose public funding often is based on how their teams perform.[78] By performance, governments of course mean wins and medals; "measures of athlete well-being do not factor into definitions of success."[79] The prioritization of athletic dominance on the world stage once again reflects global capitalist ethos related to domination and control. This isn't to say that everyone on earth has internalized this sport ethos; but in many nations it has been internalized by leadership in both the private and the public spheres, and this has downstream effects on everyone involved. As Marx explained almost 200 years ago, people may "make their own history, but they do not do it as they please. They do not make it under self-selected circumstances, but under circumstances existing already."[80]

Athletes, parents, and those wishing to take part in sport at elite levels and even recreationally almost never get to choose who the power brokers in these industries are, who governs sport federations, and who coaches them. Coaches like Brubaker, Lashin, and so many others are hired and their behavior excused because they promise and often succeed in getting good results, and in the case of sports like gymnastics, bringing athletes to the Olympics. Brubaker has now been banned from coaching sport in Canada after a Canadian disciplinary committee found fifty-four counts of misconduct and ethics violations (including physical abuse and neglect),[81] and Lashin resigned in 2010, but unless the culture around winning and high-performance changes, we could very well see coaches like this again.

Putting the onus on individual athletes to report misconduct and hoping that teams respond to market-based mechanisms and change their behavior is neither an effective nor a sustainable response or solution. Even post #MeToo, most athletes still don't report the abuse they suffer—researchers estimate the rate of reporting to be about 5 percent of athletes in men's sports and 10 percent of athletes in women's sports[82]—and if they do report, there's still no guarantee that organizations or leagues will adequately respond. More specifically, if there is no mandate from an authoritative body to force organizations to act in responsible ways, and no structural imperative under capitalism to change sport culture to prioritize worker well-being over wins and profit, there is no reason to think they *will* respond.

Win-at-All-Cost Imperatives in Sport

Unfortunately, like in chapter 2 on physical violence, the list of sexual, emotional, and psychological abuse perpetrated against athletes is nearly endless, with new reports being released seemingly daily. Abuse continues because it has been allowed to continue, because athlete well-being is not the priority for elite sport organizations under capitalism. Research has consistently shown that when winning is prioritized above all else, athlete mental and emotional well-being suffers.[83] More and more, scholars of sport are situating the problem of abuse and psychological and emotional violence in the structures of sport, rather than in individual bad coaches or management. As Sauvé and colleagues sum up in a 2023 article in the *Journal of Applied Sport*

Psychology, "various threats to Olympic athlete well-being persist as a consequence of the underpinning incentive system and priorities within elite sport."[84] The same holds true for elite and especially professional sports.

Abuse can and has happened under socialist systems like the Soviet Union and East Germany or state capitalist/socialist systems like China.[85] This abuse was based on the same issue of prioritizing winning above all other considerations, often done to elevate the prestige and reputation of the state in question, and due to sport's use as an ideological tool to demonstrate that socialist states could produce athletic excellence just as well as or better than capitalist ones. This sort of thinking must also be scrapped, if we hope to see meaningful reduction in athlete abuse. Regardless of the social system or mode of production, success in sport cannot be based only or primarily on world records, wins, and nationalist dominance over other people and nations.

However, the win-at-all-costs ethos that has existed in past socialist experiments does not *need* to exist under socialism, at least not in the way it does under capitalism. There will always be bad individual actors, regardless of the mode of production of a society. But under capitalism, the competitive ethos is built *into* the system. This is true from a nuts-and-bolts growth and competition perspective—sport organizations under capitalism have no choice but to grow and expand their fan bases and revenue streams, and the way to do this is through winning. It's also true from an ideological perspective, as sport is used to bolster claims that legitimize competition (and the subsequent inequality it produces) as the most rational way to decide how we distribute resources and rewards in society generally.

For professional sport to meaningfully reduce incidents of sexual, psychological, and emotional abuse under capitalism, the most common suggestions involve better layers of enforcement and checks on team employees and athletes, more accountability for organizations, and top-down leadership and sport governance that centers athlete well-being and harshly punishes wrongdoers. These kinds of reforms are necessary, and they can have a positive impact. But as long as structural imperatives to perform outweigh other considerations, abuse and harm will continue. It is another typical case of the need for reform and harm reduction *right now* for those athletes and people at risk, but ultimately for revolutionary change in the near future. For professional sport organizations operating in national and international markets, revolutionary socialist change may be the only way that we can truly ensure that athlete well-being is prioritized over winning and profit. If and when this kind of change happens, we still cannot rest on our laurels; the entire notion of what constitutes "success" in sport must be transformed, to a definition where well-being and athlete health is placed front and center.

The structural imperatives of *professional* and privately owned sport make it difficult to create lasting and fundamental change strictly through reform. However, these same imperatives do not need to exist for public sport organizations. Though the contemporary conservative turn of even ostensibly 'liberal' and 'centrist' political parties threatens to further privatize sport,[86] as of now, in many countries national, state, and other locality-based sport organizations are still predominantly funded by local population tax dollars, rather than through consumers and sponsors. Yes, these alternative sources of income help, but they are not nearly as necessary for the survival of these organizations, nor do they need to be. These sport organizations are not usually private businesses, and their self-described goals are usually to promote sport participation and athlete and citizen health and well-being, and perhaps also to promote excellence in the sport. It's about time they truly lived up to these aspirations. For publicly funded sport organizations, the goal does not have to be winning at all costs. But as of now it still is, and there's a long way to go.

CHAPTER FOUR

(In)Action Speaks Louder than Words
How Sport Organizations Respond to Athlete-Perpetrated Violence against Women

In the post #MeToo world, sexual violence has become such an important issue. Since Ray Rice, NFL teams treat violence against women much more seriously. Even an accusation of domestic violence can ruin a player's career. These athletes are just wild animals.

In my years studying violence against women in sports, I've heard variations of these points from colleagues, interview subjects, team management, sports journalists, friends, family, and people I've just met. I know that even for those who don't study this issue, these are common questions and topics of conversation. Some also bring up "cancel culture," ask questions about "due process," and wonder aloud about the best way to deal with accused athletes. Others mention violent spillover from the sports field to general society[1] and the lack of accountability and consequences for elite athletes. In these casual conversations, I've also heard fans both toe the line and cross the line regarding racist commentary about Black subcultures of violence.

These questions are important to consider because they show where public discourse is, in terms of identifying the roots of the problem of athlete violence, and how the general public feels this issue is and should be handled. Other than points about the lack of accountability and consequences, most discussion about the issue of professional athletes' violence against women is centered around the individual. *Athletes are just violent people; they feel entitled to women; they're wild and party too much; boys will be boys.* The role of sport organizations, leagues, and the very *structure* of elite sport in creating the conditions where athletes act in this way is ignored. The "ghost of capitalism"[2] remains just that—a ghost.

If we want to understand why all sorts of violence continue to happen in sport contexts, it is vital we understand how these sport contexts are structured. What organizations value and are forced to value under capitalism impacts the behaviors they will tolerate and not tolerate from their employees. Sport organizations do not operate based on morality; their responsibility is not to any abstract or concrete notion of the collective good. Even when they want to act benevolently in service to their communities, the cutthroat nature of win-at-all-costs elite sport systems doesn't allow them to. Professional sport organizations are profit-making organs, tasked with increasing the value of their specific organization (e.g., the Chicago Bulls) and of the league (e.g., the NBA). Management, coaches, and league executives keep their jobs because they field winning teams that produce revenue, not because they employ teams filled with the kindest and most compassionate athletes. This dichotomy—between the façade of the modern professional sports organization as a "representative of the city and hub for the community" and its true face as a cutthroat capitalist organization—is difficult for many, including myself, to come to terms with.[3]

Teams and leagues do care about pleasing their fans, but only insofar as it allows them to commodify their fandom. NBA front-office workers, in my interviews with them, noted that organizations are interested in "looking good in the eyes of the media," and "don't want to be put in a situation where [their] home fans in particular are already lined up against the player." These organizations do not want to lose fans because of the revenue they derive from them, so they (as one interviewed sport journalist explained) "lick their finger and stick it up in the air to see which way the prevailing winds are [blowing]," trying to assess the backlash they might get from acquiring a player accused of violence.

Even in cases of athlete violence against women, while the nature and details of allegations, their veracity, and the response of media and fans are important, they are only one set of factors influencing how sport organizations handle accused players. Teams and leagues must first (and second, and third) consider their bottom line. In some cases this makes releasing lower-performing players an easy decision—the public relations gains of getting rid of an accused player who is not all that valuable vastly outweigh the benefits of keeping them around. When players provide high value for their organizations through their performance, though, these decisions are not as simple. As one interviewed sports journalist explained "If you've got a guy that can shoot 60 percent from beyond the arc, but he's also a white nationalist, you've got a decision to make there."

Most of the examples, and all of the interview data used in this chapter, come from my dissertation research studying how arrests for violence against women have affected the careers of players in the NBA and NFL. I focused on these two leagues because of the interesting nexus between their sports and the criminal legal system—players in these leagues represent both an over-policed and over-criminalized racial group (young Black men) and an under-criminalized economic class (wealthy people, with the backing of even wealthier sport organizations). This is not meant in any way to give oxygen to the racist idea that Black men are more predisposed to violence or criminality than other racial groups. I focus on Black athletes in this chapter because this provides a basis for discussion of the racial capitalist dynamics of elite sports, and the complicity of capitalism and of the elite sport structures within it in the continued violence against women committed by athletes across all sports and races.

Your Quarterback's Been Accused of Sexual Misconduct by Twenty-Plus Women: Now What?

Another common question I've received in my research about athlete violence centers around Kobe Bryant—the eighteen-time All Star and five-time NBA champion shooting guard for the Los Angeles Lakers. In July 2003, Bryant—age twenty-four at the time—was accused of felony sexual assault in Colorado. In the *only* press conference he gave about the trial, shortly after the accusation, he admitted to cheating on his wife but insisted that no assault took place. After a year of evidence discovery and pretrial hearings—during which Bryant played sixty-five games for the Lakers and sometimes played and then immediately flew on a private jet to Colorado (he missed some games due to injury that season, but never due to the trial)—he entered a plea of not guilty.[4]

Bryant's lawyers tried to railroad the accuser's credibility leading up to the trial, bringing up that the accuser had sex with another man shortly after the alleged assault and claiming that the later encounter could have been the cause of her injuries. On September 1, 2004, the accuser dropped the criminal charges after transcripts from two closed hearings were "accidentally" leaked to seven media organizations and published online and the judge ruled that "evidence of the alleged victim's sexual past could be used in court."[5] Bryant was benched as a pitchman and endorser for Nike when the trial was happening but was brought back in 2005, just a year later. He signed a seven-year contract worth over $136 million with the Lakers in 2004 while the trial was ongoing and finished his twenty-year career with $323 million in earnings. Add his endorsement money to the mix, and at the time of his death in a helicopter crash in early 2020, Bryant's net worth was an estimated $600 million.[6] He is a legend in the NBA world, especially among the current generation of players.

Beyond the usual "Do you think he did it?" questions, many wonder what would happen in a similar case *today*, involving a comparable-level athlete, but in the current social and political climate post #MeToo. Fortunately for this analysis—but unfortunately for the world in general—we do have a similar case that might give us some insight into this question.

It's not a perfect comparison, but let's consider former Houston Texans quarterback Deshaun Watson. Allegations of sexual misconduct were first filed against Watson in March 2020. By the beginning of April, the number of women filing civil suits against Watson for offenses ranging from sexual misconduct and harassment to sexual assault had ballooned to twenty-two.[7] By mid-April 2020, all twenty-two women had identified themselves publicly. Most of these women were massage therapists hired either privately by Watson or organized by the Texans, the team he played for during the first four seasons of his NFL career. This was not one or two women alleging sexual misconduct (though even one allegation should be concerning enough)—*it was twenty-two*.

The number of allegations, their details, and the results of the legal proceedings in this case were undoubtedly important for the Texans and the rest of the NFL. They were just not the only important information, let alone the most important.

At the time of the allegations, Watson had just finished his fourth year as an NFL quarterback, and his third straight All-Star season. He finished the 2020 season with the most passing yards in the NFL, the second highest quarterback rating, and in the top five or top ten of nearly every important quarterback statistic. Watson was also due for a new contract following the end of his rookie deal, and as a twenty-five-year-old playing the most important position in football at an incontestably elite level, a multiyear nine-figure contract was all but guaranteed. Or at least it seemed that way until the allegations.

It was (and still is, for some) convenient to say that the allegations against Watson ruined his career. However, beyond the fact that he also negatively altered and potentially ruined the lives of the women he victimized, it is not quite clear that the allegations actually hurt Watson. Yes, he demanded a trade from the Texans following the allegations and did not play during the 2021 season as the team unsuccessfully shopped him around the league. He lost several endorsement deals, and his unofficial public approval ratings tanked.[8] But a grand jury cleared Watson of all criminal charges on March 11, 2022, and a mere week later, though still facing twenty-two civil lawsuits alleging sexual misconduct and assault, he was traded to the Cleveland Browns and promptly signed to a five-year contract worth a guaranteed $230 million. In a league like the NFL, where guaranteed money is hard to come by, this contract is staggering.

Since the signing, Jenny Vrentas of the *New York Times* uncovered that Watson had received sixty-six massages over a seventeen-month period, and that many of the other massage therapists (not part of the twenty-two-woman civil claim) also described experiences like those in the suit. One woman (who has not sued Watson yet) said that Watson persistently asked "for sexual acts during their massage, including 'begging' her to put her mouth on his penis."[9] Watson was suspended for the first eleven games of the 2022 season, and played and started the final six for the Browns. Knowing he'd likely be suspended for games during the 2022 season, Watson and the Browns structured his contract such that most of the salary would be paid out in the 2024–2027 seasons, softening any financial impact of the first-year suspensions. Browns fans may have been upset with his performance the last few seasons, but they seemed to have quickly forgotten—or forgiven—the many assault accusations against him. If this is "cancel culture," many employees all over North America are probably wishing they too were canceled.

It's easy to levy blame in these cases on the athletes accused, and they are deserving of some of it. However, there is also organizational responsibility at play. While Watson was throwing touchdowns and breaking team records, the Texans' front office was providing hotel space for him to get extra massages. At least seven women met him for massages at the team-provided hotel, including two who eventually filed lawsuits and two others who reported Watson to police. The Texans also provided Watson with the paperwork for a nondisclosure agreement when a woman who is now part of the twenty-two-person lawsuit threatened to expose his behavior.[10]

This is not just an issue in the NFL or in North American sports. Cristiano Ronaldo was accused of rape in 2018, after paying $375,000 for the alleged victim to keep quiet about an incident that happened in 2009. The victim, Kathryn Mayorga, alleged that Ronaldo "pulled her into a nearby bedroom and anally raped her while she shouted, 'No, no, no, no!'"[11] She reported the incident to police the day after it occurred (without giving the name of her abuser) and underwent a medical exam that showed that her rectum was penetrated (as she described). The case was dismissed in June 2022 after misconduct by Mayorga's lawyers,[12] but even before it was dismissed, this allegation barely made a dent in Ronaldo's reputation. None of his sponsors dropped him, and he received unconditional messages of support from his club team at the time (Juventus) and from the Portuguese soccer federation. The main fallout from the allegation was that Mayorga was railroaded in several different publications around the world, and by global football fans.[13] In 2020 Ronaldo became the first team-sport athlete to make over US$1 billion in career earnings, and his most recent contracts with Manchester United and then Saudi's Al Nassr paid him US$31.6 and US$75 million per year, respectively. He is nearly universally beloved across the soccer world, except for a small pocket of largely women activists who have tried to keep these allegations in the public eye.

Boxer Floyd Mayweather has also earned over US$1 billion in his career while being accused of violence against women *three times*, in 2001, 2003 and 2010. Now in his mid-forties, he remains boxing's most lucrative draw, with fight promoters and boxing federations making millions on his every fight. German tennis star Alexander Zverev was accused of domestic violence in 2020, and then again in 2023, for which he was ordered to pay a €450,000 fine.[14] At the time of this writing, Zverev remains unsanctioned by the ATP (Association of Tennis Professionals), and sits at no. 2 in the world rankings. Retired hockey goalie Patrick Roy was arrested in 2000 for domestic violence, again in 2022, and was a first-ballot Hall of Famer whose history of violence is barely known to most hockey fans. He now coaches the New York Islanders in the NHL. Former Bayern Munich and German national team center back Jerome Boateng was found guilty of domestic violence in September 2021 and played the season out for Lyon in French football's first division.

Though *much* more common among male athletes than women athletes, league and team protection of violent athletes happens in elite women's sports as well. WNBA star Brittney Griner pleaded guilty to domestic violence in 2015 and remains one of the top-earning women's basketball players both in the WNBA and in Europe. In 2015 US soccer goalkeeper Hope Solo was charged with two counts of domestic violence, and then allowed to play on the US World Cup team in 2016.

Powerful organizations that extract value from "talent" protecting that same "talent"—whether it's star athletes, rock stars, entertainers, or politicians—is commonplace. NFL teams are known to employ "handlers" or fixers,[15] tasked with keeping players out of trouble or keeping their trouble out of the public eye, watching over an organization's most precious "asset." One NFL journalist explained that "the Dallas Cowboys are one of the teams that are really well known for having a strong relationship with the police department. They've got essentially a fixer on their staff, that is a first person that anybody in the building calls whenever a problem arises, usually a legal problem of some sort." On the college side, an NFL front-office member explained that "schools can do their own thing—if you go to a coach instead of the campus police, nothing's going to happen. If you go to the campus police, depending on the campus, some go into the system (of recorded incidents), some don't."

While handlers might seem to some like good practice for keeping players out of trouble, it begs the question whether athletes who are so untrustworthy should be employed by professional sport organizations in the first place. Teams in college and in professional leagues are known to have relationships with local police departments, and this is known by players. These kinds of practices also send a message that athletes are above the law, and that teams will protect them at all costs if they run afoul of it. Unfortunately, this does seem to be the case for some athletes, though not all. While of course athletes still have agency over their off-field behavior, this should not shield elite sport and elite sport organizations from blame in creating contexts where violence is encouraged, tolerated, and excused. Much of the time, though, the role of these organizations and of larger sporting cultures is ignored.

Are Athletes More Violent, and Why? Research Ignoring the Structural Causes of Violence

Are athletes more violent than the general population? What about compared to those with similar demographics? The short answer is that we're not sure. Data on domestic and sexual violence complaints can be difficult to compile and acts of violence against women are often underreported,[16] and researchers have landed on both sides of this question.[17] Most athletes—regardless of the structural and cultural factors that apply to their sport and that promote or tolerate violence—do not commit acts of violence outside of their sport.[18]

In the case of the NFL, there is seemingly a constant stream of news about criminal behavior by athletes and especially by NFL players, but official crime rates of NFL players are actually lower than those for men of similar demographics, while violent crime is only slightly higher.[19] For athletes in other sports the rates of crime and violence are often lower than or similar to those for the general population.

However, considering that elite athletes often have the organizational resources to evade official arrests, crime statistics may undercount athlete violence. Those who do suggest that rates of athlete violence are higher have offered several explanations. While many of these studies hint at the role played by elite win-at-all-costs sports—structured by capitalist relations of production—in this violence, they rarely call out these relations as central, and almost never explicitly discuss the role of capitalist sport and its organizational actors.

Perhaps most common in the athlete violence literature is the link made between violence, masculinity, and sport. Much has been written about the link between sports and a specific type of "hegemonic" masculinity.[20] As explained in chapter 2, hegemonic masculinity is an often-overcomplicated term for the dominant, most highly valued form of masculinity *du jour*. For the last hundred or so years, this most highly valued form of masculinity has been based in physical strength and stature, power, and control over other men and in romantic relationships with women, and the ability to use violence and aggression to assert dominance. Men perform this masculinity through their practices, patterns of actions, and behaviors,[21] which include participation and success in (often violent) male sports.[22] To achieve higher social positioning, men must assert their masculinity not only through participating in violent sport, but also by participating in its "locker room culture" marked by sexist and misogynistic views of women. Studies of elite college athlete violence against women (VAW) have found that many college athletes are more supportive of rape myths and misogynistic views of women compared to the general student population.[23] While some recent research has optimistically suggested that sport masculinity has begun to evolve to be inclusive and less marked by misogyny and violence,[24] these sport cultures are not yet the norm worldwide.

Social-learning-based explanations for athlete violence stress that athletes are constantly learning from their sport environment, coaches, and other athletes. These learning processes interact with hegemonic masculinity, as athletes learn that violent, "masculinized sports (are) socially sanctioned stepping-stones toward privilege and power—sites where coaches, peers, parents, and the media encourage masculine identities founded on physical aggression and domination."[25] Athletes internalize the variety of messages they receive from their sport environment, which includes messages around the win-at-all-costs nature of sport, the acceptability and encouragement of violence in certain contexts, and importantly, where behavioral lines may exist and for whom.

Related to social learning theories regarding athlete violence against women, spillover explanations suggest that the violence and physical dominance athletes are expected to use in their sport spills over into general society. Other research on athlete violence looks at individual factors that may lead to violence, including alcohol and drug consumption and abuse, concussions and brain injury (discussed in chapter 3), and personal issues related to anger and lack of control.

Understanding Athlete Violence in Elite Capitalist Sport

Less common to analyses of elite athlete VAW is how sport organizations, leagues, and governing bodies respond to it, and the role of these organizations in perpetuating it. Organizational and league responses are vital to any understanding of why elite athlete VAW continues to happen, as they dictate the environment athletes live and work in, the messaging they internalize, and what they can expect to happen if they misbehave.

Most of the research in this area has looked at the one-time sanctions some athletes have received for allegations or convictions for VAW,[26] usually short suspensions or fines. Even in these studies of short-term consequences, researchers often note how lenient some of these leagues are about player VAW. Some have found that leagues cared more about illegal drug use—even for relatively harmless drugs like marijuana—than they did about VAW.[27] Others looked at how college arrests or misbehavior have impacted draft position in the NFL, but not a player's career once they enter the professional ranks.[28] Until I began conducting my PhD dissertation research on the careers of athletes following VAW allegations, specifically looking at the NBA and NFL, the material effects of VAW arrests on player careers had not been studied in any sort of systematic way.

Athlete Careers Are Not Impacted by VAW Allegations, and This Sends a Message

In the post #MeToo era, sport organizations like to talk a big game about how seriously they take player violence, and specifically VAW. There's a general narrative that sport leagues and a variety of other industries take VAW more seriously than they used to, especially following the recent #MeToo movement. Some of those I interviewed who work in the NFL also talked about the Ray Rice incident being "their #MeToo," their watershed moment where "everything changed."

Rice was arrested in February 2014 for domestic violence for allegedly striking his fiancée in an elevator of an Atlantic City Hotel.[29] At the time of the arrest, Rice was a multiple time All-Star running back for the Baltimore Ravens but had just finished a rough season on the field, with his statistics down across the board. A few days after the alleged assault, TMZ released a video of Rice from the February 2014 event, dragging his seemingly unconscious fiancée out of the elevator. Even after this video was released and a grand jury indicted Rice on a felony aggravated assault charge (which could, if found guilty in trial, carry a three- to five-year prison term), the NFL suspended him a mere two games.

Amid backlash from some media, many women's rights and domestic violence prevention groups, and a few players, NFL commissioner Roger Goodell admitted that this punishment was too lenient. Then on September 8, after the first Sunday of the NFL season, TMZ released a second video from inside of the elevator, which *showed* Rice knocking out his fiancée. Both the Ravens and Goodell denied having seen this video when they sanctioned Rice, even though both parties claimed to have completed thorough investigations, and a hotel employee stated that NFL officials *had* seen it before announcing Rice's punishment. Rice's suspension was then changed to eight games, and he was released by the Ravens. Again though, it's important to keep in mind that in the season prior, Rice had shown "diminishing performance at a position losing value in today's NFL."[30] One NFL journalist put it: "The thing about even Ray Rice, his most recent year in the NFL before that video came out was abysmal, and so it was very easy for the Ravens to be like 'you know, we don't need to deal with this.'"

While the NFL's Personal Conduct Policy (PCP) for players was updated in response to this incident and now allows for stronger sanctioning of players accused of violence, this does not tell us what happens to accused players in the long term. Those studying the NFL's application of the PCP have also found this application to be inconsistent and largely arbitrary, giving "wide latitude" to the NFL and giving "the impression that the NFL is not taking a strong stance on combating domestic violence."[31] As one NFL journalist explained, the Ray Rice case "really isn't the watershed moment that it's made out to be."

While there's been a lot of talk about the harsher consequences for athletes accused of violence, I wanted to test this empirically. In my interviews with management in the NBA and NFL, they were all quick to say that domestic violence or anything violence-related is the most severe offense that a player can be accused of, and that they try to stay away from those players. The problem is, their actions generally tell another story.

To assess whether teams "stayed away" from players accused of VAW, I didn't just look in a vacuum at the length of a player's career or their salary earnings following an arrest. Instead, I dug deeper, assessing how arrested players' careers progressed when compared to the careers of players of similar productivity, age, race, and who played the same position. In short, I compared similar players to control for the "value" a player has to their organization, which comes from the wins and revenue they help produce. This allowed me to test whether the major differentiating quality between the two players—the fact that one was arrested for an act of VAW, and one was not—really had an impact on the arrested player's career. I looked at all 31 players (and their matched pair) arrested for an act of VAW in the NBA during 2000–2019, and all 117 players (and their matched pairs) in the NFL during 2000–2020.

With the NBA, because of the relatively small group of players, I was only able to test whether salaries and careers were significantly different between arrested players and their matched pairs. For the larger NFL sample, the analysis was more sophisticated, looking again at whether NFL player career longevity was significantly different for arrested and non-arrested players, but also determining whether this difference changed over time, specifically after the Ray Rice incident.

If you've read this far, you probably won't be surprised by the results. In short, there were no significant career differences between arrested and non-arrested NBA players.[32] The NFL story is a bit more nuanced, but broadly tells a similar tale: VAW arrests have hurt NFL careers a bit more in recent years, but any negative impact is *completely negated by even average performance*.[33] Basically, if a guy is performing at an average or even just slightly below average level, a VAW accusation will have little impact, even today. To be clear, this wasn't just the James Harrisons, Xavien Howards, Brandon Marshalls, and other star players who were able to avoid consequences for an arrest. Only backup players and low-performing players saw any systematic impact on their careers, and the truth is, in the coldhearted world of the NFL, these types of players generally don't have long careers anyway, regardless of how well they behave off the field. One NBA front-office worker said that "that's why so often you see high character guys on the bottom of the roster." It is only the "bottom of the roster" athletes who are truly at risk of losing a job because of their off-field behavior. These players are—in the words of capitalist dehumanization—disposable and replaceable assets.

These statistical findings—combined with my interviews with management and journalists in the two leagues—lay bare the impact that profit-oriented sport has on even the most seemingly "moral" issues. If organizations had a zero-tolerance, morality-based policy on criminality or on specific crimes like VAW, the talent and productivity of a player wouldn't have any impact on a player's evaluation. In this non-capitalist-oriented sports world, organizations would be mainly concerned with the severity of the crime, the veracity of the allegation, and maybe the age of the player.[34] They might also consider whether the player is a repeat offender, if they were acting in self-defense, if they suffer from a mental health issue, or if they were unfairly apprehended by police. In reality, though, alleged criminality (even for violent crimes) is often considered just another "cost" in organizations' calculation of whether to acquire a player. As one NFL journalist summed up: "It's always a kind of risk-reward thing. So, if a player has enough talent, organizations are incentivized to place less importance on troubling factors." Nearly everyone I interviewed, from management to scouts to journalists, mentioned that organizations are guided centrally by their desire to field winning teams and to make money, and this *raison d'être* guides decisions related to player criminality as well.

While the NFL's Ray Rice scandal or the #MeToo movement may have brought increased media attention to the prevalence of VAW in general and in sports, teams in the NBA and NFL have not systematically stopped signing, retaining, or drafting players accused of acts of violence against women. Instead, the increased societal and media attention to the issue may be causing organizations to focus more on creating the *perception* that they care about certain social issues. One NFL journalist I interviewed made this point especially clear, linking how the league handles cases of violence against women in the post #MeToo world with their performative actions on other social justice issues.

> I think (the #MeToo movement) changed the way the NFL wants people *to think* they've looked about violence against women, which is a very subtle but important difference, right? Like, did the NFL start caring about women a lot more after Ray Rice? Maybe a handful of folks, but as an ownership group, as a league office, probably not. Same thing, NFL owners don't give a fuck about Black people a lot more after Kaepernick. No, but they need people to think they do, so they put "end racism" in the end zones. Black Lives Matter tweets and T-shirts, they've got to look like they do, right, because the league is all about perception.

Even when sport organizations seem to act on social justice issues, these acts are rooted in the protection of profit and capital. In the case of athlete violence against women, organizations use lower-performing players as sacrificial lambs to keep up appearances, releasing those players quickly and putting out a statement about how they "strongly condemn" this act of violence.[35]

There are countless examples of the different levels of leeway athletes receive for their behavior. Speaking anonymously, one NBA front-office member explained that "the biggest question (about acquiring a player accused of violence) is: Is the guy's skill bigger than his problems? Does it outweigh his issues?" Another explicitly stated that "if it's a better player, they probably have more leeway," while one NFL journalist described team decision making as "a sliding scale of how important a player is and how much (the team is) willing to tolerate." Several other people I interviewed also used sliding or weighted scale metaphors.

My statistical analyses of players in the two leagues also made this focus on talent especially clear.[36] And yet, these analyses didn't even cover all the other high-profile cases that didn't make it into my sample because either the incidents happened in college or *criminal* charges were never filed. For example, Tyreek Hill, Joe Mixon, and Kendrick Nunn were all accused of violence against women in college and have seen very little impact of this on their careers.

In 2014, Hill was arrested for domestic assault and battery by strangulation for choking and punching his pregnant girlfriend in the face and stomach. He was dismissed from the Oklahoma State football program but was picked up by the University of West Alabama for the 2015 season, and entered the NFL draft in 2016.[37] Many thought Hill wouldn't be drafted because of his checkered (to put it lightly) past, but after running an incredibly fast 4.25-second 40-yard dash at the draft combine, the Kansas City Chiefs selected him with the 165th overall pick. While Hill would have likely been selected higher without his arrest, this is a far cry from the "life ruining" that some feel happens when someone is arrested for VAW. Hill played his first six seasons for the Chiefs, though in April 2020 he was under police investigation again, this time for battery of his three-year-old son. In audio recordings released in the days following, Hill admitted to hitting his son, and when his fiancée (the same woman he had assaulted in 2014) told him that their son was "terrified" of Hill, he responded, "You need to be terrified of me too, bitch."[38] Hill was suspended by the Chiefs following this incident, but given that this suspension occurred in the offseason, it didn't amount to much. The NFL investigated the case that offseason and shocked many by not issuing any sort of suspension. Hill did not miss a single game in the 2021 season following this incident, and signed a four-year, $120 million contract with the Miami Dolphins in 2022. Using the "weighted scale" metaphor of one of the NBA journalists interviewed, it seems Hill has enough talent on his scale to balance out his negative behavior.

University of Illinois and Oakland University guard Kendrick Nunn has a similar story, as he was arrested for domestic battery in 2016 while a member of the Illinois basketball team.[39] He was suspended indefinitely by the team and eventually dismissed from the school, but he transferred to a smaller program at Oakland. After a strong senior season there, Nunn was not drafted, but was signed by the Golden State Warriors immediately afterward. He played well in the G League,[40] and was quickly (and quietly) signed by the NBA's Miami Heat. In this case, Nunn's lack of name recognition likely made it easier for the Heat to take him on. As one NBA journalist explained in one of my dissertation interviews, "(Miami) figured that because he wasn't a really well-known prospect, his arrest record didn't become a big enough story that it really polluted his reputation, so they could kind of get away with it." Nunn promptly started every game in his first year with the Heat, over 80 percent of his games in his second year, and played 22 minutes per game in the NBA Finals in 2020. He signed a two-year, $10.25 million contract in 2021 with the Los Angeles Lakers.[41]

Back on the football side, Ben Roethlisberger, Antonio Brown, and Richie Incognito were accused of crimes in civil cases or did not see charges laid against them, and also saw little change to their career prospects. Roethlisberger is perhaps the most famous example, as the Pittsburgh Steelers quarterback was arrested and charged for rape in a civil case in 2008, following his fifth season in the NFL, and for sexual assault again in 2010, following his seventh. The first case was settled out of court in 2012, and the second charge was dropped after a month.[42] While Roethlisberger was suspended six games and mandated to attend counseling by the league, he remains a fan favorite in Pittsburgh, and played all eighteen of his professional seasons with the team, thirteen of which came after his first rape allegation. Roethlisberger made over $267 million in his career, and almost $223 million since his first rape allegation.[43]

Kareem Hunt wasn't formally arrested and no charges were laid, but he was recorded knocking down a woman and kicking her at a hotel. He was cut by the Kansas City Chiefs (the team that drafted and employed Hill for the first five seasons of his career) immediately after the video was released in November 2018, but the team had known about the incident since February, nine months prior. When the video came out, the Chiefs stated that Hunt had lied to them about what happened, and once they saw the video, they cut him.[44] Hunt was signed three months later by the Cleveland Browns (the team that signed Watson to his $231million deal) but received an eight-game suspension from the NFL, one of the highest ever doled out for an act of VAW. Hunt played the remaining eight games of the season for the Browns, and then signed a two-year deal worth $10.83 million. Before the 2022 season, he signed another two-year deal, this time for $12 million.

Again, these cases were not even included in my analysis. Their inclusion may have made the statistical case even more jarring, making it clear that teams are willing to take on talented players accused of VAW. As one NFL journalist explained, the way teams deal with player criminality "depends on how good the player is. If he's a first-round-level talent, you're going to be more likely to look the other way on something than if he's a fringe talent." While teams might like to roster athletes with good reputations off the field or court, this is not what keeps organizations profitable or management in their jobs. In the words of one NFL front-office worker, "winning is the bottom line that we're all judged on in professional sport."

Paired with professional sport's general rewarding of male aggression and violence on the field or the court, the admission that teams' decisions about players accused of VAW is as much or more about their talent and productivity as the facts of their case points to team and league complicity in ongoing violence by athletes. By not intervening and holding players accountable when doing so would hurt team success and revenue, and intervening harshly when a player is less important, sport organizations are putting profits and the protection of capital ahead of those that may be harmed, which includes not just victims and those accused, but society more generally.

Professional athletes, especially in the most popular sports, are highly visible public figures who garner substantial media attention and serve as prominent role models for youth and a large population of sports fans.[45] When athletes who have misbehaved or committed criminal acts visibly pay a price for these acts, this has the potential to serve as an educational tool, setting or reaffirming social norms regarding violence against women for both athletes and the general population.[46] Starting at a young age, elite athletes often receive preferential treatment from coaches, teachers, administrators, parents, and even law enforcement in some cases. This can result in a belief that they are above the law, or that they will be protected from the consequences of any wrongdoing because of their talents.[47] Unfortunately, this belief may actually be warranted for players who reach professional or elite status.

But This Happens Everywhere, Doesn't It?

Some of the people I interviewed suggested that in any industry or work environment, lower-performing employees have lower misbehavior thresholds than higher-performing employees, and that this is not specific to sports. One NFL journalist noted, "If you are very easily replaceable, you definitely don't have a lot of leverage or wiggle room in any circumstance . . . So I think that's pretty common when you look at business as a whole. And that's essentially, at the end of the day all the NFL is—it's a business." While there is some truth to this, especially about the NFL and professional sports organizations at their base being profit-making entities, there are several important differentiators to be noted.

While star entertainers, lawyers, software engineers, and doctors may remain employed after allegations of wrongdoing, this phenomenon is most visible and most stark in professional sports. Beating your competition is of course fundamental to any organization operating in a capitalist marketplace, and profit is produced through the surplus value of workers, but the link between winning, labor productivity, and revenue is perhaps most obvious in sports. Managers, coaches, and players turn over incredibly quickly, as organizations seek every small advantage to beat their competition and secure revenue for ownership. Making or missing the playoffs can be the difference between a multiyear, multimillion-dollar deal and unemployment.

Perhaps even more importantly, talent and productivity can be measured and evaluated much more explicitly and reliably in sports compared to other industries. Over the last twenty-five years we've seen major advancements in performance analytics to assess a player's impact on team success, making it even easier to determine how important a player is to the organization. It's much easier to measure the impact that Ron Artest has on his basketball team and the value he adds to the franchise than it is to measure John Doe's value-added at his marketing firm. We also know how Ron Artest compares to an average player at his position, or even how he compares to his specific potential replacement.

The difference between an employee and their potential replacement in run-of-the-mill capitalist workplaces—if it can even be accurately measured in the first place—is also not nearly as important as the differences between players at the highest levels of sport. For leagues like the NBA, NFL, and the highest levels of world soccer, the "employees" in question are the most elite performers in the world. This makes any differences between players extremely important, as they can be the difference between wins and losses, and jobs or unemployment for management. While all workers need to produce value to remain employed, the development of capitalism has brought with it more and more specialization and Taylorization, with one of the goals of this specialization being to make employees as replaceable as possible.[48] If ownership, shareholders, and upper management of Amazon, Hilton, or Uber know they can just hire another employee (or gig-worker who gets no labor protections or benefits, in Uber's case) who will be 95 percent as productive as the one with a VAW allegation or who was caught saying racist things on Twitter, this is an easy decision. With sports, though, ownership and upper management have not yet found a way to standardize their businesses to the point that those producing the value (athletes) are easily replaceable.

Those noting that "valuable employees always get away with more" are also revealing the built-in guardrails against ethical behavior that exist under capitalism. The fact that some employees can be so replaceable that a hint of misbehavior is enough for removal, while others can be so valuable that evidence of VAW is not enough to affect them, is damning. For those who are experts in their field but have character issues outside of it, this distillation of their personhood into what they can produce for their bosses becomes a bizarro benefit. While this dehumanization is undoubtedly bad for employees (and society) in general, for people like Tyreek Hill and Ben Roethlisberger, it is the reason they made 100s of millions in their careers.

Management and ownership that see no issue with acquiring and paying top dollar for athletes who abuse women are clearly part of the problem. However, it's important to realize that this kind of callous, tunnel-vision decision making is a feature, rather than a bug, of capitalism and of capitalist sport. When success is a zero-sum game, management can feel (sometimes correctly) that they can't afford *not* to take on or retain value-producing employees, no matter how they feel about the employee as a person. This is something I heard explicitly from those I interviewed. One scout I spoke to discussed having to pick up a player the team had just signed for a tryout, and drive him across the Canadian-American border, because his previous arrests meant he wasn't allowed to fly. The player had a history of violent behavior with both intimate partners and others, and the scout said that it was "scary as heck being in a car with him." But the player was very talented and had been successful on the field wherever he went, and so the team wanted to try him out.

Several other people I interviewed mentioned that they felt they needed to be open to acquiring a talented player with a history of bad behavior, because if they didn't, someone else would. If their team then didn't perform to expectations, and/or that player ended up helping some other team instead, this could be the end of a manager, scout, or other team employee's career. A few went as far as to say that some teams even see players with a violent history or negative behavior off the field as a sort of market inefficiency. One NFL front-office member explained: "I think there's some clubs that see them as depressed assets too, where they can get them on the cheap because of their criminal background, and they're willing to live with it. And they see the upside on the fields for someone that might cost less than what the talent would suggest they should be." In the words of another NBA front-office member, "players that have some of those personality issues tend to potentially be undervalued." When all decision making is structured by the profit imperatives of capitalism, violent behavior can evolve from a negative quality to a market inefficiency to be exploited by "savvy" management, especially when teams operate under salary caps that limit how much they can spend on players.

Controlling the Narrative: "Bad Apples, Not Rotten Orchards"

How do organizations and leagues avoid blame for sending this sort of message? In short, they focus on the individual fault of athletes, rather than any of the structural or cultural issues we've been discussing. The idea that tacit acceptance of violence by high-performing athletes—coupled with privileging of aggression, violence, and domination on the field—curates an environment where athletes are more likely to engage in violent criminality outside of their sport, is not the sort of narrative floating around. They want a reputation as a league or team that "cares about women" and acts as a morale arbiter of justice, while also reaping the financial rewards of employing violent athletes who produce wins on the field or court.

To accomplish this lofty goal, it is vital that first and foremost, every case of violence is framed as an individual issue, not a structural problem. Like when a police officer caught on video[49] kills an unarmed Black person or the one time every ten years where a Wall Street trader or politician actually gets convicted of insider trading or embezzlement, the institutions that employ these actors rush to claim that this is just a case of a single bad apple and cannot possibly be seen as evidence of a rotten orchard.[50] This framing—that those who commit acts of violence are not at all a reflection of the organizations that employ them—is absolutely vital to the PR machines within sport, and is the best weapon that organizations and sport structures have in avoiding blame for the violence committed within and related to elite capitalist sport. It is also logically consistent with neoliberal logics around personal responsibility, and further solidifies and legitimizes these same logics.

This kind of blame avoidance is especially nefarious in sports with predominantly Black athletes. Scholars have detailed the way Black athletes (and Black people in general) are written and spoken about more negatively in media reports both on the field and in cases of alleged violence and criminality off it, even while white athletes in the same sport commit similar acts of violence.[51] In a 2011 article in *Journalism and Mass Communication Quarterly*, Dana Mastro and her colleagues found that Black athletes were overrepresented in criminal research compared to white athletes, and their alleged crimes were described in more explicit detail and contained language that was more "derisive, accusatory, and sympathetic to the victim"[52] than the language used for white athletes. This research is just one example of the plethora of work that has looked at racist framings of Black athletes across time, which has often used the success of Black male athletes in violent, contact, or collision sports like football to "reinforce the fixed idea that Black men are 'all brawn and no brains.'"[53] Research examining the media construction of Black masculinity during the Ray Rice case found that public displays of Black athlete violence against women were used for the maintenance of the narrative that Black men are deviant, inherently violent, brutish, and in need of discipline.[54] Similarly, in research about James Harrison—who was arrested for domestic violence in 2008 and had been punished several times for on-field violence by the NFL league office—Adam Rugg also found that the NFL and the media used discourses of "Black criminality" to present Harrison's deviant behavior and violence as "outside of the game."[55] This allows the league to "cast off the responsibility for the consequences of that violence to the footballing bodies that administer and receive it,"[56] rather than taking any of that responsibility on themselves.

Work by Black activists in the wake of the police murders of George Floyd, Breonna Taylor, Jacob Blake, and countless others has moved the Overton window of acceptable commentary *away* from explicitly blaming Black "subcultures of violence" or other racist tropes about Black genetics, parenting, or upbringings for violence.[57] However, sports organizations and leagues still engage in this kind of blaming implicitly, by ducking any responsibility themselves. Instead, they place the responsibility solely on individual athletes (of all races), to shield themselves from blame for both the social environment of privilege free of consequences that they create, as well as for their complicity for the athletic cultures that privilege violence and misogyny.

But Aren't These Just Allegations?

But these are just arrests. Let the criminal legal system do its work. They're innocent until proven guilty.

In many cases, this is the option organizations and leagues use to avoid accountability for the violence of athletes, passing responsibility off to the legal system and avoiding the need to actually deal with difficult questions about athlete misbehavior. This is especially true when it involves athletes who may have done something wrong but the team would definitely like to keep around for what they can do on the court, ice, or field.

There are several issues with this line of thinking, both with regard to the analyses I've done about what happens to players when they are arrested or convicted, and in general when it comes to powerful, wealthy defendants. First, for those who argue that players' careers should not suffer from arrests because legal systems operate under an "innocent until proven guilty" model, it's important to note that even when I limited my analyses to players who were convicted or pleaded guilty to VAW, there still wasn't a significant difference between the careers of those convicted and the careers of those not arrested at all. There also weren't even enough convicted athletes to conduct any kind of rigorous analysis.

Beyond that, it also bears repeating: the criminal legal system is not some beacon of pure objectivity. Those with wealth and advantages in political and social capital are more likely to get positive outcomes in trial, before trial, and after trial.[58] When it comes to professional athletes in elite capitalist sport (and even star amateur athletes on their way to the professional ranks), there is nearly always a clear and substantial power imbalance between these athletes (backed by multimillion- and multibillion-dollar organizations and leagues) and their alleged victims, and this makes deferring to the criminal legal system an easy cop-out for organizations that want to keep their star athletes around and avoid responsibility for condoning their behavior. Power inequalities often shape outcomes in legal cases; we know that there are "good" lawyers and "bad" ones, and that wealthy people rarely suffer in court, if their cases even reach the public eye and the courtroom at all.[59] We know that those marginalized by class, race, gender, sexuality, citizenship status, and other axes of identity are less likely to have positive outcomes in the criminal legal system. These phenomena don't just disappear when we're dealing with elite athletes. In many cases, this power differential is so great that the athletes aren't formally charged, charges are dropped, or they reach a hushed-up plea deal.[60]

But don't let just me be the one to tell you. Robert Mueller[61] was the independent investigator for the NFL's mishandling of the Ray Rice incident and had much to say on the topic. In his report,[62] Mueller stated that there are "weaknesses inherent in the League's longstanding practice of deferring to the criminal justice system. . . . Discipline should be imposed on the basis of the specific nature of the player's conduct, not solely or necessarily on the disposition of a criminal case" (8–9). He also wrote that "it is not always possible to draw precise factual conclusions from outcomes in a criminal case. . . . A prosecutor might decide not to prosecute or to accept a non-punitive disposition simply because the state cannot prove its case to the high criminal standard of beyond a reasonable doubt due to evidentiary constraints and lack of cooperation, even though the player did engage in misconduct."

Even athletes still in college or at the beginning of their professional careers, who have not yet made millions, still often have the support of these wealthy and powerful sport organizations and their legal and public relations teams. Once players reach professional status, they also become part of the league "brand" that needs to be protected. Professional leagues and teams are always concerned about their reputation, as this impacts their ability to attract commercial endorsements and sign lucrative TV contracts.[63] They need their players' reputations to remain as strong as possible, which motivates organizations and leagues to try to influence the legal system and encourage players to reach confidential settlements away from the public eye.[64] Similarly, at the college level, athletes often have the backing of coaches, athletic administrators, and fixers who work to ensure that the situation is handled at the campus level, shielding athletes from the larger criminal legal system.[65] Decision making by elite sport leagues and franchises regarding athlete criminality does not function to protect or empower victims, but to protect capital.[66]

This kind of criticism is not specific to the NFL or football, but applies to any sport league with similarly high criminal standards (which is basically all of them). While this is not to say that athletes do not deserve due process—especially young Black male athletes who are often over-criminalized in the criminal legal system—sport organizations and leagues cannot simply defer to the criminal legal system and pretend that they are doing so for reasons related to justice or fairness. This becomes especially clear when, in cases where low-performing or "disposable" (in capitalist dehumanizing parlance) athletes get accused of an act of violence, teams kick them to the curb before a shred of "due process" or investigation is done. This type of neoliberal, performative social justice capitalism is a strategy of blame avoidance and deflection used by organizations and sports league.

The work that teams and leagues do to protect players and protect capital also seems to pay off. Of the 117 NFL players arrested for an act of violence against women between 2000 and 2019, only 21 pleaded or were found guilty. This 17.9 percent conviction rate is well below even the most conservative estimates of overall conviction rates for those charged with domestic and sexual violence in the United States.[67] Of the 21 found guilty, four pleaded guilty to a lesser crime than they were initially accused of, and only five were sentenced to prison time. AJ Jefferson served 90 days, Chad Johnson 30, and Claude Terrel 30 (he was on probation for a previous arrest); Michael Pittman served fourteen days after his *third* domestic violence arrest. Willie Middlebrooks received an eighteen-month deferred sentence, but completed his probation and never had to serve any time in prison.

In the NBA, 8 of 31 were convicted, a 25.8 percent conviction rate closer to national averages, but still lower than the general population and significantly lower than the rate for young Black men, who represent 90 percent of the NBA player sample. Six of the 8 who were convicted pleaded guilty to lesser crimes, with only two convicted after trial. Only 3 of the 8 served any prison time. Jason Richardson served 93 days, Darren Collison 20, and Ruben Patterson 15.

Maybe you're still not convinced. *If the legal system decides they're not guilty, then what are sports teams supposed to do? We can't just kick people out for every allegation.* Maybe we shouldn't, and athletes do deserve second chances. To be absolutely clear, there's no social problem that can be solved by more prison, and I would never advocate for more prison sentences for athletes or for anyone. But second chances—and accountability for athletes—should be based on the facts of the case and what they do to make amends, and not on their performance on the field, court, ice, or track. When it comes to the wealthy and the powerful, accountability rarely comes from the criminal legal system, and teams and leagues are aware of this. "Letting the system decide" is one of the ways these organizations shield themselves from the responsibility they have for looking the other way when athletes act violently.

Organizations that treat violent behavior as a market inefficiency (as described above) are not only tolerating violent behavior, but using it as an opportunity rather than as a deterrent to player acquisition. While organizations granting employees second chances may seem commendable, these organizations aren't granting these chances for altruistic or morality-based purposes, but based simply on potential profit calculations.

Social Justice as Performance

One of these profit calculations is based on the positive press teams can get from actually releasing violent players, when it suits their material needs. Two examples come immediately to mind. The first is Brendan Leipsic, the former Washington Capitals, now-Magnitogorsk Metallurg (in the highest division of the KHL, the Russian professional hockey league) forward, and the second is former Seattle Seahawks offensive lineman Chad Wheeler, who no longer plays professional football.

Leipsic was released by the Washington Capitals a few days after screenshots were posted to Twitter of an Instagram group chat conversation where he used a variety of misogynistic and racist slurs, and all in all behaved like every awful stereotype of a sexist hockey "bro" (content warning for the rest of this paragraph). Leipsic called one woman a "little whore cunt," another a "slut," and compared another woman to a male football offensive lineman. He also "liked" a comment from his friend referring to a woman as a "fat native pig" and said he would "crush" or "pump" women to describe having sex with them. The release of these photos was met with outcry from the hockey world, though many (reflecting hockey's historically masculine culture) on social media also came to his defense, using discourses around cancel culture and bemoaning the fact that his privacy was attacked.[68] Responding to the social media backlash, the Capitals released Leipsic, a fourth-line player who had bounced around to multiple teams and between the NHL and minor leagues. He is no Alexander Ovechkin or Connor McDavid, which the speed of his release (without ever having been formally accused of a crime) made abundantly clear.

Chad Wheeler was arrested for several horrific acts of domestic violence in early 2021 and was released pretty much immediately by the Seahawks. Though the Seahawks released a statement "strongly condemning this act of domestic violence" and stating that their "thoughts and support are with the victim," their actions with other players may suggest otherwise.[69] Wheeler had an incident where campus police were called because he was punching windows and walls in front of his girlfriend and daughter, but the Seahawks brought him in anyway. The Seahawks drafted Frank Clark in 2015, even though he was arrested for domestic violence while in college, with considerable photographic evidence of the assault. But as longtime NFL journalist Mike Freeman wrote, "Clark is 6 foot 3, 260 pounds and runs like a car, so to teams, thumbs up, baby."[70] The Seahawks also brought in defensive back Tramaine Brock in 2017, a year after he was accused of punching and choking his girlfriend. Sure, they may have released Wheeler quickly, but he was a backup lineman, the pictures of his beaten wife were particularly jarring, and they could be seen publicly. He was expendable.

As discussions of the importance of social issues in sport (like violence against women) continue to increase, sport organizations may be incentivized to performatively express commitments to justice when it benefits their interests, without making fundamental changes to their organizational culture, structure, or the policies or systems that allow those behaviors or beliefs to perpetuate. The removal of a person like Leipsic or Wheeler is often tokenistic, used by organizations to demonstrate that they are progressive and to push a narrative that change is happening quicker than it really is. The release of expendable employees can be used by teams to "show" that they care about victims of violence, without negatively impacting their team's performance and the organization's bottom line. It really is just good ol' capitalism but responding to changing market conditions and expectations of social-justice-oriented motives and language.

CHAPTER FIVE

Labor and Violence
*American College Sports and
Minor League Baseball Exploitation*

There is only one place to start when it comes to labor exploitation in elite sport, and that is American college sports system, specifically American football and men's basketball. The National Collegiate Athletic Association (NCAA) remains one of the most naked examples of labor exploitation and of racial capitalism—the transfer of wealth produced by Black workers to white owners and managers—that exists in any sphere of contemporary life, let alone in sports.

In 2022 the schools in NCAA Division I athletics produced $15.8 billion in revenue, with football and men's basketball[1] as the highest-grossing sports.[2] The campus athletic workers who produced this revenue received none of it.[3] Until 2025, every dollar of value—including indirect value from school prestige, booster and donor payments, and campus life impacts[4]—produced by the commodity spectacle of college sports was transferred from predominantly Black athletes to predominantly white institutions, their athletic department workers, and even other athletes.

I know what many are thinking. *College athletes actually do get paid because of their scholarships and the education they get for free.* I'll get to that and other misplaced arguments from college sports fans, school administrators, those on the political right, and everyday people in due time. Before we go any further, we need to understand the link between racial capitalism and sport, as this structural formation underlies the exploitation of campus athletic workers in college football and men's basketball, and of so many workers the world over.

Racial Capitalism

Professional and elite sport has long been a prominent example of racial capitalism[5] and a site of structural harm,[6] both for those directly involved in sport and those outside of it. Zooming out, racial domination and racial hierarchies have always been a key component of capitalism itself.[7] But racial capitalism is not just about who is the exploiter and who is the exploited. The transatlantic slave trade of African people and the genocide of Indigenous peoples in the Americas did not simply occur alongside capitalist expansion, but played a vital role in its development. As Black Marxist scholar Cedric Robinson explains, the theory of racial capitalism does not simply *describe* the fact that capitalism has generally been marked by white capitalists extracting value from Black and other minoritized groups' labor, but shows also that these race-based extraction patterns necessitated an ideology of racial hierarchy that remains inextricable from capitalism even today.

As Robinson writes, since "the development, organization, and expansion of capitalist society pursued essentially racial directions, so too did social ideology."[8] Capitalism requires a belief in different human abilities and human values, in order to legitimize the inequalities that it necessarily produces. How else could capitalists justify why they and others have so much, while so many have so little? The legitimacy of the system has always been based on "fictions of differing human capacities, historically race."[9] Therefore, as Africana studies professor Jodi Melamed explains, racial capitalism isn't a version of capitalism, it *is* capitalism. Capitalism is and has always been racial capitalism. "Capital can only be capital when it is accumulating, and it can only accumulate by producing and moving through relations of severe inequality among human groups—capitalists with the means of production/workers without the means of subsistence, creditors/debtors, conquerors of land made property/the dispossessed and removed. These antinomies of accumulation require loss, disposability, and the unequal differentiation of human value, and *racism enshrines the inequalities that capitalism requires.*"[10] The effects of capitalism's racial character have downstream effects on all the elements of our superstructures, both past and present. As Robinson writes, "racialism inevitably permeated the social structures emergent from capitalism,"[11] including sports.

Racial Capitalism and the Plantation Dynamics of College Sports

In college football and men's basketball, we see the exploitation of Black laborers by largely white management and athletic departments—as well as the "disjoining or deactivating of relations between human beings."[12] This "disjoining of relations" is the process whereby athletes are evaluated, judged, and discussed as "assets" whose value consists only in their ability to produce value for their employers or bosses. Though campus athletic workers are not even paid for their labor, they still produce the commodity-spectacle of a college football or basketball game; in the words of sport scholar Bero Rigauer, "the spectator-consumer (still) receives the material object called for."[13] It should already be clear why many scholars see the college sport context as modern-day, sport-specific manifestation of racial capitalism and plantation-like social relations.[14]

Even at its inception, the creation of the term "student-athlete" was used for the express purpose of obfuscating the true labor relationship between campus athletic workers and universities, under the guise of "protecting" athletes from exploitation and securing the "sanctity" and "purity" of college sports.[15] For decades, sport scholars like Bero Rigauer, Eric Dunning, Billy Hawkins[16] and so many others have been calling out the use of "amateurism" (or shamateurism, in Dunning's words)[17] as a framing tactic to avoid having to treat athletes (many of whom are young Black men) properly as workers. In football and men's basketball, these sports have been professionalized to such an extent that they make any claims to "amateurism" completely laughable. Just like in professional sports, college athletes are expected to work forty hours per week on their sports and follow team rules and training regimens, and team revenue is earned from sponsorship, merchandise, ticket sales, and television rights deals. The only difference between professional and elite college sport is that colleges hide behind the veneer of "amateurism" to avoid paying their workers and offering them the labor protections they deserve.

While recent hard-won legal battles have *finally* resulted in campus athletic workers being able to profit off their name, image, and likeness (NIL),[18] this did not yet change the underlying exploitation at the heart of athletic departments revenue production. Fortunately, in late 2024 *House v. NCAA* forced college athletic departments in the Power Five conferences (the Atlantic Coast Conference, Big Ten, Big 12, Pac-12, and Southeastern Conference) to create a revenue sharing plan (set to begin in 2025)[19] where campus athletic workers could share in up to $20 million of revenue yearly.[20] As of this writing, this revenue sharing deal has not been enforced, however, and athletic departments are still not paying for the athletic labor of their workers. They are just "allowing" their unpaid workers to get paid by *someone else*, following the NIL case. Schools are simply forced to grant athletes the *privilege* (heavy sarcasm italics) of doing gig work on the side. What business wouldn't take this deal?

Consider for a moment how strange it is that NIL was something that had to be "won" by athletes in the first place. For more or less every other person, the ability to profit off our name, image, and likeness isn't even something we think about, because it is a right we obviously have. We can all go seek sponsorship with brands, get paid for other work we take on, or become a social media influencer. Of course, some jobs might include noncompete-type provisions that limit our ability to do some other kinds of work, but these are (a) rare and (b) part of a contract with a job that actually *pays*.

The NCAA "granting" players the ability to profit off NIL is like if years ago, your government decided to restrict a certain group of people from working in a particularly lucrative industry, and then finally decided to loosen that restriction after tons of public pressure. Sure, it's great that they finally did it, but why did this restriction exist in the first place? Should we really be applauding people for putting out fires in houses they themselves set fire to? While obviously not to the same level, this is reminiscent of some contemporary people in colonial states like the United Kingdom or the United States who bring up how their countries "ended" slavery. In reality, enslaved people's resistance is what ended slavery, and the only reason this resistance was even necessary was because of their enslavers and those who benefited from slavery, who then take undue credit for their liberation.

For the NCAA, granting NIL rights to athletes is also a delay-and-distract tactic, to avoid them bargaining for their right to a portion of the lucrative media rights contracts signed by schools and athletic conference, a right that they've finally begun to give some ground on starting in 2025. As the general public has become more receptive to the idea that campus athletic workers should be paid for their athletic labor, NIL offers a way for the NCAA and its institutions to claim that athletes can now profit, while ensuring that they aren't the ones footing the bill. This allows schools to continue producing the revenues that pay for huge athletic departments, help attract students (and their gargantuan tuition fees), and bring in donor dollars and school prestige.

Understanding how revenue is used by NCAA institutions, as well as the indirect benefits of athletics described above, can help rebut one of the main arguments that the NCAA and its apologists like to use against paying players, which is that athletic departments aren't profitable and don't have the money to pay athletes. While this may be true in a literal sense right now, it is only because of how athletic departments spend the surplus value that they expropriate. For Division I schools, especially those in the Power Five conferences, revenue is reinvested in luxurious athletic facilities meant to attract future athletic stars, and used to pay the many employees in university athletic departments. To give you an idea: in 2022 the Ohio State University athletic department reported $251.6 million in revenue, including $48.9 million coming from media rights and $59.6 million from ticket sales, $30 million from sponsorship and licensing agreements, and $62.9 million from donations and "contributions." The remaining revenue comes from the NCAA,

"Football Bowl Generated Revenue," parking, programs and concessions, conference distribution, sports camps, and "other" revenue.[21] While much of this revenue was paid out to athletic department staff, none of it went to athletes.

While athletic department staff racial makeup has improved in recent years, these athletic department staff are and have historically been predominantly white, and their salaries are paid for off the backs of the unpaid labor of campus athletic workers.[22] For example, in 2023, in Division I men's football and men's basketball—the two highest revenue-producing sports—48 percent of athletes in football were Black and 54 percent of athletes in men's basketball were Black,[23] while 16 percent of head football coaches were Black and 33 percent of head coaches in men's basketball were Black, 12 percent of football offensive coordinators and 24 percent of football defensive coordinators were Black, and 38 percent of assistant coaches in men's basketball were Black. At the Division I level, only 5 percent of head athletic trainers were Black, and only 6 percent of other trainers were Black. It is the same story at all the different positions of Division I athletic departments.[24] The framing of athletic departments as unprofitable both operates as an excuse for why schools "can't afford" to pay their athletes, and also obfuscates the still very real racial wealth transfer between predominantly Black athletic workers and their institutions.

This racial wealth transfer is especially stark, and given the nature of the sport, especially heinous, in college football. College football produces the most revenue of college sports, and it also produces the most injury and harm. These athletes are the most exploited in terms of pure dollars and cents, while also suffering the harshest long-term consequences to their bodies.[25]

We've already gone over the bodily harm and long-term brain injury that arises from football (chapter 3), so I won't belabor the point here. While (explicitly) professional players are more likely than college athletes to suffer debilitating injury, CTE, and brain trauma (simply because they've been playing the sport for longer), college athletes are not spared from these potential consequences. CTE is caused by repeated hits to the head, and for college players who practice nearly all year round for several years, they are still very much at risk.

Beyond this long-term injury risk, college football is also home to the biggest racial wealth transfer from workers to management of any sport. Remember the $59.6 million in ticket revenue that Ohio State athletic department received in 2022? $47 million of it came just from football.

So where does all this money go?

To coaches, for starters.

USA Today's 2023 annual review of coach compensation for Division I college football found an average salary of $2.7 million[26] for head coaches. In 2017 a football coach or men's basketball coach was the highest-paid public employee in 39 of 50 states.[27] Of the fifteen highest-paid NCAA football coaches for the 2023 season, Nick Saban topped the list at $11.7 million; Ohio State head coach Ryan Day sat in the seventh spot with $9.5 million. Clemson coach Dabo Swinney—who vehemently opposes paying campus athletic workers and anything related to athlete unionization, and once kicked a player off his team simply for "having a bad attitude"[28]—came in just below Saban at $11.5 million.

It's not just head coaches benefiting off the labor of campus athletic workers. Per a 2017 NCAA survey, the average college football coaching staff for Power Five schools had 29.9 paid staff, while non–Power Five schools had 21.7.[29] These numbers are surely even higher now. While non-head-coach pay is lower, assistants are still often making six to seven figures, with the top 10 Division I college football *assistant* coaches in 2021 making $1.5 million to $2.5 million annually.[30]

Data for 2022 from the US Department of Education shows that NCAA Division I Football Bowl Subdivision (FBS) schools[31] pay an average of $253,046 to all their men's full-time assistant coaches. Keep in mind that this average is from all universities with football programs, but includes coaches not just from football, but from all other men's sports. Assistant football coaches are likely paid an average much higher than this $253,046 (especially at Power Five schools), as this average is brought down by coaches from other sports. For further proof of this, consider the average assistant coach salary for Division I schools *without* football, which sits at $78,039, a $175,000 decrease. And when teams win their conference championship, particular "Bowl Games," or the National Championship (or simply make the National Championship playoffs), coaches can often accrue large bonuses, sometimes totaling in the hundreds of thousands or millions. Athletes receive nothing, except maybe a bag of sponsored merchandise and plastic trinkets branded with the Tostitos or Lockheed Martin logos.[32]

Racial Capitalism and Coercion in College Sports

Coaches are also free to leave their current job—as all employees should be—and seek greener pastures and higher salaries whenever they want to. While this isn't a problem in and of itself, it is an opportunity historically not afforded to players. If a coach recruits an athlete to a particular school and then leaves, until recently the athlete was not able to switch schools without penalty. Until April 2021, to switch workplaces campus athletic workers had to wait a year before being eligible to play (and still not get paid) at another university.

Recent changes to transfer rules now allow players to change universities and play immediately, but there are still potentially negative consequences for athletes who exercise this right. Many coaches have loudly and publicly complained about the transfer portal and players using it. In just one example, Michigan State head men's basketball coach Tom Izzo called the transfer portal "ridiculous," saying that giving kids this kind of freedom will hurt them in the long run, and that he will try to "protect" his athletes from leaving. In a classic example of "saying the quiet part out loud," he finished this rant by explaining that he and his staff "put a jail around all the kids on our campus to try to keep people from poaching our kids."[33]

This is common coach-speak at the elite college level, with coaches using patronizing language around "protecting" their "kids" as justification for asserting control over the lives of the athletes whose labor pays their salaries.[34] This rhetoric has led to parallels drawn with slavery, where owners of enslaved people would justify their ownership and exploitation as benevolent, saying that they were providing safety and security (and room and board) for people who were unable to make decisions for themselves. While college athletics is, of course, not as brutal or as legally entrenched as chattel slavery, the justifications used are similar. Writing in *The Atlantic*, Taylor Branch also likens college athletics to colonialism, with the same kind of paternalism-masked-as-care that was used by colonial powers to justify their exploitation of colonized people's labor and the expropriation of their resources. These parallels are further crystalized by the racial makeup of college athletics management (majority white) and its exploited labor force (majority Black), which once again mirrors colonial hierarchies.

In college sports, the "protection" offered by universities and coaches also often manifests in what coaches call "tough love" or "tough coaching," which is ostensibly done *for* athletes rather than being done *to* them. This includes harsh discipline and tight control over schedules and athlete behavior, even including off-the-field conduct and social justice activism. In the wake of the George Floyd murder and more conversation about racism and white supremacy in American society,[35] University of Texas students petitioned for the university to stop singing "The Eyes of Texas"—the school's "fight song" that debuted in minstrel shows in the Jim Crow South. When predominantly Black football players left the field while the song played later that year, University of Texas donors came out in droves calling for the school to stand up to "cancel culture" and threatened to stop donating to the school and to athletics. Here's a sampling of these messages, from a 2021 *Texas Tribune* article:

> "The Eyes of Texas is non-negotiable," wrote another graduate who said they've had season tickets since 1990 and whose name was redacted by the university. "If it is not kept and fully embraced, I will not be donating any additional money to athletics or the university or attending any events."
>
> "It's time for you to put the foot down and make it perfectly clear that the heritage of Texas will not be lost," wrote another donor who graduated in 1986. Their name was also redacted by UT-Austin. "It is sad that it is offending the blacks. As I said before the blacks are free and it's time for them to move on to another state where everything is in their favor."

The school still plays "The Eyes of Texas" today. In 2016, when some Black athletes refused to stand for the American national anthem in protest of police brutality and racial inequality, Clemson coach Dabo Swinney (2024 salary: $11 million) called these protests a distraction, saying that athletes should not use their platforms for activism and that some of those protesting police violence "need to move to another country."[36] Remember, this is what the coach is willing to say in public, at a news conference. It's not hard to imagine what he might say behind closed doors.

Beyond asserting control, this kind of school oversight and "tough" coaching reifies long-held beliefs around the purpose of sport as a tool of cultural indoctrination, to instill cultural values conducive to capitalist relations of production and to the white, heterosexual masculinity that has long been hegemonic in American sport and society more broadly. This ideological environment stresses ultimate obedience by players, where "questioning authority (is) a radical act, one of insubordination, rather than evidence of critical thinking cultivated in academic environments elsewhere on campus."[37] As sport scholar Andrew McGregor writes: "Authoritarian 'my way or the highway' tough love operates to police cultural values and reorient athlete behavior to conform to the values of middle-class whiteness whose lineage dates back to the Muscular Christian legitimization of sports. The white, capitalist, heterosexual masculinity that has long structured American society demands authoritative fatherly figures to hold the line against intellectuals, who, conservative coaches suggest, through their anti-intellectual rhetoric, embrace a cultural relativism that undermined traditional sources of authority."[38]

If students are supposed to be receiving an education as payment for their academic labor (more on that soon), shouldn't this kind of questioning of authority and critical thinking be lauded by universities and coaches, who are ostensibly educators? In the short term, coaches also don't want players engaging in activism or entering the transfer portal because of how it might affect their team's performance, and because it reduces the power they have over players. If there is no penalty for players leaving their schools (functionally, their workplaces), coaches are forced to actually care about the way they treat players, rather than knowing that these players are structurally coerced into playing and staying with that school and coach.

The new transfer rules have helped shift some of this balance of power, but coaches have not lost huge aspects of their control. While campus athletic workers can leave, coaches still determine playing time and player reputation, both of which are extremely important for athletes' prospects of playing professionally once they leave college. A bad word from a coach about a player's "loyalty," "discipline," or "character" can affect whether an athlete is drafted or signed to a professional team, and for how much. If a coach decides not to give an "unruly" athlete playing time, this can hurt that athlete's chances of playing professionally, and can even impact their NIL opportunities.[39]

This is an example of coaches exercising *status coercion*, a concept developed by sociologist Erin Hatton that describes the way that workers, especially those without labor and state protections, can be coerced into their labor.[40] Hatton uses examples from precarious workers across different fields, including prison laborers, graduate student workers, and college athletes, to explain how these workers are coerced into labor and into performing this labor under difficult conditions, due to the power that their overseers (usually coaches, in the case of athletes) have over their work privileges and benefits. The immense power that coaches wield over collegiate and amateur athletes include the very chance to play and showcase their talents in order to move up and earn money from their athletic abilities.[41]

In my research interviewing NFL and NBA scouts and management, nearly all of them spoke about the importance of player "intel" when it comes to assessing the "character" of a player they might want to sign or draft. The intel that management takes in almost always comes from coaches at lower levels, be that college, high school, or AAU (in basketball only). As one NBA front-office worker explained, "It's a very connection-based industry. So [it's about talking to] managers, coaches, teammates, somebody that grew up with them. It's not even as much about seeing the person in person or the player in person. It's about talking to people around the arena, coaches, assistant coaches, other scouts, and then kind of gathering that information."

Status coercion is especially effective in the context of college sports because athletes are not getting paid, and because this status coercion also interacts with elements of *structural* coercion for many athletes. As explained in chapter 3, structural coercion involves "the ways in which broader context acts upon individuals to compel them"[42] to make certain decisions and behave in particular ways. College athletes are spread out across the country, and their careers only last a few years, making collective organizing difficult. Add in the ideological environment that many athletes have grown up in (and that is reinforced by coaches), where college sports are framed as just a "stepping stone" and the athletes themselves are framed as amateur "student-athletes," and many athletes have historically not even seen themselves as workers. This may be changing though, as unionization efforts have begun in different corners of the college football landscape; and as explained above, the recent decision in *House v. NCAA* may compel schools in the Power Five conferences to compensate athletes. As Nathan Kalman-Lamb, a coauthor of *The End of College Football*, explains,[43] athletes are more and more aware of the exploitative dynamics of their sport, though they still feel hindered to speak out due to the status coercion they face: "[Athletes] are conscious of the fact that there is a disproportionately racialized workforce in a sport like football, and they are extremely conscious of the fact that the coaches and athletic department administrators are predominantly white. These kinds of dynamics are all symptomatic of racial capitalism and are things that frame and shape their everyday lives. And they notice them, but they also know that it's not safe to talk about those things in many contexts, because of the status coercion that they face."

Beyond this, the simple fact that university tuition rates are so high, and that many American athletes feel (rightly in a lot of cases) that athletic excellence is their best and sometimes only chance for upward mobility, means there are huge structural constraints on athletes. This is particularly salient for football players, who are more likely to come from disadvantaged economic conditions.[44] One Black college football player explained, in Kalman-Lamb and Silva, *The End of College Football*:

> Where we're from, you end up dead or in jail. It's literally a place full of statistics. When we left, my parents were just so motivated by being in a new place. It was just, the verbiage was more along the lines of, "Hey, we can't pay for you to go to school, but here's some options for you,

academics or athletics." I don't think I'm not intelligent, but I just knew that I had a better chance playing sports . . . [and] I had to get a scholarship. If I didn't get a scholarship, I wouldn't have been going to school. I would've had to apply to work somewhere, because my parents could not afford it, period. Even then though, I was sending money back when I got my stipend and little things just to help. Like I said, I'm the oldest and it was always tight around the house. Anything I could do to make it less tight or make my parents worry less, or just aim that direction into the other kids and not me kind of thing, that was always my goal.

In football especially, players know that they have no choice but to participate in the NCAA system, even when they know the system is unfair. Another athlete from Kalman-Lamb and Silva, *The End of College Football*:

So when you take college football and look at it from that point of view you see that the whole thing is built to make money—money for universities, for coaches, for ads, for ESPN and CBS and shit. Everything in college football is about making money . . . except if you're a so-called student-athlete. Then you can't make any money. You're not allowed to. You're told you're not a professional and can't take a share of the money you are part of earning, you know? But the fucked-up thing is, bro, there's nowhere else to go. They have created this system where you can't go nowhere [else] to play football because there ain't any options. So if you want to be a professional and get paid, you have to play in college or nobody going to notice you. How is that fair?

Rather than being seen as a constraint for athletes, the disadvantaged circumstances of these athletes is even used by coaches to extract more value from them. In his 2012 book *Play Their Hearts Out*, which looks at youth sports, George Dohrman spoke to one white coach who told him matter-of-factly that "the perfect team is a team of all single moms,"[45] because these players are easier to control and may play with a "chip on their shoulder."

This type of thinking is also not limited to white coaches. Former NFL star and now University of Colorado coach Deion Sanders recently explained, to laughter from the other panelists, that while he wants his quarterbacks and offensive linemen to come from dual-parent households and have high grades, "defensive linemen is totally the opposite. Single mama, trying to get it, he's on free lunch. He's just trying to make it, to rescue mama."[46] While Sanders came under fire for these comments, he was perhaps just saying out loud what many football coaches already think: they want players who come from poor backgrounds with no other options for upward mobility and financial security, because these athletes will be "willing" (more like structurally *forced*) to sacrifice their bodies and brains for their teams and for the chance to make it professionally.

The structural coercion of college athletes also serves another purpose. Beyond ensuring a steady stream of athletic labor to universities and those who expropriate and materially benefit off this labor, it is also used to sell false notions around the American Dream and meritocracy in "post-racial" America. As David Leonard and C. Richard King write in *Commodified and Criminalized: New Racism and African Americans in Contemporary Sports*, the commodification of Black athletes as athletic labor "functions as an ideological and discursive commodity used to sell the American Dream and color blindness in post-civil rights America."[47] Though Black athletes are in reality economically exploited by college sports—while suffering bodily harm and injury that often stays with them for life, and not truly benefiting from the education that is supposed to be their wage—their inclusion in these sports is framed in a completely opposite way, as evidence of a postracial meritocracy that has *allowed* them the privilege of university and potential upward mobility.

Dispelling the Myths of College Athlete "Payment"

In football and men's basketball, often termed the "revenue-producing" sports for college athletic departments, the teams are filled predominantly with Black athletes, who are brought into predominantly white universities solely for their value as athletic laborers. Though they are not paid for their labor, it is made very clear to them at multiple points in the recruiting process and in their time on campus that their athletic ability is why they're welcomed at this school.[48] Such athletes have described feeling like "they are perceived as mere interlopers within the academic domain."[49] As sport scholar Billy Hawkins, author of *The New Plantation: Black Athletes, College Sports, and Predominantly White NCAA Institutions*, writes: "The dehumanization of Black athletes takes place when these institutions value Blacks more as athletes than as students, especially when output (athletic performance) does not equal input (educational opportunities)."[50]

This dehumanization and commodification of Black athletic labor lays bare both the exploitation of these athletes' labor, as well as the ways that "institutions continue to support racial hierarchies of intellectual and physical superiority,"[51] where Black athletes are brought in for their physical prowess but are not expected or given the opportunity to perform intellectually. This commodification makes athletes feel replaceable and alienated.[52] A 2011 study by sport scholar Derek Van Rheenen found that most athletes in revenue-producing sports felt exploited by their institutions, and Black athletes were most likely to feel this way. "83% of 4th year revenue college athletes reported feeling exploited by their university. By comparison, 73% of first year, 63% of second year, and 75% of third year revenue college athletes tend to feel exploited by their university.... Black non-revenue college athletes are 3.23 times more likely to feel exploited than their White peers, and 2.76 times more likely to feel exploited than members of other racial categories."[53]

They have good reason for feeling this way, considering that they are not paid for their labor, and do not receive a *meaningful* education in lieu of the wage they're owed. In a 2018 report by Shaun Harper and the University of Southern California Race and Equity Center, the authors found:[54] "Black men were 2.4% of undergraduate students enrolled at the 65 [Power Five] universities, but comprised 55% of football teams and 56% of men's basketball teams on those campuses. Across four cohorts, 55.2% of Black male student-athletes graduated within six years, compared to 69.3% of student-athletes overall, 60.1% of Black undergraduate men overall, and 76.3% of undergraduate students overall."

These kinds of statistics also help counter one of the primary arguments against the notion of campus athletic worker exploitation, which is that "they are paid in scholarships." Many sport scholars have shown why this kind of argument does not hold water.

First, if athletes are being "paid" with their scholarships, then what we really mean is that they are being paid with *education*. As sport scholar Kalman-Lamb, coauthor of *The End of College Football*, explains:[55] "What they [college athletes] are promised—it's not a degree, it's not a piece of paper. No, you are promising that athlete an education, you're promising that you're going to teach them and provide them with skills and value that is commensurate with the work that they're doing for your institution." Athletes are ostensibly receiving an education in exchange for their athletic labor, and this education is valued at the cost of tuition and (some) living expenses. This is why you'll hear many claim that athletes are being paid the equivalent of $40,000 to $50,000 per year, in scholarships and expenses.

The first, obvious point about this should be that only in the United States does education cost this much. No other country in the world charges as much for education—in Canada, tuition averages around CA$6,700 per year (about US$5,000),[56] while in many countries in Europe, costs are in the low thousands or free. The only reason athletes' scholarship "pay" is ostensibly "worth" so much is because tuition is so exorbitant in the first place.

More than this, athletes are also not receiving all the benefits of this education, which is supposedly their wage. As Kalman-Lamb explains, they can't pick the classes they want, and are steered toward particular classes and majors—"athletic departments deliberately and systematically funnel athletes into majors that the university is perceived to be less onerous in order to place lower demands on them academically, so that they can put more of that energy into their athletics."

Sometimes it isn't even a matter of steering them toward or away from majors, but the simple constraint that athletes have sport-related commitments twice a day—practice and film study in the late afternoon, and lifts in the morning. Many classes are simply out of the question for athletes. Some athletes are even lured to a school and told they could study a particular subject that they're interested in, or that the school is known for, only to find out that they're actually unable to study in that program if they want to keep their scholarship. Kalman-Lamb again: "Often athletes are going will come to a university with a particular major in mind because that university has a strength to that area, and the academics have been used to seduce them in the recruiting process. Then they are told when they arrive on campus, they are not allowed to take the very major they were recruited to take." When college athletes are able to take some of the classes they want, they have much less time and energy than nonathlete students to spend on them. Add up practice time, film study, lifts, games, and travel, and athletes are working forty-hour weeks. In sports like football and basketball, athletes travel midweek and at the end of the week for games, which results in either missed class time or once again being forced not to take certain classes. Because of NCAA regulations around how many "official" days of school athletes can miss, they are also very often traveling at night, which eats into any remaining time they have to sleep or study. It is hard to imagine how college athletes can be expected to perform in the classroom and get the most out of their education (again, their supposed "payment") under these conditions.

Even when athletes do receive (air quotes) "preferential treatment" by professors and university staff, it is only because of their ability to produce value for the university as athletes. It is also most often the kind of treatment or aid that does not help them as learners or enrich their college experience, but instead allows them to just scrape by, pass a class, and stay eligible for sports. One Black football player explained, "I would purposefully not wear any team-issued gear to class for the first few weeks in order to not be labeled as an athlete. Attending a PWI [predominantly white institution] like I did brought enough negative assumptions about me without football adding to it... professors didn't treat Black athletes the same. They looked down on us... like we didn't deserve to be there."[57]

The University of North Carolina (UNC) academic scandal is a particularly egregious example of this. For almost twenty years, UNC provided fake classes and automatic grades to many athletes to ensure their eligibility.[58] While some may say this is a "benefit" to athletes (*they didn't have to go to class!*), it directly takes away from the education that is ostensibly their wage. Adding more racial capitalist fuel to the fire, many of these "paper classes" were part of the school's African American studies department, which offers the added benefit (for institutions) of cheapening and delegitimizing what is a vital area of study. Unsurprisingly, the 2013 USC Race and Equity Center report found that Black men represent 2.8 percent of undergraduate students at UNC, but 62 percent of the school's basketball and football players, and that these athletes graduate at a rate of 45 percent, compared with 72 percent for all athletes, 74 percent for Black males, and 90 percent for all students.[59]

None of these revelations about the education environment are groundbreaking. But it is important to understand that if athletes are being ostensibly paid through the value of the education provided, then this education should be top-notch. Every loss to athletes' education experience should be considered lost wages, under the logic of the "paid in scholarships" crowd.

Another important question to ask ourselves when thinking about college athletes and pay is: When was the last time anyone accepted payment *in kind* for their work? There is no other sector of the economy where people are expected to do a job and be paid in some sort of service or good that isn't money. Everyone is paid in money. Thankfully, we long ago moved away from Rockefeller and Carnegie factory towns where workers earned factory credits to buy food at the factory store and pay for their factory house rent, all but shackling them to their employer (who also happened to be the store owner and their landlord).[60] This sort of factory-town arrangement is actually closer to the college athlete experience, for those who believe they are "paid" through their scholarships. Athletes are "paid" in their education, credits for the dining hall and meals on the road, and housing on campus or close to it, but they are not paid a wage that they can spend as they please.

The exploitation of college athletes in revenue-producing sports like football and men's basketball also has the perverse effect that the unpaid labor of these athletes is effectively subsidizing college athletes in other sports. In a 2018 *Los Angeles Times* editorial, sports historian and former college Division I runner Victoria Jackson wrote about this phenomenon, explaining how the dollars generated by and then withheld from revenue sport athletes in football and basketball are used to "subsidize idyllic student-athlete experiences" like hers. Calling the college sports system "21st century Jim Crow," Jackson explains how she was able to compete as a college runner on scholarship, while never spending more than twenty hours a week on her sport, and with coaches that prioritized academics. She eventually went on to earn a PhD. "Thanks to the labor of football and basketball players, I did not pay for college, took full advantage of attending one of the top public universities in the nation, and traveled to cool places on the school's dime."[61]

Jackson also notes the racial breakdown of this wealth transfer. It's not just white coaches and management earning salaries off the unpaid labor of Black football and basketball players, but other white *athletes* in non-revenue-producing sports that also benefit. According to NCAA data, 20 percent of Division I athletes are Black and 55 percent are white. However, Black men constitute 55 percent of the athletic labor force in men's basketball and 48 percent in football, compared to just 23 percent and 36 percent, respectively, for white men. These are the sports that produce revenue, and this revenue is used to pay for the college athlete experiences of so many others.

Professional Sports: Wrestling and Minor League Baseball

Labor exploitation is not limited to college sports but includes cases of explicitly professional sports. As with all labor exploitation under capitalism, it is those on the margins of any industry that are most at risk and most harmed. The most visible athletes—the Cristiano Ronaldos, Mike Trouts, and John Cenas of the sporting world—are not those at risk of harm, and are propped up as examples for why athletes are not exploited. Just like how those who benefit from contemporary systems of inequality will point to individual barrier-breakers—*There's no more racism in the USA, Obama was president. What do you mean sexism, our CEO is a woman*—many will point to those at the top of sport system as evidence that exploitation cannot be occurring.

But as Varda Burstyn writes, "while the earnings of the top players glitter at the top of the sport pyramid, the economic reality for the majority of boys and men who play and train in the broad feeder systems of professional sport is generally grim."[62] Like with every form of violence and harm in this book, there are too many individual cases to explore all of them. There are young soccer players recruited into youth academies and spit out years later with no education or employable skills to show for it,[63] journeyman boxers and other combat sport veterans underpaid for their fights and with no pensions or medical insurance, and even unpaid youth athletes playing in tournaments and competitions that produce revenues for organizers and governing bodies. We don't have time to explore all these issues with the specificity they deserve. Instead, we will look specifically at professional wrestling and professional baseball, as these industries provide case studies for the various mechanisms of exploitation used by ownership.

Professional Wrestling and WWE

While professional wrestling (think light shows, suplexes, and chairs as weapons, not Olympic wrestling) is of course a performance, and the athletes don't compete against each other in the same way that athletes do in other sports, these athletes are nevertheless workers, and their labor carries significant risk. Brain and head trauma is common, as are all sorts of other ailments and injury. These result from the stunts these athletes perform, as well as their near-constant travel and performance schedule, which often sees athletes performing and traveling every day without a break for weeks at a time.[64]

Though wrestlers produce revenue for corporate entities like World Wrestling Entertainment (WWE), they often receive little of the profits they produce. According to Forbes, in 2016 WWE finished with revenues of $659 million, of which only $50 million (7.6 percent) went to the athletes in the ring.[65] As with many entertainment industries under capitalism, even this small slice of revenue is then divided inequitably, with top performers earning huge sums and those on the margins fighting for scraps. Of this $50 million in revenue, $31.4 million went to the top ten wrestlers, while the rest of WWE athletes earned the remaining $18.6 million split between them. This means that apart from the top ten earners, all the remaining WWE wrestlers earned *2.8 percent* of WWE revenue.

Sport scholar Karen Corteen has conceptualized the labor-related violence and exploitation of wrestlers by WWE as a form of white-collar crime, where workers are harmed in pursuit of corporate profits.[66] As Corteen writes, "WWE does what corporations ordinarily do: they pursue profit and put the economic health and well-being of their shareholders over and above the health and well-being of their workers."[67]

Corteen's conceptualization of this exploitation as a form of white-collar *crime* relies on a zemiological, harm-based approach to understanding criminality.[68] Rather than focusing strictly on the *legality* of a certain behavior, zemiological perspectives focus on the harms produced by actions and even by the omission of certain actions, with particular attention paid to the actions of powerful actors[69] like WWE. Social-harm-based approaches to criminological inquiry are meant to counter completely legalistic approaches to crime, which can advantage powerful sectors and people in society who cause harm without contravening any explicit law, as "the social injuries and harms resulting from the corporate pursuit of profit, capital accumulation and power are not subjects for criminological inquiry."[70] While zemiology has grown as an academic subdiscipline in recent years, focusing on social harm or social violence committed through acts of commission or *omission*, this understanding of deviance and criminality has long been a part of Marxist analysis.: As Engels wrote in 1845, in *The Condition of the Working Class in England*:[71]

> When one individual inflicts bodily injury upon another such that death results, we call the deed manslaughter; when the assailant knew in advance that the injury would be fatal, we call his deed murder. But when society places hundreds of proletarians in such a position that they inevitably meet a too early and an unnatural death, one which is quite as much a death by violence as that by the sword or bullet; when it deprives thousands of the necessaries of life, places them under conditions in which they cannot live—forces them, through the strong arm of the law, to remain in such conditions until that death ensues which is the inevitable consequence . . . its deed is murder just as surely as the deed of the single individual; disguised, malicious murder, murder against which none can defend himself . . . because no man sees the murderer, because the death of the victim *seems* a natural one, since the offence is more one of omission than of commission. *But murder it remains.*

While this passage describes state and capitalists' responsibility for the death of working-class people, the same mechanisms of harm (ostensibly "legal" acts, done in pursuit of profit) are present in a variety of sport sectors, WWE included. WWE's monopoly on wrestling, the deregulation of the industry, and the dehumanization and commodification of its athletes has resulted in extensive harm for these athletes and their families, both through crimes of commission and omission. Corteen again: "Work-related harms in this industry are individual, familial, and social. They entail premature deaths (as a result of enlarged hearts, heart attacks, accidental and intended fatal drug overdoses) and nonfatal drug overdoses. They also comprise: wrestler mistreatment; short, long and permanent injuries; addictions to, and use and abuse of, painkillers, alcohol, and other drugs including heroin, anabolic steroids and human growth hormones; chronic physical ill-health and poor mental well-being; individual and familial breakdown."[72]

Many wrestlers have died prematurely, with 2004 research indicating that wrestlers have a death rate seven times higher than the US population. Even when compared to pro football players, wrestlers are 20 times more likely to die before age forty-five.[73] The case of Chris Benoit was perhaps the most disturbing example. Benoit died by suicide at age forty, after killing his wife and son in their home. Like some of the football players discussed in chapter 3, Benoit took repeated hits to the head during his training and performances in WWE, and his autopsy revealed that he had a brain like that of an eighty-five-year-old Alzheimer's patient when he died.[74]

In WWE, wrestlers have little to no say over their work conditions—they are told their wages and how much they're expected to work and told to take it or leave it.[75] Worse still, they are technically classified as independent contractors with WWE, which does not pay for their travel expenses or health insurance.[76] In many ways, their position within WWE resembles others in the so-called "gig" economy, where companies like Uber, Lyft, and Door-Dash have been able to flout labor laws by classifying their workers as "independent contractors," even when most of the company's labor is done by those who work full-time hours. Boxers and other combat sport athletes face similar gig-type work conditions. The fact that this kind of gig-economy work has remained legal in so many North American jurisdictions speaks to the legal system's subordinate, superstructural role in relation to capital.

Without health insurance, paid time off, or any other employee benefits, wrestlers have no real "offseason." Some have reported working 300 days a year, with constant travel, in order to earn a living.[77] To keep up their larger-than-life appearances, wrestlers are also expected to put on massive amounts of weight and muscle, which often requires using steroids or other performance-enhancing drugs. The nonstop schedule and performance expectations have also led to a culture of painkiller and other drug use, often necessary for athletes to keep performing while injured or worn down. To keep expanding and raking in profits, WWE has also continued to push the limits in terms of the acrobatics, stunts, and overall dangers the wrestlers must subject themselves to.

The only attempt real at unionization and improving labor relations for wrestlers came in the 1980s, as wrestling and WWE were reaching new heights of popularity. WWE and its infamous owner Vince McMahon behaved exactly as any industry-leading corporation would over this period, using its profits to grow, expand, and suck up any smaller wrestling federations, to thwart any viable competition and thus any bargaining power for wrestlers.[78]

WWE also pushed for deregulation of WWE and the wrestling industry more generally. For example, by classifying itself as "entertainment" rather than "sport," WWE was able to "escape regulatory oversight by the state athletics commission(s),"[79] including requirements around physical exams for wrestlers. McMahon and WWE "effectively established a monopoly over the industry,"[80] which nearly always spells trouble for workers.

With little real alternative available, wrestlers were forced to continue taking short-term contracts with WWE, all the while knowing that huge disparities existed between most wrestlers' wages and those of the biggest stars. While quiet plans were being discussed among some wrestlers about a union, nothing major materialized. When these wrestlers tried to get Hulk Hogan, WWE's highest earner and marquee draw, involved, he reported on the union stirrings to McMahon, not wanting to risk cutting into his own huge earnings. With the boss aware and angry, union efforts floundered, with wrestlers rightfully concerned that McMahon would take his anger out on them by barring them from WWE and obstructing whatever income they could still earn as wrestlers.

In situations where athletes have little leverage, due to either legal constraints like their employee status or structural ones like a lack of competition in their industry, their choices are generally either to form their own leagues or to try to unionize. The barriers to creating a financially viable and competitive professional league that can compete with established leagues are monumental. They require not only vast amounts of capital that 99 percent of athletes do not have, but also complete buy-in from the best athletes in a sport. Asking professional athletes who've worked their whole lives to make money through their sport to risk being blackballed from established leagues for joining an upstart league with no guarantees or track record is a serious request, and even the most labor-conscious and radical athletes would have a hard time making this choice. Start-up leagues also need buy-in from media, who are vital to increasing support and ensuring the viability of young sport and entertainment properties. These media have a vested interest in keeping established leagues on side, as they too would be taking a risk by supporting an upstart league and especially by writing critically about established leagues.

This leaves unionization and collective bargaining, the path generally taken by professional athletes. Until 2023, minor league baseball players were some of the last nonunionized professional team sport athletes and suffered the consequences for it. Their recent unionization demonstrates the power of worker solidarity and workers' voices, as the union was immediately able to win huge increases in pay and improvements in working conditions, after forcing organizations to actually sit down at the negotiating table.

Sowing the Seeds of Its Own Destruction: Working Conditions and Eventual Unionization in Professional Baseball

For so many Minor League Baseball (MiLB) players, the 2023 season marked their first year as unionized workers, improving on years of exploitative, awful working conditions marked by long, cramped bus rides, three-to-a-room housing, fast food, and extremely low salaries paid only from April to August (that didn't include mandatory spring training). Though MiLB is the primary pipeline to the multibillion-dollar MLB, until players actually had the ability to collectively bargain and fight for their rights as a collective, these athletes suffered. As Garett Broschius, a career minor leaguer, explained in a 2018 SBnation.com article:[81]

> Very early on in my career, I looked around and noticed things didn't seem quite right. You have the bat boy in some cases making more money per game than the first baseman is making. You're cramming six guys into a two-bedroom apartment, just to make ends meet and split the rent as many ways as possible. You have players sleeping on futons in people's basements, because a host family saves you a lot of money. Host families are great, but why are we asking people in the community to take in professional baseball players in a $10 billion industry?

Jack Kruger, who played seven years in the minors before retiring in 2022, told similar stories in a self-posted Twitter thread in February 2022. "I've had teammates who were homeless. I've had teammates skip numerous meals. I've had teammates get called up & down more than 20 times in a season. I've missed weddings. I've missed events. Besides my signing bonus, I've made very little money." Players lived in two-bedroom apartments with three to five teammates and worked part-time jobs in the offseason. They lived a transient life without any financial or social security or stability. And they hadn't organized or unionized, in short, because they were scared.[82] Broschius again: "Fear is the predominant issue for players. When I was talking to players [about organizing], it's not that they didn't recognize the benefits of a union, but they were scared. They looked at me as if I might as well have been asking them to jump off of a cliff with me. They are so fearful of those owners, and what they might think about it, and how the owners might judge that decision to act collectively."

These athletes have been working their whole lives to make the majors. For some, especially those plucked out of Central America and the Caribbean (some as young as sixteen), this is their "way out," much like for college basketball and football players. Many of these athletes grew up in poverty and would have to leave the States if they quit baseball.[83] Like athletes afraid to lose their spot if they miss games to a hurt knee or concussion, or wrestlers afraid of being blackballed by Vince McMahon, MiLB players had been hesitant to rock the boat, feeling like they couldn't risk becoming a pariah to their organization or to baseball kingmakers more generally. Their status in their organization and in the whisper networks of baseball's clubhouses was at stake.

These pressures are felt especially by Latin American players. These athletes are "discovered" and put into academies at young ages in the Dominican Republic, Panama, Venezuela, and other Central American and Caribbean countries. Though the MLB's Attachment 46 clause prohibits negotiating or signing contracts with children under sixteen, teams frequently make "handshake deals" with players even younger than this, promising a lucrative signing bonus when they turn sixteen. However, they can back out of these deals at any time if the athlete doesn't perform or develop as they expect. These handshake deals also often tie a young athlete to a particular club, reducing their negotiation leverage.[84]

Athletes may also be approached by *buscones*, "independent, unregulated scouts who scour Latin American countries 'in search of young talent and notify MLB scouts when they believe they have discovered noteworthy players.'"[85] These buscones often house and train players in their own baseball academies, with young athletes forgoing any education to train relentlessly. A place in these academies is often paid for through a loan, meant to be paid back to the buscones when the athlete "makes it." If they don't develop as expected and receive a lower signing bonus (or the team backs out altogether) when they hit sixteen, young athletes and their families can find themselves in debt. There have also been reports of buscones providing performance-enhancing drugs to players, as their own income is dependent on the player's success and progression in baseball.[86]

Even for athletes signed legally, while the big-name prospects and players make the headlines, most Latin American players are paid small signing bonuses and forced into the same exploitative working conditions and low pay as other minor leaguers. Adding to this, many of them don't speak English, they are far away from home, and many are expected to send money back to support those at home.[87] The cultural mythology of the American Dream and the rags-to-riches stories of Dominican and other Latin American baseball players also impacts players' willingness to put up with horrible working conditions.[88] These players have often been fully devoted to baseball since they were twelve or thirteen, with no other skills or education and little family wealth to fall back on.

The MLB has consistently gotten away with underpaying players in the minor leagues because its owners have tons of money and powerful friends in Congress who've historically protected them from antitrust legislation and from paying minimum wage.[89] But most importantly, they were able to do this because athletes have historically been unable to organize, and with this, unable to negotiate collectively and threaten to withhold their labor without improvements to their working conditions.

That is, until now. In September 2023, a majority of minor league players signed their union cards, concluding years and months of collective struggle. In 2023, minor league baseball players played their first season as unionized workers.[90] Initial gains to working conditions and pay have been dramatic—with minimum salary increases of over 100 percent. ESPN reported:[91]

At each level, the pay structure will see annual minimum salaries go from:

Triple-A: $17,500 to $35,800
Double-A: $13,800 to $30,250
High-A: $11,000 to $27,300
Single-A: $11,000 to $26,200
Complex league: $4,800 to $19,80

Small increases are scheduled for 2025, 2026 and 2027, and workers will also be paid nearly all year round. Instead of only receiving their wages during the four- or five-month season, players will be paid from January 2 until mid-November.

Beginning in 2024, players in Triple-A and Double-A are also guaranteed their own bedroom, with special accommodations for players with spouses or children. In the other leagues, teams will provide transportation to stadiums and team meals. The union also won expanded medical rights and injury expense coverage, as well as name, image, and likeness rights (which will allow for group licensing for things like video games). While these benefits might not seem like much, they are monumental increases for minor league players, and will provide drastic differences in quality of life. They will also give more players without independent wealth or a hefty signing bonus the chance to continue on in baseball.

None of this would have been possible without a union. In many ways, none of it would have been possible without the horrid conditions and greed of MLB owners as well. MiLB unionization is a case study in dialectics, and in the contradictions between workers and ownership under capitalism. Marx famously wrote that capitalism carries the "seeds of its own destruction,"[92] and union organizers often say that "a bad boss is the best organizer." Whichever quote you like better, this is exactly what we see here.

For years, MLB ownership has been hell-bent on squeezing every ounce of profit possible out of their organizations, and realized that the easiest way to do that was to continue spending money on their Major League club while cutting every possible corner in the minor leagues. Ownership assumed (rightly, for many years) that the legislative context and their political connections would protect them from legal trouble, that narratives framing athletes as "just overgrown children playing a game" rather than workers would hinder public support for their cause, and that the structural position of MiLB players as transient workers with short careers, obsessed with the dream of striking it big in the majors, would stunt their collective power. Ownership thus responded to the profit imperatives of capitalism by creating such abhorrent working conditions that they essentially paved the way for increased public support for players, and eventual unionization.

In the mid 2010s, players began leveraging the open nature of the internet and their own social media profiles to broadcast their minor league horror stories to the public. One of these articles—a *Washington Post* feature with Matt Paré (who started his own blog called *Homeless Minor Leaguer*) and Garrett Broschius (mentioned above)—caught the eye of a union organizer and activist Bill Fletcher Jr., who took on the MiLB players cause.[93] Fletcher, Broschius, and Harry Marino—a former minor league pitcher turned lawyer—began speaking to players, teaching them about unionization and collective action, and gathering support. This support may have started slow—players are scattered across 120 teams around the United States and change teams constantly, and precarious athletic workers generally are understandably reticent to stand out in any off-the-field way—but MLB decisions and unfair legislation acted as powerful recruiting tools.[94]

In March 2018, Congress quietly passed a spending bill that incorporated provisions from the previously failed *Save America's Pastime Act*. These provisions allowed for minor league teams *not* to compensate players beyond forty hours a week, even if they spent more time than that traveling, practicing, and preparing for games. This provision also classified minor league athletes as "seasonal apprentices," which was particularly insulting for players. As Trevor

Hildenberger, who played in the MLB for the four-year period 2017–2021, explained, "We sacrifice weddings and funerals and births to be here, and they don't even want us to make minimum wage. That was a big eye opener for me and many other players."[95]

The MLB then cut forty-two minor league teams in 2019, effectively firing over 1,000 players overnight, and did not pay players for the canceled 2020 COVID season. Between these cuts, the insulting congressional spending bill, and players sharing their experiences both with each other and with the public via social media, blogs, and in mainstream publications, fires were now stoked among players. The MLB Players Association (MLBPA) agreed to allow affiliation with minor league players in August 2022, and just seventeen days later MiLB players signed their union cards and joined.[96]

Structural Coercion and the Romanticization of Sport and Play

This importance of public support is essential. When it comes to capitalists justifying exploitative labor conditions, it is not just about lobbying lawmakers and making sure everything is legally aboveboard. Management, ownership, and executives in nearly every sport, from baseball and football to tennis and diving, need to win not only the legal battle but the narrative, ideological one as well. They try to ensure that people do not think about athletes as workers, but as overpaid divas that are *paid* to *play a sport*. As we've seen all throughout history and in all capitalist economies, it is vital that ownership and management cut off as many avenues for labor solidarity as they can. I'm sure many of you have heard the arguments.

Athletes get paid millions to play a children's game. You know that sport that you pay money to play once a week with your friends? They get paid to do that! These athletes are living the dream. They're so spoiled. They never work a day in their life.

It's true that *some* athletes make millions, and it's also true that if we paid people according to their objective worth to society, many professions (teachers, nurses, doctors, sanitation workers, miners, and so on) would make more money than athletes. Of course, objective worth to society and to the fulfillment of human needs is difficult to quantify and requires philosophical debate and econometric calculation that I don't have time for here.

In response to the argument about athletes' salaries, though, this sort of profession/worth calculation illustrates that under capitalism, people do not earn salaries according to their relationship (however hard to quantify) with a normative social good, but according to their relationship with profit.

Anyone making the argument that athletes should not earn high salaries because they do not produce any social good or because they're "playing a game" should be asking the same question about a variety of other industries and jobs, many of which pay highly and do not produce any social good. Some of these industries even actively produce social harm,[97] and yet high-earning executives or workers rarely receive the type of interrogation that high-earning athletes do. Perhaps even more importantly, when athletes are accused of being paid too well for the social value of what they are doing, this critique rarely extends to a wider critique of the capitalist system that underlies it. Instead, it is often used as a racist or classist dog whistle to call out athletes as lazy, pampered, or entitled.[98]

This critique also rarely extends to ownership and upper management. If people are so concerned about wealth related to sports, why doesn't the same critique also apply to ownership? Is it okay to make money off the work of athletes playing a children's game, but not for the athletes playing the children's game themselves to make money from it? Perhaps questioning the relationship of wealth accumulation to social good and "worth" is a step too far, as it logically leads down a rabbit hole of interrogation into all of capitalist relations of production, and many people do not have the desire or the energy to engage with these questions.

Even if one does not interrogate the logics of capitalism, do athletes not deserve protection from unfair labor practices just like other employees do? Under society's current capitalist construction, many professional sports teams and leagues make lots of money, as do a variety of other industries. Regardless of whether the workplace in question is a steel mill, a software development company, or a professional sports league, from a Marxist perspective, one's position as a worker or as a capitalist is not based on any arbitrary wealth or income threshold, but on one's relationship to capital. The athletes—the workers in the wealth production equation of professional sports—are the ones who *produce* this wealth. Fans come to watch A'ja Wilson and Luka Doncic, not Mark Davis and Mark Cuban.

Sport media helps preserve the fiction of sport as a fun and frivolous activity and helps muddy the relationship between consumers (fans) and the real people and athletic labor behind sport's commodity spectacle. Instead of fans seeing athletes as workers, they often understand their sport fandom as a "relation between things"[99]—between their consumer dollars and athletic commodity spectacles. This kind of commodity fetishism (see chapter 3) obscures the exploitation and harm suffered by so many athletes.

Don't get me wrong, sport in and of itself is not always labor, and it can be lots of fun—I would even argue that we should be trying to get back to a place where sport, even at the highest level, is a site of fun and play. And plenty of professional athletes enjoy their labor, just like many other employees enjoy their labor. Liking your job does not mean it's not a job. The classification of an activity as labor is not based on how much fun it is or can be; it is based on whether the activity produces surplus value for yourself or the business you work for, which undoubtedly applies in the case of athletes.

Management and ownership can't have it both ways; they can't operate a cutthroat capitalist enterprise, where winning and revenue are the only goals and players are conceptualized as "investments" and "assets" like stocks or iPhones, while also pretending that these same "assets" are just overgrown children playing pickup hoops with their friends. While some journalists have begun to push back on this pro-ownership narrative in recent years, this view remains pervasive, especially in more conservative political circles.

Minor league players shouldn't have to suffer through a grueling 140-game schedule on $25 per diems and $1,000 per month, just because they are playing a sport rather than working in a warehouse or an office.[100] College football players shouldn't be forced to work thirty to forty hours per week, unpaid, for their college team, while also having that college team pick their major and their course schedule, just because kids love football and choose to play for free in high school.[101] All workers deserve a living wage and good working conditions, regardless of what the content of their work is. While athletes have begun to recognize their power as the primary producers of value and fight for better working conditions for themselves and their peers, narratives that they are just playing a children's game and that they should feel fortunate for their sport opportunities remain a persuasive tactic used by organizations and leagues to deflect blame for poor labor conditions.

The romanticization of sports even extends to the sport industry itself, and to low-paid (or unpaid) workers off the field. Mythologizing around "dream jobs" and the "privilege" of working in sports has created a work environment, especially in North America, where those trying to break into the sport sector at any level are often expected to work crazy hours for little or no pay.[102] Those trying to "break in" to the sport industry are victims of what Lauren Berlant, a University of Chicago English professor and cultural theorist, termed *cruel optimism*: "[A] relation of cruel optimism exists when something you desire is actually an obstacle to your flourishing."[103] Drawing on interviews with young sport interns and employees, Matthew Hawzen and his research team found that these workers—especially those working in a sport that they grew up watching or for a team they grew up rooting for—often feel an affective attachment to their work that makes them more likely to deal with difficult and exploitative labor conditions.

The relationship these young workers have to their sport industry labor is one of cruel optimism, and it is part of what allows these poor working conditions to continue. The other part of what allows these working conditions—and it is an important aspect less often discussed—is the material conditions of sport industry work.[104] Many of the jobs in this industry are low-paid entry-level positions, seasonal service work, or unpaid internships. Young workers accept these positions out of cruel optimism, but also because they have no choice. Undergraduate sport management program enrollment continues to grow rapidly, with new programs being developed and starting every year. These programs result in a growing "reserve army of labour"[105] for sport organizations, where they (and their employees) know that there are more unemployed and freshly graduated sport management students ready to fill their low-paid positions. These students may also feel after they've completed their sport management education that they're stuck in this field, structurally forcing them to take any position in the industry, no matter the working conditions or pay. As one of Hawzen and colleagues' interviewees explained: "The problem is if I want to work somewhere else other than sports what's the likelihood... someone wants to hire somebody like me with a sport management degree? This is the toughest thing. I feel pigeon-holed a bit."[106] Finally, many of these undergraduate programs require internship participation as a condition for students to graduate, creating another imperative for students who want to graduate with their sport-related degree.[107]

In my own interviews with NBA and NFL management, one front-office employee told horror stories about his position as a manager with the men's basketball program at a prestigious, extremely wealthy university. Though the athletic department at this university produces over $100 million in revenue yearly, and the school had a 2021 endowment of over $36 billion, this employee was paid $1,200 per month while working seventy to one hundred hours per week, often sleeping on the couches of the basketball team offices. He described an environment where the players and members of staff feared losing games because of how they would get "reamed out" the next day at practice, creating an environment of high stress—"I really can't stress the extremely high stress (environment) enough"—where my interviewee lost weight, couldn't sleep, and felt his "body was disintegrating." He was yelled at in public, and his manager was yelled at to the point of tears several times throughout the season, often in public.

And yet this employee stressed that this is what the working and living conditions are for many managers at the highest level of college basketball, and that the job he and the unpaid student managers had were in extremely high demand. At Duke University, the "tryouts" for the position of unpaid manager of the men's basketball team have hundreds of applicants every year, and are glorified by media.[108] Expectations of abuse, mistreatment, low or no pay, and 24/7 on-call working hours are the norm in these programs, and they are still the clearest route to success for those wanting to work in sports. The employee I interviewed also emphasized that though his time working as a manager for his prestigious university was awful, it is the reason he had his current job working for an NBA team.

The fact that these conditions are accepted by so many is based in the material conditions described above, the lack of labor protections for workers in the United States, and the cruel optimism of sport industry workers. The mythologizing and romanticization of sports and the sports industry play an important part here as well, as organizations weaponize the perceived glamour of sports to exploit both athletes and off-the-field staff. This is common in other entertainment-based industries as well; stories of interns who work seventy-hour weeks and abuses by those in power are endemic to the fashion, film, and music industries.

When you consider all these factors, it is no surprise that sport is still rife with labor exploitation. Athletic labor and work in the sport industry exist in an environment of structural and status coercion, with a lack of labor protections, and a culture that glorifies overwork and working through pain and suffering—or perhaps even worse, a culture that doesn't even consider work in sport as "real work." This is an exploitative recipe, and one that organizations and sport leagues are all too happy to cook up and serve to their workers and to anyone forced to accept it.

CHAPTER SIX

Crowd Violence
Winning at All Costs and Imagined Communities under Capitalism

When I say the words "spectator violence" many might think of drunken football (the European kind—we're using "football" to mean soccer in this chapter) hooligans spilling out of stadiums or viral videos of fans fighting in the stands at large arenas. But spectator and fan violence are not just an elite, professional sport problem. It is a fixture at all levels of sport. In this chapter, we're going to take a deeper dive into this phenomenon, looking at both professional *and* youth sports.

Whether it's fan riots in the early and mid-1900s, the football hooliganism crisis of the 1980s, the NBA's Malice at the Palace in the early 2000s, or parental harassment and violence in youth sports today, spectator violence and harassment remains pervasive, and shows no signs of abating. Professional leagues, national and international sport bodies, and youth club presidents, coaches, and parent groups know it's a problem, and often talk about fixing it, but still it persists.

While youth sports played in small, dingy gyms and arenas and on local pitches and fields may seem like a context completely different from the professional and elite competition we see on TV and pay to attend, spectator violence and harassment manifests in these different contexts in shockingly similar ways. Whether it is parents frothing at the mouth when their daughter gets tripped without a penalty being called, or lifelong Manchester United fans watching in horror as their team loses to their archrival City, the heightened importance and meaning of sport to those who watch it still frequently results in harmful behavior by sport spectators.

Explanations for Spectator Violence in Elite Sport

As explained in chapter 1, just because this chapter and this book focus on the structural conditions and factors that influence violence and harm, this does not mean that we lose complete sight of individual, interpersonal, and situational factors. Many studies on spectator violence—which sport scholar Kevin Young defines as "acts of verbal or physical aggression (threatened or actual), perpetrated by partisan fans at, or away from, the sports arena that may result in injury to persons or damage to property"[1]—have focused on individual demographic factors for this behavior, including lower socioeconomic status,[2] age (young), and gender (male),[3] and the presence of alcohol. Researchers have also investigated the myriad situational and psychological factors that might fuel fan violence. They have conceptualized this violence as a response to triggering events,[4] a manifestation of overinvolved parenting or overidentification with the team,[5] or based in a desire to wrestle back some control of an ever-uncontrollable social world.[6]

Early research on spectator violence began in the 1970s and 1980s, focusing on football "hooliganism" in England and in Europe more generally. This research often conceptualized hooliganism as a specifically working-class phenomenon,[7] though scholars differed on *why* this was the case. For Marxist criminologist and sport scholar Ian Taylor, working-class spectator violence was a manifestation of class-based revolt against the constant and near total commercialization of sport.[8] In this sense, working-class spectator violence was theorized as a response to worker alienation and commodification of culture and leisure.

Similarly, but without the same revolutionary zeal, British sociologist Peter Marsh explained spectator violence among working-class fans as a way for these spectators to assert some control over their lives and over the outcomes of sporting events, as a response to their lack of control in other spheres of life, including their workplaces and work outcomes.[9] As Irving Goldaber, founder of the now-defunct Centre for the Study of Crowd and Spectator Behavior, explained: "There are increasing numbers of people who are deeply frustrated because they feel they have very little power over their lives. They come to sporting events to experience, vicariously, a sense of power."[10]

Interestingly, this thinking mirrors some of the explanations for higher rates of domestic and intimate partner violence (IPV) in working-class families, especially violence perpetrated by men. Though IPV and domestic violence are, of course, multifaceted phenomena, some early studies of lower-income and working-class IPV explain this violence as "compensatory violence,"[11] a way for men to assert dominance and control in their personal lives, to make up for their lack of control and power in their workplaces and "public" lives. This compensatory violence hypothesis also links to theorizations around "masculine capital," as male compensatory violence against their wives and partners was and still is sometimes seen as a way to assert hegemonic masculinity. This is especially salient in a world where working-class men often aren't able to assert the control needed for this masculinity anywhere else.¹²

Under this theorizing, IPV and spectator violence have an instrumental, goal-oriented purpose. The potential results of this violence are both explicit and implicit; they allow men to feel some sort of control over their lives (explicit), reify hierarchies that place men above women, and legitimize violent behavior as a natural and rational emotional regulator and response to adverse conditions (implicit). As Kevin Young writes, football hooligans' "relatively deprived social condition [are seen as] instrumental in the production and reproduction of normative modes of behavior, including strong emphases on notions of territory, male dominance and physicality."¹³

These explanations of spectator violence as a purely working-class problem sound neat and tidy, and might strike many as intuitively sensible and correct. Like with many sociological questions, however, it's not simple. As I tell my students, sociology is the study of our very complicated social world, and when you ask complicated questions, you get complicated answers. If you want straightforward, yes-or-no type solutions, try math.¹⁴

Early work by scholars like Taylor, Marsh, and many others lacked strong empirical backing, relying more on anecdotal and media reports of spectator violence that villainized working-class people as the sole deviant sport fans. This framing was often based on classist tropes about the "unsophisticated" and "wild" lower classes, narratives that were all too eagerly eaten up by middle- and upper-class people.¹⁵ In the years since, it has become clear that spectator misbehavior is undoubtedly not just a working-class phenomenon, but instead can involve sports fans of all stripes.¹⁶

This realization has brought with it other explanations for spectator violence, many of which are more social-psychological in nature and less directly related to socioeconomic status or class. Sport psychologist Daniel Wann has done lots of work on spectator behavior, emphasizing how crowd violence "emerges in a process where fans 'overidentify' with a particular team,"¹⁷ often trying to fulfill their social and psychological need for community and group identification. This explanation suggests that fans who have stronger team identity—defined as "the extent to which individuals perceive themselves as fans of the team, are involved with the team, are concerned with the team's performance, and view the team as a representation of themselves"¹⁸— are more likely to respond with violence when their favorite team loses.

Similarly, Wann and others have also focused on the effect of rivalries between teams, as well as group antagonisms between fans along other (class and nonclass) identity lines like political affiliation, region, religion, or ethnicity.[19] This can help explain the rivalries and subsequent fan violence and abuse between fans of teams like Real Madrid and Barcelona (political and regional), Celtic and Rangers (religious and political) and the Duke Blue Devils and North Carolina Tar Heels (regional and class-based), among so many others. To solidify their own group identification with their team and other supporters, fans may also construct a discursive "other" or "enemy" out of the fans of opposing teams, which impacts the likelihood of berating or physically attacking them.[20] This type of fan fervor is reminiscent of the way politicians and governments have historically whipped up anti-"other" sentiment among populations, usually for the politicians' or government's own political or geopolitical aims.[21]

The unpredictability of sports and the ability for spectators to impact the outcome also adds more gasoline to the potential spectator violence fire. Unlike other events with crowds (concerts, theater, even political rallies), the results of sporting event are unknown in advance and to be determined,[22] and spectators in sports crowds also have a vested interest in these results.[23] Adding to this, fans may feel that their cheering, jeering, and passion can actually positively impact their favorite team, providing support for them and their fellow fans while helping to vanquish the out-group "enemy."[24] Given that referees do on the whole tend to respond favorably to home crowds,[25] they may actually be right.

But this still doesn't tell us *why* fans care about their favorite teams so much, and why sports have such a hold on them.

Let's Get Structural

The demographic and individual factors and the psychological processes described above are vital for understanding some of what make spectator and fan violence more likely. But they do not explain the social structures, material reality, and sport cultures where all of this happens.

As sport scholar Kevin Young[26] explains, psychological and individual explanations "are clearly limited in their explanatory scope and potential" because they "provide next to no insight into the sociological dimensions of crowd violence."[27] Sport scholars like Ramòn Spaaij, Kevin Young, and Jay Coakley have all noted that this phenomenon must be understood holistically, as a result of "the dynamic interplay between individual, interpersonal, situational, social environmental, and social structural factors."[28]

Spaaij's ecological model explains how factors at all of these levels influence the likelihood of spectator violence and harassment, and all levels act in relation to one another. Spaaij argues that the challenge and goal of explaining spectator violence is "to ascertain how macro-social factors are mediated or moderated by social environmental, situational, and interpersonal processes to produce sports crowd behaviors."[29] To put this in more concrete terms, an overtired parent who just had a bad day at work may be *individually* more prone to violence, and the fact that the games involves intercity rivals and that everyone is drinking are interpersonal and situational factors that also make violence more likely. A bad call by a referee may be another situational element that ultimately sparks violent or harassing behavior. But all of this happens within a larger social environmental and social structural context, and none of the above-mentioned individual, interpersonal, and situational factors—either in and of themselves or combined—tells us why sporting events are so prone to violence and harassment more generally.

For the rest of this chapter, we will focus on the social structural and social environmental factors. It's not just about the spark, or the kindling, but about why the whole damn thing is so flammable in the first place.

Alienation, Social Reproduction, and Why We Care So Much about Sports

There comes a time in every big sports fan's life when someone asks you the worst and most awful question, usually *right* after your favorite team misses a penalty, free throw, or forgets to cover[30] the other teams' best player: *Why do you care about this so much?*

Many sports fans meet this question with a teenager-level eye roll, a "you just don't understand" shake of the head, and maybe even some anger at even being asked the question. But it's actually a good question. Unless we have money on a particular game or team,[31] why *do* we care so much? Many (maybe even most) sport fans feel more identified, and are more knowledgeable and passionate, about their favorite athletes and teams than they are about their local politics and political representatives or any other religious or class-oriented group. If you ask a random sports fan—and I'd argue, maybe even just a random person—who their local team's striker or quarterback is, you're more likely to get a correct answer than if you asked them about their local elected representative.[32] Is this just because sports are exciting and interesting, and the results are immediate and clear? Are we just less religious than we used to be, and less socially engaged and conscious, and politics and politicians are the worst?

As discussed in chapter 2, sport has long been used as a pacifying and moralizing tool for ruling classes. In late nineteenth- and early twentieth-century Britain, as well as in North America, sport opportunities (for men) were considered an effective strategy for steering the working class away from antisocial behavior, which usually meant drinking, petty crime, or most frightening for the ruling class, collective organizing and unionization.[33] When factory workers and other underpaid laborers went on strike or demanded better working conditions, one of the concessions made was often for access and opportunities to participate in sports clubs.

Sport was also historically thought to be a useful and safe way to ensure that workers were in proper physical condition to wage war against other nations, without provoking the kind of class consciousness that would make workers revolt against their *own* ruling classes. For ruling classes all over the world, sport has acted and still acts as both a "reward" for obedience and deference, and as a distraction to draw attention away from the inequality that persists under capitalism. While not as explicit, you could argue that even today, sport diverts people away from class struggle and revolutionary political work and toward sport fandom that is either apolitical or politically oriented toward national chauvinism, patriotism, and "victory" over other nations and discursively constructed "others."[34]

This diversion of attention away from political struggle and toward the apolitical or the politically beneficial (to ruling-class interests) is not accidental. It is used to solidify the hegemony of the capitalist class, and it is so successful at doing this *because* of the alienation so many feel under capitalism. Just as the material effects of industrial capitalism paved the way for commercialized sport to grow—bringing people into cities, regimenting and standardizing economic activity and labor time, and providing workers with small amounts of leisure time[35] that ruling-class interests wanted to ensure was filled with "productive" (for the purposes of capitalism) and apolitical activity[36]—the alienation of workers under industrial capitalism is vital to sport's *continued* hold on the population.

This ideological role is especially vital today, as workers continue to feel the alienation of life and work under capitalism. As explained in chapter 2, alienation is the lack of emotional and spiritual fulfillment so many workers feel. Forced to sell our labor and often not seeing the fruits of this labor in any meaningful way, work becomes "only a means for satisfying other needs,"[37] and loses any intrinsic meaning. This is especially problematic when so much of our days are spent working, and from a young age we are told both explicitly and implicitly that our identity is tied to our job. For many workers, the lack of meaning in work has gotten consistently worse over time, as work processes have continuously standardized and workplaces have become more bureaucratic, labor has become more repetitive, and workers have even less space for creative expression or for any decision-making power over what they do and why they do it.

This alienation is also a product of a hypercommodified society, which will be discussed in further depth below with regard to youth sports. In a world where even our very personhood has been commodified (as our "brand"), contemporary capitalism has in many ways turned into the most extreme version of Marxist commodity fetishism; except for a few relationships with our closest friends and family, so much of modern life feels transactional. In Marx's words, the relationships we have with others exist more as relationships between products of exchange (like our labor, or our brand) than as relationships between people.

But what does all this have to do with sports? Quite a bit, actually. In this hypercommodified world devoid of genuine human interaction, emotional fulfillment, and meaning, sports (along with other elements of consumer and leisure culture) help fill the gap. This is where we also see links to another concept brought up in chapter 2, social reproduction.

For bosses and capitalists, the alienation and lack of fulfillment that workers feel under capitalism is worrisome, but not because of some altruistic desire to have happy employees. Rather, capitalists know that an unhappy and unfulfilled workforce is much more likely to be an unproductive, disloyal, or worse (for them), a militant and fighting workforce. All of these possibilities are bad for business.

Capitalists pay workers the wages that workers need to *reproduce* their own labor. This reproduction includes not just food, shelter, clothing, education, and work-related skills, but that spiritual and emotional fulfillment we talked about above. If workers feel complete alienation, this will impact the quality of their work and their ability and desire to work, not to mention that they might not procreate and raise the children needed for the next wave of workers.

Similar to how women's unpaid domestic labor was for so long exploited by capitalists—as this labor was vital in reproducing workers, but not paid for by capitalists or by anyone else—athletic labor and athletic commodity spectacle provides the meaning and emotional and cultural significance that so many people are missing.[38] As Nathan Kalman-Lamb explains in his work on athletic labor and social reproduction,[39] in a world devoid of community, sport provides an "imagined community"[40] where emotions can be felt collectively, experiences shared, victories celebrated, and defeats mourned.

Even for fans who are not together in an arena or watching in the same room at home, sports and athletic commodity spectacle—which, it bears repeating, is produced by the *labor* of athletes—delivers feelings of fulfilment and community, or at the very least excitement. The effects of sport spectacle on fans is also not just something discussed by Marxist scholars. Sport sociologist Jay Coakley writes that fans "may be living lives so devoid of significance and excitement that they want to create a memorable occasion they can boastfully discuss with friends for weeks and years to come."[41]

This understanding of one of the key roles of athletic commodity spectacle helps explain why physical violence *in* sports is so necessary (see chapter 3), how athletic labor can be exploited both directly and indirectly (chapter 6), and lastly, for our purposes here, why spectator and fan violence is so pervasive. When we understand that for so many people, sport spectacle, sport fandom, and individual athletes and teams hold this outsized importance—due in large part to alienation in work and in life more generally—it starts to make a lot more sense why fans fight in the stands, riot after lost championships, or scream at referees and coaches at the top of their lungs. While alienation under capitalism and sport spectacle as social reproduction do not explain *everything* about why fans behave violently, they are vital *preconditions* to all of the other factors we see, and act as the structural scaffolding for fan violence in both elite and youth sports.

Spectator Violence and Harassment in Youth Sports: The Case of Canadian Minor Hockey

In my research interviewing people involved in Canadian minor hockey[42]— parents, coaches, administrators, and referees, with many of my interviewees wearing several of these hats at the same or different times in their lives— spectator violence, harassment, and abuse were said to happen so frequently that they weren't even worth mentioning. By about my eighth interview, I realized that the first question of my interview guide—"Have you ever witnessed a case of spectator violence or harassment?"—was basically a waste of time and, if anything, may have had the unintended negative effect of signaling to my interviewees that I must not know anything about hockey and youth sports if I was even asking it. The next ten seconds usually went something like this:

Of course I've witnessed spectator violence and harassment. How often? Oh, basically every game.

These parents, coaches, administrators, and referees would often laugh as they said this—*it's just part of the game*. And they're right. Spectator violence and harassment has existed for so long in Canadian minor hockey—and in so many other youth sports—that at this point, most people involved in these sports consider it just background noise. Somehow we've reached the point that parents and spectators at sport events played by children and teenagers— which are ostensibly about fostering teamwork, promoting exercise and healthy life habits, and learning lessons in hard work and responsibility—are so likely to yell at each other, the athletes, the coaches, and the referees, that everyone seems to consider it normal. They might even engage in physical acts of violence, and even *that* would barely be noteworthy.

But this shouldn't and doesn't need to be the case. Spectator violence is extremely detrimental to everyone involved, and we *know* this. At just the youth level, this kind of behavior results in harm to athletes, coaches, referees, and other fans, and can result in damages to sport facilities and even increase the costs of sport provision. Athletes hate when their parents behave this way,[43] and this kind of behavior can make it difficult to recruit and retain volunteer coaches and even paid referees. Beyond the direct financial, physical, and emotional costs of spectator violence and harassment, this kind of fan behavior also teaches athletes the exact *wrong* lessons and values about handling adversity and about responsible behavior in a cooperative society, contrary to the ostensible ideological benefits athletes supposedly imbibe from supposedly "meritocratic, inclusive, and equal" sports.

So, if we know that all this harm comes from spectator violence, why does it continue to happen? While my interviews with Canadian minor hockey stakeholders cannot be generalized to all hockey contexts or to all minor league sport contexts, they do give us a glimpse into this question. For those with any involvement in other youth sports, especially in North America, I think you will also find that the issues and explanations for fan misbehavior sound familiar, and speak to the problems of a larger sport culture obsessed with winning and performance, and where parents derive so much meaning from the athletic performances of their children that they will do nearly anything to see that child succeed.

Performance, Professionalization, and Pressure: Minor Hockey and Beyond

> The biggest problem is . . . Everything is performance-based, and they try to identify the elite players at seven, eight years old and then treat them

like NHLers. . . . The children have enormous pressure. The parents are seeing their retirement fund on the ice, and everything is performance-based—winning, winning, winning, winning . . . that philosophy brings the worst out of parents because all they want is to win.[44]

Even at the minor league levels, hockey parents, like many sports parents, are obsessed with winning and performance. In the research on youth sports and in my own interviews, the rampant win-at-all-costs culture of sports was consistently cited as a primary cause of misbehavior by fans in the stands.[45] When parents are so focused on their child performing at the highest level and their team winning, tensions run high and fuses are short. This can result in altercations between fans of the same team or fans of opposing teams, or harassment directed at the coaches, players, and referees in the game.

According to those I interviewed, referees are the most frequent targets, followed closely by coaches. In an environment where parents and fans have attached high stakes to the game, a perceived missed penalty call by the referee can result in verbal harassment and even physical violence, either during the game or after the final whistle. As one parent and coach explained: "I've seen a cowbell thrown at referees. I have seen coffees thrown at referees, verbal assault at referees. I've seen banging the glass, picking up sticks and smashing. They've taken their child's stick and swung it at the glass near a referee's head."

The frequent abuse of referees has created recruitment and retention issues in a variety of sports.[46] This phenomenon is also not limited to any geographic area, as referee abuse is a problem anywhere that sports are played, and seemingly at every level.[47] One parent, coach, and former referee told me, "I've seen coaches in a novice tournament . . . just losing it for no reason whatsoever—Novice B [a lower level of six- to seven-year-olds], screaming at the referees." While some of this abuse may be a matter of individual fans or coaches running hot, or higher levels of tolerance for this kind of behavior in different sport leagues, it nevertheless speaks to the extremes that fans are willing to go to in youth sports.

Parental obsession with performance and winning also creates a vicious cycle of financial investment, personal investment, and anger that can prompt spectator violence and harassment. While middle-class and upper-middle-class parents have long invested time and effort into their children's sports and activities,[48] this kind of investment has reached stratospheric heights in recent years. Parents pay for sports league fees, equipment, extra training sessions, and travel and tournaments. While fees and equipment costs have long existed, these costs have ballooned. Parents also invest more *time* and energy on their children's athletic pursuits, as sport specialization and higher levels of commitment are now expected earlier and earlier. As all these costs and investments increase, so does parent intensity, and the cycle of investment and anger begins. As one parent, coach and administrator explained:

> These kids are on the ice five, six times a week now. Plus, your hockey season, the tournaments.... On average a hockey season for a child is anywhere between $500 to $1,000 because of equipment, travel, restaurants, the tournaments ... it's an easy trap to fall into [psychologically] where you're saying, "I paid for three months [of] training or a couple of courses on stick handling to try to get my son better. I'm paying this for him to make that level." The parents are seeing this as an investment.... Of course, that kid gets hit. That kid doesn't get a penalty called on him. The other coaches bench him because he was disrespectful on the bench. Parents are seeing their investment being wasted and they get mad.

Beyond capitalist ethos of competition infecting sport parents with the initial win-at-all-costs virus, the market has also provided an opening for vultures to come in and prey on the dreams of young athletes and their parents. Personal trainers, private training centers and camps, and even social media brand ambassadors and managers have been popping up for years now, and show no signs of slowing. For the modern sports parent in North America, there is seemingly always another tournament, personal trainer, or camp advertising that they are the missing piece to take their child to the next level.[49] Another hockey parent, coach, and administrator: "Hockey has become more of a business. Instead of it being a winter sport, it's turned into a 12 months of the year activity. Development has become a key to people's successes, so they're seeking out professional trainers, more development. It's more commercialized now than it used to be. Then, you go into the equipment aspect of it, where no one really wants that $30 wooden stick ... They're looking at that $300, $400, $500 stick, and $1,000 skates."

This is, of course, not just a hockey problem. For youth sports where the top professional leagues pay big bucks (and even for sports where they don't), the youth sport systems below have thoroughly professionalized.[50] Looking at the "Big Five" North American professional team sports (American football, basketball, baseball, soccer, and hockey), private instructors, tournament circuits, training and identification camps, and 24/7 training expectations have become the norm for anyone with hopes of playing their sport professionally.[51]

In many ways we've seen something similar happen with private school attendance, private tutors, test prep, and other efforts from parents trying to ensure that their children get into the best universities. Perhaps it's always been common for wealthier families to pay for private instruction in high school or to pay (sorry, "donate to") top universities to make sure their children get in, but these processes are now happening earlier and earlier. As school disparities continue to widen in places like the United States and the United Kingdom,[52] it is not uncommon to hear about parents and children stressing about getting into the right middle school or high school, with the understanding that this could impact the rest of their school and career trajectory.[53] These moves to private services and schools by wealthy parents also takes funding and resources away from the public system,[54] a phenomenon also mirrored in youth sports.[55]

The thorough and complete commodification of competitive sports—I don't even want to say "elite" sports, because the bar has gotten lower and lower for when this commodification starts—is especially stark in North American youth basketball. By now, anyone who follows the NBA or WNBA or really any level of elite basketball knows about the Amateur Athletic Union (AAU) basketball circuit.

Touting itself as "one of the largest, non-profit, volunteer, multi-sport event organizations in the world, dedicated exclusively to the promotion and development of amateur sports and physical fitness programs,"[56] AAU and specifically AAU basketball has expanded well beyond its humble beginnings as a small tournament and event organizer. A 2015 ESPN report[57] found that just the AAU's national tournaments produced upward of $20 million a year. This number has surely risen since and does not even account for the often-huge sums changing hands between coaches, agents, apparel companies, and even content creators and advertisers.

While old-school coaches and curmudgeonly analysts[58] bemoan the effects of AAU basketball on the game and players, it is impossible to deny its importance. For many high school basketball players, the summer AAU season is more important than their high school season and team, as it is where they play against the best players in North America, and get valuable exposure to collegiate and NBA scouts and to social media. AAU games determine the all-important high school player rankings, which can make or break early careers. The Season Ticket[59]—a site specializing in youth sport content—found that in 2021, of the 305 American-born NBA players who were of AAU age during the period of the three dominant AAU circuits (Elite Youth Basketball League, Adidas 3 Stripes Select Basketball, and

Under Armor Association), 77.1 percent of them played on one of these circuits.

But the exposure and free shoes and apparel come at a cost. Some of these curmudgeonly coach complaints are actually quite valid. Beyond the (perhaps subjective) negative aesthetic and performance effects of AAU basketball on the game—players barely practicing and only playing games, focusing too much on one-on-one play and individual accolades, relying on athleticism over skill, and trying to go viral rather than caring about team success—elite AAU circuits like the EYBL, 3SSB, and UAA have basically turned players into professional athletes when they're teenagers, at least in terms of their schedules and expectations, and the attention they receive.

Similar professionalization exists in the other big-money North American team sports. To give you just some idea, as of May 2023, Football Camps USA, which "works with prestigious college camps across America,"[60] lists 1,219 upcoming football events, all of which are pay-to-participate. This is just a fraction of the private and public, invite-only and open-training and "exposure" camps available for young football players. Seven-on-seven football has also grown tremendously in recent years, creating another revenue stream and competition circuit for aspiring football players. Baseball has travel teams and tournaments, which often cost thousands of dollars and have priced out lower-income athletes. The Greater Toronto Hockey League, the biggest youth hockey league by player registration in the world, charges parents to attend games, has paid coaches (some officially, some "off the books" through sponsors) in the top divisions, and had $8.8 million in revenue in 2022.[61] Youth sports is a growing industry and getting more professionalized and commodified by the day.

Returning to basketball, AAU players on the top circuits,[62] many of whom just barely finished middle school, are shuttled around across the country to tournaments all summer, playing multiple games every weekend and sometimes twice in a day. Even though the best players' *financial* costs are often covered through team sponsorship with shoe and apparel companies (hence the circuits being sponsored and run by huge apparel companies), these miles add up and can take a physical toll on young athletes. Many have started to notice rising injury levels among players (even while having undoubtedly better medical knowledge now than we used to), and have begun to connect the dots.[63] In a story with ESPN, pediatric orthopedist Dr. Nirav Pandya described seeing young athletes with all sorts of overuse-related injuries, repairing ACLs torn three times before the athlete in question could legally vote, and speaking to parents whose first questions were about when their child could get back to playing their sports.[64] Beyond the physical effects, top AAU players (and top players in other sports) are also living under intense public scrutiny, starting from a young age.

This early professionalization and commodification are especially common for young Black athletes.[65] As with many supposedly irrational "choices" made under capitalism, Black Americans' (and minoritized youth in other countries) perceived "obsession" with sports is still often wrongly blamed on bad parenting, mistakes in socialization, and misplaced values, rather than on the social structures and inequities that make sports one of the only true "ways out" for many Black youth.

Theresa Runstedtler, an American Studies professor, explains that the athletic industrial complex (AIC) and the powerful actors within it take advantage of Black Americans' lack of access to formal political channels, along with their continued social and economic marginalization,[66] to make money off the labor of these youth athletes and off of the commodification of youth sports more generally.

> The likes of Nike, the NCAA (and its members), the NBA, and media companies benefit from young Black American boys' lack of access to good-quality public education, their diminished job prospects, and their early exposure to the criminal justice system in the post-industrial United States.... Moreover, the continuing race to the bottom with the expansion of AAU basketball sponsored by multinational sporting brands has spawned a host of new markets, as coaches, consultants, scouts, bloggers, tournament organizers, and entrepreneurs have moved in to make money at every layer of the system. For the AIC as a whole, capitalizing on the precarity of Black youth for the sake of profits has become business as usual.[67]

Beyond the profits made off youth athletes, the commodification and professionalization of youth sports brings with it incredible pressure and potential harm. Add to this the intense scrutiny of our modern mediascape, where every move athletes make has the potential to go viral on social media, and you get a destructive cocktail of scrutiny and commodification.

I remember watching Zion Williamson highlights when he was in tenth grade, and a viral mixtape of Seventh Woods when he was fourteen. While this kind of attention can have some financial benefits, especially as marketing teams continue to mine social media for eyeballs and dollars, it can also have drawbacks. Williamson rode this initial attention and fame (and his otherworldly talent) to a dominant one year in college basketball and then to hundreds of millions in the NBA, but Woods has not had the same path. Though Woods's relative lack of professional basketball success (so far) may just be a matter of his talent and height plateauing soon after his age-fourteen mixtape, the pressure that this brought didn't help. From a 2022 *Sports Illustrated* article on Woods:[68]

> The proverbial gift and the curse of attention produced a magnifying glass that he couldn't shake with even his best crossover. It created a dark cloud of doubt in his head that loomed for years.
>
> "I thought I had to be perfect; I really did," Woods says. "If I got a turnover, all I could think was that people were gonna think I wasn't that good. I really questioned every mistake. In hindsight, I was trying to live up to people's expectations and I couldn't shake that."

AAU and "hoop mixtape" culture has commodified young athlete performance, with the age of this commodification seemingly dropping by the day. If you scroll Instagram, TikTok, or Snapchat and have ever shown the algorithm that you care even a little about sports, you will be met with fifth-grade "hoopers" trash talking their ten-year-old opponents, kids touted as "the BEST 13-year-old in the NATION" (only to be apparently unseated by other kids next week), and teenagers throwing down thunderous warm-up dunks or canning deep threes. The other day I saw tennis "highlights" of Carlos Alcaraz's eleven-year-old brother on Instagram, and a video of "the biggest 8th grader in America" playing offensive line for his middle school team on Snapchat.[69]

The commodification of youth sports is bad enough from a labor perspective, and for the harm it causes. Professionalizing and commodifying sports at such a young age can turn athletes off from their sport, and can result in burnout, stress and anxiety, disordered eating, and other mental and physical health consequences that follow athletes around for the rest of their lives.[70] Beyond this though, this commodification is also responsible for so much of the fan violence, harassment, and misbehavior we see today, even at younger ages. At the more competitive levels, youth sports are no longer just kids playing a game, making friends, and trying their best. Romantic ideas of sport-as-play (while being something that we actually *should* strive for) is not what we have in contemporary North American capitalist sport systems, and because of this, the same life-or-death stakes that permeate professional and elite adult sports also exist in youth sports. These youth sports also act as a site for the same parents and fans alienated under capitalism to act out.

When thought about from this perspective, we might even expect *more* spectator misbehavior in youth sports than in elite sports. In youth sports, fans have a real material interest in the performance and health of the athletes, beyond even their emotional fulfillment. These athletes are their sons and daughters and children who, though they may commit to their sport like it's a full-time job, are not yet being paid for their athletic performance. Parents also might have a more personal (nonfinancial) stake in their children's performance. As much as some fans like to use first-person plural pronouns when talking about their favorite teams—*We traded for her. We won the championship. I can't believe we lost that game*—most fans have no material impact on the results of their favorite athletes and teams and can't sincerely take any credit for their successes. Their children, however, are another story.

Living Vicariously through Athletes:
The Search for Meaning under Capitalism

In the never-ending quest for meaning and fulfillment under capitalism, living vicariously through others is another dangerous but common path. This is especially true in sports, where fans internalize and overidentify with their favorite teams, resulting in extreme reactions to results. This phenomenon intensifies exponentially when the athletes in question are family or are people you helped raise.

It shouldn't come as any surprise that tons of parents try to live vicariously through their children. This isn't even necessarily a bad thing; finding joy in the success of your children is natural and can be a truly selfless experience. But like anything else, it can also reach extreme levels that have detrimental effects for youth athletes and everyone involved. While wacky stories of "crazy sports parents" may prompt laughs and some light condescension, it is this kind of obsessive behavior—again structured by performance expectations, hypercompetitive capitalist values, and a search for emotional fulfillment—that is in large part responsible for the toxic spectator environments we see in youth sports.

In my minor hockey interviews, coaches and parents frequently talked about how parents often live vicariously through their children and consider it a "badge of honor" for their child to play on a high-level team, regardless of whether it is the right level for them. This obsession with performance and especially *status* among young athletes (but really among parents) results in shocking and irrational behavior. One parent, who worked as the president of his local hockey association and was also a coach and parent in the region, said that he knew of "six or seven times" where "mothers [slept] with coaches picking the kids on the team." This was done even in cases where the athlete had no real chance of playing the game professionally, of earning a college scholarship, or of financially benefiting in any real way from the sport.

Less salacious but no less obsessive examples include parents emailing and messaging coaches at all hours to suggest strategies and line combinations, yelling at and confronting coaches and referees in hallways and after games, and even timing how long players were on the ice and hand-charting statistics. As one parent and coach explained: "We're playing a game of four-on-four novice (ages 6–7) hockey, where there's no scores, no nothing, that structure.... The one game that we played, one guy had a pad. I peeped over, (asked) "What the hell are you doing?" He was counting shots and scoring chances on four-on-four mini hockey, where they don't count goals."

Sport's hegemonically masculine culture—as well as its existence as a "relatively autonomous social world ... (where) normative codes relating to the use of violence in sport are different from those that govern most other societal domains"—also makes violent fan outbursts more acceptable, and therefore more likely.[71] In other words, as one of my minor hockey interviewees explained, "You can't allow [your anger] to boil over at your kids' school. You can't allow it to boil over at your office. A lot of people don't want it to boil over at home. The arena is this place where suddenly, I can let it rip." Many still consider sport environments acceptable places to let out their anger or frustration, due to a sports culture that both accepts violence broadly and has normalized extreme investment and passion in the outcomes of games.

Avoiding Blame for Spectator Violence

This brings us to our usual end-of-chapter question: How do sport institutions, leagues, and structures get away with letting this kind of violence and harassment persist?

The first and easiest answer is that most people don't even consider these leagues and institutions at fault. Given that the links between elite capitalist sport's structure and fan violence are less obvious than the other relationships between sport and violence explored in this book, these institutions have less work to do to avoid blame.

First, sport organizations don't even consider overzealous and overly attached fans to be a problem. Leagues and teams are always seeking more ways to "connect" with their fans, be it through social media, phone apps, fan research, or targeted advertising. They aren't concerned with the negative "outside the lines" consequences of fans living and dying by whether a twenty-five-year-old point guard has a good shooting game, or a keeper chooses the right place to dive on a penalty kick. As capitalist enterprises, they don't have to be. Their job—under the current imperatives of capitalist sport—is to increase revenues for ownership, stakeholders, and the league. The best way to do this is to increase ticket sales, merchandise sales, and viewership numbers, leading to bigger television contracts, sponsorship deals, and gate receipts.

When fan violence becomes too hard to ignore—think the NBA's Malice at the Palace, English football's Luton Riot and Heysel Disaster, or more recently, the death of 125 fans crushed at an Indonesian soccer match[72]—there is always another culprit to blame. For the Malice at the Palace—the 2003 caught-on-camera brawl between players on the Indiana Pacers and Detroit Pistons fans—much of the blame was levied against the players on the court, who were called every racist epithet in the book (thugs, gangsters, hoodlums) by media.[73] The NBA and the two teams—the Pacers and Pistons—were blamed too, but only for employing these players. Only recently, after a 2021 Netflix documentary presented the players' side of the story, was any blame levied on fans and on extreme fandom.

Similarly, though the 1985 Luton football riot—which left a trail of destruction including eighty-one injured—prompted Margaret Thatcher to declare her own personal "war on football,"[74] little blame was placed on the team, the sport, or capitalist society. Instead, in typical Thatcher-fashion, law-and-order style regulations were put in place to limit opposing team fans and increase police presence, and the day after the Luton riot, brash Chelsea chairman Ken Bates suggested he would electrify the fences around his team's home pitch.[75] During that same 1985 season, as English football hooliganism reached near its apex, forty people were injured and more than a hundred arrested when Chelsea fans rioted after their team's loss to Sunderland. In response, Football Association (FA) Secretary Ted Croker offered "little more than (saying) 'It's the clubs we feel sorry for,'"[76] both showing a lack of ability to properly deal with the problem and demonstrating that the main priority of the governing body of English football was protecting clubs (capital).

This year of hooliganism hell in English football culminated in the Heysel Disaster, where drunk Liverpool fans caused a wall to collapse before their European Cup Final match against Juventus, killing thirty-nine people, mostly Italian Juventus supporters. This resulted in European football bans for English football and Liverpool FC. However, this tragedy was mostly depicted and discussed as a problem "attributed to the irrational, bestial and military qualities (of) participants,"[77] with media calling them hooligans, animals, mindless morons, and other names. The media also showed a "preoccupation with threat(s) and calls for tougher measures (meeting violence with violence)"[78] rather than interrogating the irrational passion that fans have for their team. These depictions of fans also echo preconceived ideas about football hooliganism as a predominantly working-class behavior, reifying biological or "natural" hierarchies between working and ruling classes. In all these cases, and in more recent cases of spectator or fan violence, there is rarely any discussion of the perils of extreme fandom, and even less (read: zero) about the role of capitalism in creating the conditions of alienation where this kind of search for meaning is necessary.

Alcohol is another frequently cited cause of fan violence. Make no mistake, the relationship between alcohol and violence is about as clear as the one between scoring more goals and winning more games—but it is not the only factor to consider. Perhaps more importantly, while sport organizations and governing bodies are quick to blame hooligan fans for their drunken behavior and will institute alcohol bans when things get too out of hand, the marketing and sponsorship they engage in on the business side tell a completely opposite story. Alcohol sponsorship has been a part of world football—and many other sports—for years. The English FA still partners with Budweiser, Arsenal has three official beers for three different countries, and Manchester United has an official wine and an official whisky.[79] Guinness is a principal sponsor of Six Nations Rugby,[80] Anheuser-Busch is the official beer sponsor of the NFL, and Australian Open partners include Canadian Club whiskey, Gordon's gin, Grainshacker vodka, Peroni beer, Piper-Heidsiek champagne, Pure Blonde organic cider, and Treasury Wine Estates. I'm not even nitpicking sports or leagues that are particularly bad. If you threw a dart at a board of sport institutions, you'd be all but guaranteed to find alcohol sponsors.

While sport may have been initially "given" to the masses in hopes of curbing "antisocial" or "unruly" behavior, now that it has become a business focused primarily on profit, alcohol moved from the back alley to center stage. The profits from alcohol are nearly endless and extend to all parts of the elite sport environment. Not only do alcohol sponsorships for leagues and teams bring in money in the initial deal, but in many leagues where alcohol can be served at the event, teams make huge profits on alcohol sales in their stadiums. A 2021 Statista survey[81] found that fans of the NFL, MLB, NHL, UFC, and NBA spend, on average, more than $54 *per person* on alcohol at sporting events, with NBA fans topping the list with an average of $66 per fan. We are seeing the exact same process right now with sports gambling, as the once-taboo behavior is now seemingly part of every sport league's sponsorship package, and it is impossible to watch professional sports without being inundated with gambling content.[82]

The structures of elite capitalist sport are more than complicit in excessive consumption of alcohol and gambling products. Placing the blame on fans for their alcohol consumption is like a parent putting candy and chocolate in front of their kids, telling them how delicious it is all day, keeping thirty bags of the stuff at home, and then getting upset that the kids were on a sugar high and didn't go to sleep at bedtime.

Conclusion

The win-at-all costs nature of elite sport, even at youth levels, can push crowds into a frenzy of anger, harassment, and ultimately violence toward other spectators, coaches, referees, and officials, and even athletes themselves. Parents of elite youth athletes see dollar signs everywhere while watching their sons and daughters on the court or field, and these expectations create difficult environments for everyone. At the professional and elite college levels, there is often an added layer of fan identification, as fans and spectators (at live events, in bars, and even at home) latch onto their favorite sports teams as a response to their alienation as workers under capitalism. With little ability to find meaning and community in capitalist society, fans grasp onto the imagined communities of fandom around sports and sports teams, giving them elevated importance and expectations that, when unmet, lead to violence.[83]

CHAPTER SEVEN

Mega-Events and Mega-Harm
Structural and Environmental Violence, Sportswashing, and Celebration Capitalism

Seizing land and homes, running roughshod over the rights of those of African and Indigenous descent, opening the doors for foreign plunder, enabling the buzzsaw development of the Amazon, exporting Brazil's culture, declaring an end to public space, militarizing the cities: all of these incursions on people's democratic rights can be facilitated through laws described as "states of exception," like those historically passed for the Olympic Games, in which the usual rules (and constitutions) no longer apply.
—Dave Zirin, *Brazil's Dance with the Devil*, 2014

This chapter, like many, could be its own book. And many journalists and authors have done exactly this, documenting how the sport organizations, private companies, and governing bodies that host, build, and run mega-events engage in extreme levels of *structural violence* against mostly low-income and often racially marginalized communities, as well as against the natural environment.

To reiterate, structural violence encompasses the "social arrangements that put individuals and populations in harm's way."[1] Structural violence expands violence perpetration from an individual acting in a way that directly and immediately harms another person (e.g., physically hitting someone) to a broader definition that includes decisions that ultimately lead to harm. An individual or group acting in such a way that harm eventually occurs (e.g. building a waste disposal plant right next to a community), creating the conditions for harm to occur (e.g., giving police extended surveillance and preemptive arrest powers), or causing harm by *not* acting (e.g., not building hospitals or health care clinics in a neighborhood) are all examples of structural violence. Structural violence can also occur even when the offending party isn't necessarily *trying* to cause harm, but the situation created causes harm nonetheless.

The social arrangements producing harm here are mega-events, defined by French sociologist Maurice Roche as "large-scale cultural (including commercial and sporting) events, which have a dramatic character, mass popular appeal and international significance."[2] The social arrangements and harms include those from when the event is happening, as well as all of the decisions and actions done in preparation for the event and that linger long after the trophies and medals are handed out. Given the many different ways sport mega-events can harm both people and planet, as well the especially detrimental impact of the two most expensive and most widely watched sports mega-events—the FIFA World Cup and the Olympics—these two events will be the main focus of this chapter.

Whether it's forced displacements and gentrification, rising rents and costs of living, raiding and emptying public coffers to pay private businesses and friends, hypersurveillance and securitization, sportswashing and greenwashing, or the environmental devastation that these events bestow upon cities and neighborhoods, the World Cup and the Olympics have a hugely detrimental material impact on so many, while only benefiting a select very rich and very powerful few. As critical sports journalist Dave Zirin writes in *Brazil's Dance with the Devil*, a fantastic book on the impacts of the World Cup and Olympics on Brazil and Rio in 2014 and 2016: "The countries change, but the scenario stays the same: a profit orgy and a tax haven for corporate sponsors and private security firms, obscene public spending on new stadiums, and then another round of brutal cuts that fall on the backs of the poor when the party's over."[3]

Before we go any further, I need to make something clear, and preempt any argument that *I just don't understand how great these events are*. I understand that the World Cup and the Olympics can be a ton of fun for fans, and a crowning achievement for athletes. These are clear benefits and positive impact that these events absolutely have. I grew up loving the Olympics, and still enjoy watching. I get it. The point of this chapter is not to say that international sporting competitions must be completely abolished, or that nothing good comes from them. Rather, it is to clarify what the costs of these events are, not just in terms of the final dollar figures, but in the real-life impacts on local communities and on working people in hosting countries and abroad.[4] This allows us to determine if the benefits we derive from these events are worth it; and if they are not worth it, it provides a roadmap for how to fix them. It is still possible to celebrate and compensate athletes, without our current mega-event structures.

Beyond this, we must also avoid falling prey to the corporate and state propaganda of mega-events, which often frames any benefits that do happen around these events as *only* possible because of the event, and because it was run the way that it was. This wrongly assumes that the way these events are run is the *only* way of doing business, or that the benefits of these events are derived *from* their harmful practices, rather than occurring *in spite* of these practices. World Cups, Olympics, and our favorite large sporting events can still provide the same and even greater benefits—excitement, joy, community, pride, city investment, and renewal—without so many of the harmful practices and exorbitant costs. We can do sport events differently, but the longer we pretend otherwise, the more the people and the planet will continue to be harmed.

Mega-Events: What Are They Good For? Sportswashing and Celebration Capitalism

As long as we have mega-events, someone will have to host them.[5] They are expensive, require significant planning and resource allocation, and more and more, citizens aren't all that excited by the prospect of hosting. So, from a country's or city's perspective, why do they even want them in the first place?

Organizing committees and local politicians may wax poetic about their wholesome desire to "show off their country/city on the world stage," to "bring sports to the masses," and to "invest in their city,"[6] but based on everything we've seen over the past hundred years, these are not the true reasons. This is just what politicians and lobbying industries and organizations sell to the media and to local populations before, during, and even after events. Explanations for why countries bid for and want to host mega-events like the World Cup and the Olympics can be broadly grouped into two categories: sportswashing and profiting from celebration capitalism.

Sportswashing

One easy way to understand sportswashing is as a metaphorical cousin of money laundering. Instead of "cleaning" "dirty" (i.e., illegally obtained) money through a legitimate business, sportswashing involves state governments, organizations, and even individual people using sports to launder or "wash" away" their poor reputations, diverting attention away from wrongdoing (both inside and outside sports) and toward sport spectacle, amazing athletic feats, and (often) nationalistic pride. Jules Boykoff, a former professional football (we're using "football" to mean soccer in this chapter) player and now activist, writer, and political science professor who has written extensively on mega-events and sportswashing, "define(s) sportswashing as a phenomenon whereby political leaders use sports to appear important or legitimate on the world stage while stoking nationalism and deflecting attention from chronic social problems and human-rights woes on the home front."[7]

In Western media circles, there are a few mega-events that always come up in the sportswashing conversation, and they might even be the ones you are already thinking right now: the Qatar World Cup in 2022, the Sochi Winter Olympics and World Cup in 2014 and 2018, and the Beijing Summer Olympics in 2008 and 2022. While these were undoubtedly attempted cases of sportswashing—each of these countries has a variety of social problems and human rights violations that they would love to distract from—it is important to stress that sportswashing happens not just in non-Western or authoritarian regimes,[8] but in ostensibly "democratic" Western countries as well.[9] I put "democratic" in brackets here because many Western capitalist nations today could more accurately be termed dictatorships of the bourgeoisie, beholden to the wishes, influence, and lobbying power of the corporate class and structured to protect private property rights at all costs, with little meaningful opportunity for the vast majority of workers and people to influence policy and decision making, and especially to compel revolutionary change.[10] Regardless of one's views on the democratic or participatory nature of different political systems and contexts, The use of sport to launder a country's or government's reputation can and has occurred in a variety of places and in all manner of different states, from the earliest games in ancient Greece, to Hitler's 1936 Nazi Olympics, and up to now, in countries like China, Russia, Qatar, and yes, the United States, Canada, and the United Kingdom.

Sportswashing is a tool of "soft power," a term coined by political scientist Joseph Nye to explain the ways states can compel others into certain behaviors or beliefs without needing to threaten or use physical force or coercion ("hard" power).[11] Soft power overlaps with notions of "hegemony" used in previous chapters, as both of these concepts (soft power and hegemony) rely on noncoercive actions to shape the values and beliefs of others. They are ostensibly nonviolent—at least in terms of physical violence—ways of shaping public perception and asserting control over public narratives.

While some scholars critique the effectiveness of soft power due to the need for the *receiving* person or entity to accept the values that they are presented with, others note that those using soft power do not actually need to *persuade* their target audience. Rather, they need to present receivers with their vision of events and social relations, "sociolinguistically construct(ing) 'reality' not through evidence-based argument but through representational force."[12] This makes mega-events—and especially global mega-events like the

World Cup and the Olympics—ideal stages to wield soft power. They offer state governments and corporations the opportunity to present global audiences with the exact representation of their country that they would like them to see, all shined up by the glamour and good vibes that come from events like the Olympics, where (and this is taken directly from the Olympics website) "the world comes to compete, feel inspired, and be together."[13] For many states and corporations, mega-events are the ultimate shaking-hands-and-holding-babies goodwill tour, broadcast to millions of people around the world.

Sportswashing allows state governments and corporations to obfuscate the harm they are causing outside of sports, as well as the harms caused by the mega-event itself, behind a veneer of sport and spectacle. In the Vancouver 2010 Winter Games, which were played on unceded and stolen Indigenous lands, organizers often emphasized and touted the value of the games to Indigenous groups in Canada, as well as the official partnership between the Games and Indigenous people, the first of its kind. There was a small uptick in Indigenous employment around the games—from 1.5 percent of workers in the organizing committee to 3 percent, before decreasing again to 1 percent in 2009[14]—but this improvement disappeared quickly, and even before the Games, 80 of the 203 Indigenous bands (groups) in the province refused to participate. Promoting short-term employment and arts and culture opportunities for Indigenous people to draw attention away from the contemporary and historical mistreatment of these groups is an example of "redwashing," which Clayton Thomas-Müller of the Mathias Colomb Cree Nation defines as: "An attempt by a corporation to paint itself as 'benevolent'—a good neighbor—through sponsorship schemes for Indigenous education, art and culture. It is the process of covering up the detrimental effects of corporate initiatives with friendly slogans and lump sum donations to Indigenous communities."[15] If this sounds like performative activism, that's because it is. Sportswashing either has an apolitical character—relying on the excitement, fun, and the performances of athletes to simply make people forget about any unrelated harmful practices of the same state government or sponsor that is hosting or funding the event—or tries to lean into some of its past or contemporary harms, providing some crumbs to marginalized groups in an attempt to dissuade would-be critics.

Sportswashing is also used for both international and local audiences. While many in Western countries may look at Sochi, Qatar, or Beijing as failed sportswashing projects—given the torrent of negative press that happened before, during, and after these mega-events, at least in Western countries—the events may have still had positive reputational impacts on the local populations within these countries. In Russia, even though critics lambasted the Sochi organizers for putting on what at the time was the most expensive Winter Games in history (costing $55 billion), and less than half of Russians surveyed before the Games thought that they would yield economic benefits, 62 percent said they were proud to host the Games and the 2018 World Cup.[16] While it's still too early to assess the social impact on Qatari residents post–World Cup, research on the Beijing Olympic Games and on Chinese sporting prowess more generally has also shown positive effects on national pride and self-esteem,[17] though results have not been completely consistent.[18]

Reputation laundering through sport is not just about hiding negatives but also about trying to elevate a country's or corporation's international status. The Qatari royal family surely hoped that the glitz and glamour of the World Cup would make Qataris forget about their country's horrendous treatment of migrant workers and draconian treatment of women and LGBTQ+ people, but the event was also about elevating Qatar and marking its ascendance as an economic power and player on the world stage. The Olympic Games in Beijing and Vancouver were also good examples of this sort of status-making mission, as was the 2010 World Cup in South Africa. In nearly every World Cup and Olympics, local politicians and business leaders will tout the reputational gains that the mega-event will bring and the positive spotlight it will put on their cities, even as research continues to show little long-term positive impact.[19]

Status-based sportswashing is also now a commonly used strategy by ruling elites in the Gulf petrol-states, especially in elite world football. For just a few examples: Qatar Sports Investments, the state-run company headed by Qatari ruler Sheikh Tamim bin Hamad al-Thani, owns Paris Saint-Germain and tried to purchase Manchester United; United Arab Emirates deputy prime minister Sheikh Mansour owns Manchester City; Saudi Arabia's Public Investment Fund—chaired by Saudi crown prince Mohammed Bin Salman—owns majority shares in Newcastle United; and Qatari businessman (and member of the ruling family) Abdullah Al Thani owns the Spanish club Malaga. Many of these states have also inked expensive sponsorship deals linking their state-controlled airlines with some of Europe's most famous clubs, including Qatar Airways with Barcelona and the UAE's Emirates and Etihad with Arsenal and Manchester City. All of these sponsors are advertised prominently in the center of each team's jersey, and Arsenal's home pitch is even named after its sponsor airline.

It should also be noted that beyond the authoritarian nature of these states and state-run companies, the wealth of these ownership groups and sponsors is based on their oil and gas resources. As climate change continues to worsen and pressure mounts against fossil fuel companies and states, investing in high-level sports may become even more prominent as a form of preemptive sportswashing and *greenwashing* (which will be discussed in depth below).

Petrol states involving themselves with globally celebrated mega-events like the World Cup and Olympics and with the most popular sports clubs in the world has a dual purpose. It can cleanse their reputation and public perception—just look at the photos of Newcastle fans costumed in traditional Saudi Arabian dress after the Crown Prince's purchase of their beloved team—while also further enmeshing themselves in the global sport economy. This immersion into the global sport economy will allow these states and companies to hold important sway in sport-related decision making, and more than this, perhaps lead sports fans to consider them "too-important-to-fail" if and when our economies move away from fossil fuels.

There is so much more that can be said about sportswashing, its effectiveness, how we talk about it, and the many cases worldwide. Though it is not within the scope of this chapter and this book, I want to make it clear once again that neither sportswashing nor greenwashing is a uniquely Arab or Gulf state phenomena. Western countries and brands—including fossil fuel and chemical companies like British Petroleum and Dow Chemical, and junk food and plastic purveyors like McDonalds and Coca-Cola—have also been doing this for years.[20] It is obvious that less attention is paid to the sportswashing practices of Western countries, and issues of human rights and political violence are brought up *much* less often when these countries host mega-events.

The negative attention and media coverage of Qatar (some of it warranted) for the 2022 World Cup dwarfs anything we've seen for past mega-events, regardless of the negative actions of other host countries. The 2002 Salt Lake City Winter Olympics happening amid the illegal American invasion and destruction of Iraq, the Vancouver Games being played on Indigenous land, even the human displacement and ecological devastation brought about in Rio and in Brazil—these did not receive the same mainstream Western coverage as issues in China, Qatar, and Russia. Western "democracies" rarely get accused of sportswashing, even as they put on similarly expensive spectacles that distract from their wrongdoing and do not provide substantial benefits to local populations. There are also different expectations for athletes to speak out against non-Western versus Western host countries; consider the calls for athletes to boycott or speak out against the government in Qatar in the most recent World Cup, compared to the relative silence when these events happen elsewhere. Nathan Kalman-Lamb explained: "We don't hold an equivalent standard for [Western] athletes to advocate around injustices at home, let's say in North America, or perhaps in Europe, [even though] Europe and North America are not ultimately arbiters of global justice.... But injustice is everywhere.... We see forms of imperialism and colonialism around the world. These phenomenon are not some kind of exotic thing that we can parachute in on and then suddenly seize the moral high ground.... These problems are with us all the time."

While we can debate the relative atrocities of individual nations and companies forever, what we must understand is that sportswashing is not the work of any one type of government or business. Rather, it is the product of a system where profit is paramount, and when that profit is extracted in nefarious ways, reputations need cleansing. And under a global capitalist system where inequality between and within countries grows by the day, and huge profit can be extracted only through exploitation of either workers, the planet, or both, the only countries and corporations profitable enough to pay for mega-events and premier sports clubs are often engaging in other business practices that need a reputational uplift.

Sportswashing is also what happens when sports are transformed from activities performed for enjoyment, community, and health into the basis of commodity spectacle, used to extract profit from consumers and distract from other pressing social issues. Viewed from the perspective of politicians, profit-oriented state governments, and private corporations, rather than from the perspective of the local population, mega-events provide a double benefit: a chance to sportswash, and a great opportunity to make some money along the way.

Celebration Capitalism and the Neoliberal Trojan Horse

Celebration capitalism[21] is another term used by Boykoff, this time to describe the state of affairs brought about when states, their governments, and a variety of corporate stakeholders work together to host mega-events. "Celebration capitalism is disaster capitalism's affable cousin. Both occur in states of exception that allow plucky politicos and their corporate pals to push policies they couldn't dream of during normal times. But while disaster capitalism eviscerates the state, celebration capitalism manipulates state actors as partners, pushing economics rooted in so-called public-private partnerships.

All too often these partnerships are lopsided: the public pays and the private profits. In a bait and switch that's swaddled in bonhomie, the public takes the risks and private groups scoop up the rewards."[22]

Sport mega-events are fertile ground for all sorts of corporate profit. This includes opportunities for those in construction, hospitality, security, and the police. When we say that the World Cup cost Qatar $220 billion[23] or the Sochi Olympics cost $50 billion, this is where this money is going. They are not "costs" that disappear into the wind, but instead money that goes directly into the pockets of powerful stakeholders in these key industries. In many cases, the awarding of these contracts presents an opportunity for corruption; in Sochi, two of Vladimir Putin's childhood friends—Arkady and Boris Rotenberg—"received twenty-one government contracts worth seven billion dollars—more than the entire cost of the 2010 Olympics in Vancouver."[24] But even when there is no clear corruption, celebration capitalism offers profit opportunities for tons of businesses, often at the expense of local communities.

When new stadiums are built at warp speed with exploited, underpaid, and (often) migrant workers, construction firms, concrete suppliers, and even migrant labor middlemen all profit. When states pay for added security, in the form of both technology and human guards, tech and security firms sign huge contracts. When police forces are asked clear out homeless encampments, they get more funding and additional legal powers. These may strike most working people as *costs* of mega-events, but they are actually seen as benefits by organizing committees, and especially for those lobbying these committees. Zirin writes, "Countries don't want these mega-events in spite of the threats to public welfare, addled construction projects, and repression they bring, but because of them."[25]

Sport sociologist John Horne, who has also written extensively about the Olympics and mega-events, explains how mega-events provide an opportunity for host nations to modernize and expand their technological apparatuses, as these events "provide an opportunity for power plays by states, civic authorities, and groups for and against the event."[26] Zirin also refers to mega-events like the World Cup and the Olympics as "neoliberal trojan horses," because they are brought in with the promise of providing exciting sports and communal, societal benefits, while in reality they bring further privatization of common space and resources, community displacement, and wealth transfers to private corporations and powerful people. As Zirin explained in an interview with Democracy Now! about the World Cup: "It comes in, and people are supposed to be excited about soccer and hosting this big party, but in reality it pushes through a series of development programs, which are mainly for the benefit of big construction, big real estate and tourists—and the tourist money coming in, [it's] not for the people who actually have to live here once the cameras have left and once the confetti has all been swept away."[27]

The way sport is used to justify private profit and governmental and corporate overreach is reminiscent of the creation and implementation of other "special exception" legislation. This includes the Patriot Act, introduced in the United States less than a month after the 9/11 terrorist attack in New York City. The post-9/11 political climate in the States was used as justification for this far-reaching legislation, as the US government and media constructed this time as an exceptional period where civil liberties and restrictions needed to be put aside in the name of "national security." This led to extreme levels of government overreach, restriction of civil liberties, and racial profiling and racist policing, the effects of which are still felt today.

Boykoff, Zirin, and many others have shown that mega-events are framed as another version of this sort of "exceptional period" (or "state of exception," in their words), which states and political and economic elites use to impose and justify violent policies against the poor and unhoused, neoliberal budget cuts, and hypersurveillance of residents. Rather than being strictly in the name of national security, however, it is "in the name of sport," "safety," and "showing the best version of our city/country to the world."[28]

This "state of exception" thinking permeates every mega-event. When South Africa hosted the World Cup in 2010—the first time the Cup was hosted on African soil—organizers claimed that any critiques of the event and its organizing were a form Afro-pessimism and European prejudice. They even claimed that the games needed to be a success at any cost, because, as Zirin writes, "if the World Cup 'lost,' they argued, then Africa would also lose."[29] While European sport federations and European political structures do often show prejudice and condescension toward Asian and African sport and political leaders, in this case, "this argument was aimed at squelching dissent, not challenging European prejudice."[30]

For locals, even those who love the sports that have come to their city, mega-events become associated more with the harms they cause than the competitions themselves. Spectators in the stands—separated from locals either due to displacement or even physical barriers—and those watching on TV may remember the glittering stadiums and world records. Locals remember the mismanagement, displacement, silencing of activists and rights groups, and violence. And they remember how this was "justified" by football, or the Olympics, or for "unity," or because "the world is watching." As Larissa, a

Brazilian (Sao Paulo) activist explained: "Some of us are in jail, others are just being cautious. During our latest protests at Rio's Maracanã Stadium, fifteen of us were arrested and are now in jail. The police beat many of us.... I love football. I actually play football myself. I just hate the whole industry around it, which—in the name of FIFA—has been eating up whole neighborhoods here in Brazil. They think they can do anything in the name of football."[31]

Displacement and "Cleaning Up the Streets"

Perhaps the most common form of harm stemming from mega-events like the World Cup and the Olympics is the displacement of local communities. This happens in nearly every city and country that hosts one of these events, either as part of a mission to "clean up the city," or to make room for some piece of infrastructure deemed "necessary" for the games.[32] This "necessary" infrastructure includes stadiums and sports venues, of course, but also hotels and hospitality infrastructure, and roads and even parking lots.

I say "deemed" necessary, because if you ask the people on the ground, many of the "necessary" improvements made for mega-events are not actually all that necessary for those who live in these cities. Rather, the alterations are done for the short-term tourists and for the cameras. In FIFA's case, it is not sufficient to simply have enough stadiums to host the many matches in a World Cup; they must be "FIFA-quality stadiums," with FIFA-quality parking, amenities, and of course, prices. Beyond pricing out most of the local fans, this expectation leaves many countries, even those with enough stadium infrastructure, with only two expensive options. For Brazil, Russia, and South Africa, this meant building new stadiums and stadium infrastructure, and displacing hundreds of thousands of residents. Qatar, a country of about 2.7 million people, didn't have nearly enough stadium infrastructure (of any quality), and this meant a $220 billion dollar World Cup price tag, and huge payday for many of the construction and real estate firms that so benevolently joined in on the fun.

The number of people displaced for these events is staggering. The Centre on Housing Rights and Evictions, a Geneva-based NGO, found that 720,000 residents were forcefully evicted in the lead-up to the 1988 Seoul Olympics, and that 300,000 houses and apartments were demolished for the Beijing 2008 Summer Games. In the 1996 Atlanta Olympics, 30,000 residents were displaced for construction works,[33] and according to the World Cup and Olympics Popular Committee of Rio de Janeiro, 100,000 people were displaced from their homes due just to the 2014 World Cup. Street market sellers in Rio, Cape Town, and Johannesburg were moved out of their usual selling spaces, functionally taking away their jobs and ability to put food on the table.

The unhoused are an especially common target for mega-event organizers hell-bent on "cleaning up their cities" and putting on a shiny show for the world. One Johannesburg city councilor, saying exactly what so many politicians try to *avoid* saying, explained: "Homelessness and begging are big problems in the city. You have to clean your house before you have guests. There is nothing wrong with that."[34]

One of the first documented cases of this kind of cleansing was in the Berlin Nazi Olympics of 1936, where police "rounded up eight hundred Roma people living in the Berlin streets and put them in an internment camp."[35] Organizers and city governments followed the Nazis' lead (never a good thing) in future events. Avery Brundage,[36] who was in attendance for the 1936 Games and was IOC president from 1952 to 1972, oversaw deportations in both Tokyo (1964) and Mexico City (1968). Things didn't change much when Juan Antonio Samaranch took over in 1980 (or in the intervening years), as Samaranch was a proud Francisco Franco supporter whose main goals for the Olympics could basically be summed up as money, money, and more money.

In recent World Cups and Olympics, unhoused and mentally ill people, refugees, and asylum seekers are still rounded up and removed from city centers, often moved hundreds of miles away. In Atlanta, 9,000 people were arrested for "begging" and "loitering" in the lead-up to the Games, and homeless people were sent nearly 300 kilometers out of town.[37] Following Atlanta's lead, the city of Sydney, Australia, made it possible to arrest and charge people with causing a "social nuisance," and privatized a public park, kicking seventy unhoused people to the curb.[38] In 2004 many refugees and asylum seekers joined the unhoused and mentally ill as targets for Greek police,[39] and Vancouver's large unhoused population was harassed by police for a variety of petty offenses, while gaining nothing from the Games.[40]

These kinds of displacement, done in service of mega-events that are ostensibly supposed to benefit cities and the people in them, are a clear form of violence against residents, both housed and unhoused. Residents are ripped from their homes, often forced to move to areas where they do not know anyone—often moved far away from family, friends, social support systems, and crucially, their jobs.[41] Beyond the pure economic cost that comes with longer commutes and potential lost employment, residents lose their informal ties and community. These kinds of ties are especially vital to lower-income and already marginalized people, who may live on the fringes of organized society and the organized welfare state (if one even exists in the first place). They are often more reliant on mutual and community aid and solidarity. Losing these formal and informal ties due to displacement not only exacerbates financial losses, but it can also cut into the very essence of what makes life worth living—shared experience, connection, and a sense of home.

If the displacement of locals wasn't enough, the construction that they are displaced for is itself often violent and wasteful. In past mega-event construction blitzes, workers have been forced to work extreme hours in brutal working conditions, with many suffering and some dying—forty in Greece, twenty-one for the Russian World Cup, and eight in Brazil. Though public pressure fortunately forced Qatar to remove their exploitative Khafala work migration system in 2008,[42] thirty-seven people died directly building stadiums and 6,500 total migrant workers died between 2010 (when Qatar was awarded the World Cup) and 2020.[43]

These deaths are caused directly by the all-out sprint to build new stadiums, and real estate and construction firms trying their best to both build quickly and make as much money as they can. This leads to underpaid and overworked staff; two of the Brazilian worker deaths, for example, happened when an overworked crane operator, on his eighteenth straight day of work, made a mistake that caused the crane to crash down. The only reason the human damage wasn't more substantial was that it, fortunately, happened over the workers' short lunch break, so most were not on the construction site. FIFA knows about these kinds of risks when they award tournaments to hosts that will need to build quickly, and yet they did nothing to prevent this from happening in either Brazil or Qatar. This would be a clear case of a crime of omission—where the absence of action creates the conditions for harm to take place—except it's worse than that. In Brazil, FIFA actually pressured the government to crack down on the worker strikes[44] that were happening and speed through or work around any safety regulations that would slow down construction.

The treatment of "favelas" and their residents in Rio and in Brazil encapsulates this violence and the way it touches all parts of displaced people's lives.[45] It is also a microcosm of how mega-events are weaponized against locals more generally. As Zirin explains in *Brazil's Dance with the Devil*, people who have never been to Brazil and have only seen or heard of favelas through news outlets or the odd colonial-gaze documentary might think of favelas as a version of tent encampments or temporary housing for poor people. But in Rio and Brazil they are so much more than this. While Zirin emphasizes that it is important not to romanticize favelas and favela life, or poverty in the Global

South more generally, he notes that the "favelas of Rio . . . are a different and very specific kind of community."[46]

Built onto the hillsides of Rio,[47] on common land that historically never belonged to any one person or entity, the property structure of favelas is reminiscent of past living arrangements, before the (still very recent, historically) advent of private property. They are community-organized and community-run, with community associations, often called Neighborhood Associations, that meet to discuss and decide on key issues. Plumbing and sanitation, building of housing and infrastructure, even policing, legal disputes, health care, and child care are often dealt with by the community itself with little outside oversight. Some public services, like streetlights and garbage collection, are still handled by city governments, but most of what favelas need is provided by the people of the favelas themselves.

Rio's favelas are places where neighbors look after each other, children play together, and adults cook and work with one another. Multiple generations of families live together or close by, and these families have lived in the same favelas for decades. They are not temporary camps, but real *homes* for people, built up over years. Many put in great effort to build up and decorate their small homes, making use of every inch of space and creating warm, welcoming environments for themselves, their families, and anyone else in the community who might need them. It is not an ideal living arrangement, and there are still issues of sanitation, overcrowding, security, and crime—though they are not nearly as bad as the voyeuristic and gruesome media representations shown on Brazilian and International news make them seem—but favelas have a vibrant culture and strong social and communal importance for so many people.

In the lead-up to the Rio Olympics, many of the cities' favelas were slated to be demolished, with different favelas offered different options for what would come next. Some were offered relocation, others compensation, and others nothing. The justification for the removal and relocation of favelas was, predictably, to make the city "safer" for visitors, using laws passed specifically for the "state of exception" of the coming mega-events, which allowed police and city government officials to bypass constitutional and civil rights requirements. To convince and coerce people to leave, city governments withheld key services like garbage collection and streetlights, and removed trees. They offered small amounts of money to people to leave and even offered higher payouts if they were able to convince others to leave, often pitting (or at least trying to pit) community members against one another.

A propaganda and media blitz also followed this legislation and early plans to remove favelas and their residents, with media showing scenes of squalor and destruction to illustrate why favelas needed to go. In reality though, these scenes were often actually depictions of what the favelas looked like *after* the citizens were displaced and removed or the demolition process began. People were seeing the *results* of displacement, not a reason it needed to happen.

Other favelas and housing were removed to be replaced by parking lots, stadiums, and hotels. In some cases, like the former site of Favela de Metro, the favela was demolished and the people removed, only for a pile of rubble to be left in its place, with nothing even built for the World Cup or Olympics.

While community organizing and resistance (through the Neighborhood Associations and other activist circles) helped repel some of the most egregious and potentially disastrous demolishing and relocations—such as in the Vila Autodromo community, which was forced to move only 1 kilometer away[48]—Brazil's mega-events forced 100,000 out of their homes and their favelas.

People's former homes, health centers, and areas for recreation, ritual, and community were either destroyed or turned into luxury property and infrastructure that they could never rent, own, or enjoy as visitors. In many cases, previously commonly held favela land was turned into nameless, faceless, and memory-less property commodities, to be sold to the highest bidder. Instead of spaces for people to live, to share, and to help one another, these mega-events gave real estate tycoons and corporate interests the opportunity and justification to turn the land into a moneymaker, with little care for how profits would be made and who would be hurt along the way.

Some favela residents acquired property rights in the short term, but in the medium and longer term, marketizing these areas will remove all of those who once lived there, through pricing them out and gentrification. Setting aside the physical loss of property, and the financial and employment ramifications of long-range displacement, the World Cup and Olympics destroyed entire communities and an entire way of life for thousands of people. While we might try to calculate this sort of harm, the complete upending of entire communities' lives and collective history and memory is incalculable.

Squandered Money and Wasted Funds

Even when brand new stadiums are successfully built, they often remain underused, with costs that are astronomically higher than the use that people get out of them. This is most egregious for lower-income and working people, the same groups who are either displaced for them to be built, or who actually put in the energy and time to build them.

It's not even just the working class who cannot realize any of the benefits from the huge outputs needed for mega-events. Nearly every mega-event host has horror stories about abandoned hotels, ghost towns, unused parking lots, unsold apartments, and stadiums that cost more to keep open than they can garner in revenue. In the years following the 2018 Pyeongchang Olympics, the Olympic Stadium and the Olympic Sliding Centre[49] sat mostly empty,[50] as does Montreal's Olympic Stadium. In advance of the 2014 World Cup, Maracanã Stadium in Rio, famous for its hostile crowds of 175,000 standing-room-only fans, was transformed into a cookie-cutter 75,000-seat stadium fit with the usual North American mega-stadium moneymakers, including luxury boxes and VIP sections. All of this was done to increase the profit-making potential of the stadium and turn it into a "FIFA-quality stadium." But what this did instead was sap the energy and uniqueness from the venue, transforming it "to sell its 'Brazilianness' at the expense of actual living, breathing Brazilians: another economic example of a Brazil treating its very culture as an export commodity to market abroad."[51]

After renovations that cost $500 million, the stadium sat vacant for several years after the 2016 Olympics, racking up millions in energy bill debts as the city of Rio and the Rio Organizing Committee fought over who was responsible for these bills and repairs. The stadium is now owned by the Rio government and managed by professional clubs Flamenco and Fluminese, but it's hard to argue this was money well spent. Many of Brazil's expensive World Cup football palaces are also withering away or sit unused. As Zirin wrote in 2016: "In Brasília, the $550 million stadium is now a being used as a 'parking lot for buses.' In Natal, the stadium—again, built with public funds—can be rented out for weddings and kids' parties. In Cuiabá, at the new stadium, it was found that the locker rooms had been broken into and were being used by the homeless, just as homeless people in Greece had repurposed structures from their 2004 Olympics."[52]

The Sochi Olympics are another particularly vivid example of wasted money, resources, and infrastructure, with some corruption thrown in for good measure. Like all Olympics, Russia's went vastly over budget—originally pegged at $12 billion, the Games ultimately cost $55 billion.[53] This was more than all other past Winter Olympic Games budgets *combined*, and a lot of this cash went to Vladimir Putin's oligarch friends.[54] The returns for the Russian people have been negligible, including in the use of facilities built or restored specifically for the Games, and in the lack of economic returns for the investment put into the city and area around Sochi.

A curious choice for the Games when it was announced, Sochi is a coastal a city of only about 500,000 people. Though it is known within Russia as a tourist spot along the Black Sea, it has never had this reputation for tourists abroad, and the Games haven't changed that. The city is not well connected to the biggest airports, tourists require a visa to enter the country, and for those who want sun, beaches, or mountains, there are many better options relatively close by.[55] Hotels and beachfront tourist infrastructure built and restored for the Games remain underused (except for once a year during the F1 Russian Grand Prix), not bringing even close to commensurate return on the huge investments made by the Organizing Committee and Russian government. Again, these were investments that could have been made in so many other areas of Russian society, and could have helped so many.

Beyond the lack of tourism, Olympic facilities also mostly lie dormant, with little use by locals and Russian people. Some have been converted into centers for children's sports, concert and entertainment venues, and a tennis academy, but "the majority of them are either abandoned or underutilized."[56] As urban planning scholar Simona Azzali explains, quoting one of the Sochi Olympic experts she interviewed, the Adler district (the coastal area in Sochi where the non-mountain-sport facilities were built) "is too tiny and far from Sochi Central to justify the presence of six iconic and large-capacity sports venues for winter sports." The 40,000-seat Olympic stadium built just for the Games was used only for the opening and closing ceremonies, and then for the World Cup. Now it sits mostly empty, which is unsurprising—the old football stadium for the local team in Sochi had seated 10,000, and was rarely full.

The Olympic Park is far from the city center and sees few visitors, and the Athlete's Village—turned into luxury condos—remains mostly unsold and unused, with international buyers looking elsewhere and Russians unable to afford them. Occupancy rates for the many new hotels in the area sat at 20–25 percent in 2017, with Russian tourists choosing (or only being able to afford to choose) cheaper hotel and vacation options.[57] While the construction boom of the Sochi Olympics and Russian World Cup may have helped line the pockets of business elites in both Russia and abroad, while giving Putin a few glamorous photo-ops, it seems to have done next to nothing for everyday people.

But what about the few cases, or potential future cases, where organizing committees actually do manage to stay on budget, and all the venues, new construction, new and restored transit, and hospitality services are maintained and benefit all people, including working-class people? Other than this being a pipe dream that has yet to become a reality, this should lead us to another question: Even if this pipe dream were to become a reality, aren't there bigger problems, and better uses for all this money?

As Zirin writes, again about Brazil: "The stories that emerged out of Brazil also speak to the irony and oddity of building stadiums in cities where there are other, far more pressing needs. . . . In a city with immediate health care and education imperatives, where the absence of hospital beds, overcrowded classrooms, and high rates of illiteracy are facts of life, the effort and attention devoted to the new stadium(s) struck many residents as obscene."[58]

It's vital to remember that this is not a uniquely Brazilian problem. In every country that hosts the Olympics, World Cup, or other mega-events—even countries generally considered relatively stable like Canada or the United Kingdom—there are social problems that could use the funding that is instead spent on hosting. This is not to say that public funds should not be spent on sports. Rather, it is that the people in a particular country or city should have more say about how this funding is used, and this money should be spent on sustainable sport that provides benefits to country or city residents, rather than to wealthy spectators, politicians, and corporate interests.

In Brazil and South Africa, billions were spent on new football facilities, even when each country had perfectly usable stadiums and a litany of other social problems, including education, health care, and inequality. Brazilian activists, mocking FIFA head Sepp Blatter's constant calls for "FIFA-quality stadiums," began proclaiming the need for "FIFA-quality hospitals and schools" instead. In Japan, while the organizing committee framed the Olympics as a chance for the country to recover and heal following the 2011 earthquake, tsunami, and Fukushima nuclear disaster, Olympic efforts were actually materially diverting valuable money, resources, and labor away from these recovery efforts.[59] Athens and Vancouver racked up huge Olympic bills, well over their projected and agreed upon budgets, all while both cities had and continue to have tons of unhoused people.

Of the past twenty-one Olympic Games over the past fifty-five years (since we've had sufficiently good data), only one (Los Angeles in 1984) has come in on or under budget. It is also the only Games to turn a profit, owing largely to its many already-existing stadiums and the influx of private sponsorship and television revenue. Every other Olympics has overrun its projected costs; on average, final costs finish at more than 2.5 times their initial budgets.[60] Unless we have solved all social problems (we haven't), and each of these hosting countries adequately provides for all of its citizens (they don't), then it is likely that the funds from these extremely ballooned budgets could have been effectively used elsewhere. As Brazilian soccer star Romário explained in *Brazil's Dance with the Devil*:

> FIFA got what it came for: money. Things like transportation that affect the public after the tournament is over? They don't care. They don't care about what is going to be left behind. . . . You see hospitals with no beds. You see hospitals with people on the floor. You see schools that don't have lunch for the kids. You see schools with no air-conditioning. . . . You see buildings and schools with no accessibility for people who are handicapped. If you spend 30 percent less on the stadiums, they'd be able to improve the other things that actually matter . . . they found a way to get rich on the World Cup and they robbed the people instead. This is the real shame.[61]

Surveillance and Securitization

The last piece of the mega-event puzzle is the creation and maintenance of Big Brother levels of surveillance and security against residents of host cities and countries, which often persists long after the event. To put on mega-events with the expected glamour, cities and organizing committees need to "clean up their neighborhoods" and "ensure safety" for tourists and visitors. This means not only displacing local populations and building new stadiums and hotels that these displaced people will never be able to enter, on top of the rubble they used to call home, but also that host cities and countries must beef up police forces, install new security provisions, and circumvent existing civil liberties to ensure that tourists and those watching on TV get a shiny, spotless, and ultimately distorted view of the place and the event.

These presentations of safety and security, however, are not for residents. Canadian scholar Anne-Marie Broudehoux writes, "Symbolic transformations of urban environments to fit global expectations of modernity—expressing security, order, and economic success in vibrant, exciting, safe, places (that are) 'open for business'—tend to impact on the quality of life of inhabitants and most negatively on poor and marginal populations."[62] In short, while corporate stakeholders may benefit from this security and safety, these benefits do not trickle down to poor and marginalized people; instead, they do the opposite, creating new forms of exclusion and harm.[63]

The is especially ironic in the Olympic and World Cup contexts, as these events are ostensibly put on to "bring the world together" and foster community and openness "through the power of sport." In reality, as sociologist Vida Bajc explains, mega-events create a new, temporary "social order" that is directly opposed to these values, transforming "everyday life to a security-sanctioned order in which civil and human rights, interpersonal relations, and democratic principles are overshadowed by the needs of security."[64] New legislation gets passed, more military and police personnel are brought in, and personal information and human behavior are treated as commodified data to be gathered and eventually sold, all for sake of commodity spectacle.

We see this at every World Cup, at every Olympic Games, and at many other mega-events; the difference only varies in level. The 2004 Greece Olympics, the first Summer Games post-9/11 and therefore the first in our more mass-surveillance, hyper-securitized world, saw egregious displacement of vulnerable populations and civil-liberty-destroying hypersurveillance. Overriding the country's constitution, Greece brought in 50,000 military troops from Israel, Britain, and the United States to patrol the streets in Athens. Refugees and asylum seekers were rounded up, as were other unhoused people.

In London in 2012, missiles were set up on apartment buildings, 48,000 security forces were brought in, and laws were passed giving police additional public order powers. Beyond confusing locals in under-resourced East London (where the Games mostly took place), local youth described more frequent police harassment both during and after the Olympics, made possible by exceptional powers for police in Stratford and the areas around the Olympic venues. These powers allowed police "to move on anyone considered to be engaged in antisocial behavior, whether they are hanging around the train station, begging, soliciting, loitering in hoodies or deemed in any way to be causing a nuisance."[65] According to Canadian sociologist Jacqueline Kennelly, for youth in Stratford "the Olympics triggered the implementation of dispersal orders that restricted their freedom of movement and assembly in their own neighborhood. Police behavior heightened their anxieties, especially among the Black men, who were often the targets of unwelcome attention from officers. Ultimately, many concluded that the enhanced policing and security for the duration of the Olympics were designed for foreign visitors, not for Stratford resident."[66]

The South Korean government similarly used their Olympics to install more CCTV cameras and facial recognition technology and add to their fleet of drones. These technologies and added police resources were kept after the Games.[67] In Vancouver, police used enhanced powers to round up and move houseless people out of downtown, aided by 1,000 new security cameras placed around Olympic venues and downtown.[68]

More recently, in the lead-up to the 2020 Tokyo Olympics, "Japanese legislators rammed anti-terrorism legislation through the parliament, justified by the need to protect the Olympics."[69] This legislation added hundreds of new crimes and police powers to the docket, including anti-protest, anti-privacy, and media censorship legislation; the UN special rapporteur on the right to privacy expressed "serious concern" about these bills, given their risk of "arbitrary application of this legislation given [its] vague definition[s] and overbroad range of crimes."[70] While residents and human rights groups consistently come out in protest against these kinds of measures, these "necessary" security enhancements and the provision of additional police forces are extremely profitable for security technology manufacturers and other corporations linked to the wider security-industrial complex.

Not only do these kinds of security measures infringe on human rights, prompt more arrests, and subject people to more constant surveillance, but they also present a manufactured view of reality and of how people in host cities feel about the mega-events. While more critical scholarship and critical journalism have made strides in recent years, if you were to only watch Olympic or World Cup coverage on TV, you would think that everyone in each host city is ecstatic about the event. Much of this positive coverage is due to the reciprocal profit-making relationship between broadcasters and the events, and these broadcasters' ultimate desire to continue showing and making money off of these events. The hyper-securitized atmosphere helps them tremendously in presenting this illusion. It's a lot easier to depict happy fans and blissful sports when the protestors are either muzzled or confined to areas miles away and only those with tickets are allowed anywhere near stadiums.

Broken Promises and Legacy Mythology

This brings us to our next point, regarding why so few people know about the harms of Olympic Games (unless they've come to your city), and how organizing committees and corporate sponsors mostly escape public scrutiny. Elite sport structures have two main strategies for avoiding blame for the harms that mega-events cause: exaggerating legacies and breaking promises.

In the sport event and mega-event context, legacies are defined as "all planned and unplanned, positive and negative, tangible and intangible structures created for and by a sport event that remain longer than the event itself."[71] While this definition might sound needlessly complex (it is an academic definition, after all), we all know and have heard legacy arguments.

These games will offer a platform for Vancouver to show itself off on the world stage. There's going to be an amazing rise in physical activity in Tokyo in the years following the Games. We're going to "revitalize" downtown Rio. We're building affordable housing in London. Tourism will flourish. The city will receive a "boost." Little girls will know that they can accomplish their sport dreams!

To be clear, many of these potential "legacies" of a sport event are objectively good things—if, of course, they actually happened.

I was born and raised in Montreal, and like many Montrealers, I grew up hearing about how we were "still paying for the Olympics," which cost 13 times the original estimated budget. It took Montreal taxpayers thirty years to pay off the debts incurred for the 1976 Games, and all they were left with was an ugly, mostly unusable, and falling-apart stadium far from downtown, and some interesting-looking apartment complexes that no one can afford to live in.[72] As explained above, this gargantuan debt also forced the city to ignore years of crumbling infrastructure and other city issues, which still impact Montreal today.

Tales like these—of excited bidding by elites and politicians, followed by games that come in way over budget, and culminating with post-games hangovers felt by working people—are common across Olympic and other mega-event host cities. Organizers promise a suite of positive legacies before, during, and after nearly every mega-event, regardless of whether there's evidence to support these claims.[73] They also often conveniently ignore any negative legacies the event may also bring.[74] For every story of a beautiful new low-cost swimming pool or long-term tourist bubble,[75] there are many other stories of barely used million-dollar athletic facilities and impossibly expensive housing that's priced out the former local community.[76] Cities and local populations are sold the dream of revitalized economies, new infrastructure, and "intangible" social and civic pride—but the reality is often much different. Researchers at the University of Minnesota found that event organizers and local officials only use the word "legacy" in reference to positive outcomes, with no clear or consistent term for the vast and sometimes overwhelming impacts that are negative.[77] This is unsurprising, when you consider that organizers and officials often serve as de facto boosters for mega events and therefore need to amplify the positives and bury the negatives.

Before the 2012 London Olympic games, organizing committee leader Sebastian Coe promised 30,000 to 40,000 new homes near the Stratford Olympic site area, "much of which will be 'affordable housing' available to key workers such as nurses or teachers."[78] Twelve years later, only 12,400 homes had been built, and less than 10 percent of these are affordable to people on average incomes, according to the London Legacy Development Corporation.[79] "Much" is a vague term—and was probably chosen by Coe for that very reason—but I don't think 10 percent qualifies. In the surrounding boroughs 75,000 families are currently on the waiting list for council housing,[80] while the areas promised as affordable housing sites are filled with "luxury living" estates charging (in 2022) over £1,700 (more than US$2,000) for a studio apartment.[81] The organizing committee also promised positive sport participation legacies, though in the years following the Games, there are no indications that sport participation has increased.[82]

Overpromising and under-delivering (or not delivering at all) are common in the stories of mega events and the people they leave behind. London and Montreal are more the rule than the exception. In Rio, over 22,000 families were "resettled" (evicted) as far as 50–60 kilometers from the city center to prepare for the Olympics; many were moved from areas they and their families had lived in for generations.[83] Atlanta residents were similarly given one-way bus tickets out of the city in advance of the 1996 Olympics, with an estimated 30,000 displaced and 6,000 evicted from public housing.[84] Plans for using biodegradable fuel, reforestation, and building low-income housing in Rio crumbled before they even began. Sochi and Krashaya Polyana are now mostly summer ghost towns, and many of the Winter Games venues that cost so much to build and still cost so much to maintain are barely used.[85] The activist Los Angeles organization NOlympics LA was created with the express purpose of ensuring that the Olympics don't come to Los Angeles[86]—and this is in the one city that actually made a profit on their Olympics. Similar groups exist in cities like Boston, Chicago, and Calgary.[87]

Beyond the fact that legacies related to mega-events or publicly subsidized new stadium builds often don't come to fruition, these supposed social benefits are also wrongly framed as inextricably linked with events or stadiums, which is far from true. Hosting a massive sport event isn't a necessary prerequisite for investment in public infrastructure, better health services, or new affordable housing. Local governments and city elites can help build a new light rail or put more money into better hospitals without hosting the Super Bowl or the X Games. Framing an Olympic Games, a World Cup, or a World Championship as the only way to get the funding needed to revitalize a city or community is disingenuous and even predatory, as sport governing bodies and business elites implicitly withhold necessary public funding and social improvements by tying them to sport projects that ultimately won't even benefit those they purport to serve. Tim Kellison—a sport scholar who researches sport in urban environments, urban planning, and sport event and climate legacies—explains, "These improvements could have happened without the 10s of millions (or billions) of dollars to host a three week- or month-long event . . . it's not necessarily the best use of money."

And yet, sport events and the governing bodies that promote them continue to beat the same legacy drums. Once again, the mechanisms of capital are to blame. Olympics, World Cups, Super Bowls, and a variety of other large sport events are in fact quite an economic boon for some people—just not working people. Like politicians claiming that the project that just so happens to hire their buddies' real estate development firm is going to *serve the people*, those who promote mega-events use false narratives of "positive legacies for working people" to justify filling the coffers of the powerful and their own pockets. As Nolympics LA so eloquently sums it up, "These games and other sporting mega-events threaten to destroy communities and cement cities as playgrounds for the rich." It is much easier to get the funding to build luxury condos in London[88] if you dress it up in Olympic pageantry and promises of social and economic revitalization than if you just say you'd like to build more luxury housing because that's where the money is made.[89]

Beyond "wealthy business elites," Kellison also notes that "political leaders see this as an opportunity to cement their own legacy," promoting their success in bringing a large event to their city or area, with the hopes of moving on in time for someone else to be left to pick up the pieces "when the bad stuff starts to occur." Mitt Romney, a Republican senator from Utah and one-time Republican Party presidential nominee (losing to Barack Obama in 2012), used his success leading the 2002 Salt Lake City Winter Olympic bid to catapult himself into the conversation for the Republican nomination. On the campaign trail, he also constantly touted the lessons he learned and the skills he developed in his oversight of the project.

But how do organizations get away with pie-in-the-sky promises and outlandish claims about the legacies of large events, when there is so much evidence to refute them? The first way is through—in the words of Kellison—"sheer saturation of the media narrative, by focusing on the positives, so they basically overpower or outlast (other) claims on the political or environmental or economic downsides with hosting these events." By pumping positive news stories into the media sphere and ensuring access for reporters who want to write positive stories about these events, sport governing bodies and event organizers can ensure a steady stream of good press. The media are also complicit in this coverage, as broadcasters benefit from the advertising boost that comes with showing large events. In the age of streaming, live sports have become even more vital for broadcasters because they secure advertisers, and these broadcasters know that their contracts with the IOC, FIFA, or the NFL are unlikely to be renewed if they are critical of the event or its impact. The IOC is notorious for blacklisting journalists and academics who cover the Games in an unfavorable light, including activists-scholars like Jules Boykoff.

Kellison also notes that those living in host cities can get "caught in the euphoria of the games," especially people who don't see their negative impacts (forced displacement, homelessness) firsthand. This lack of knowledge links back to the positive press buildup, and the fact that although academics and some journalists have consistently delivered evidence of legacies as false promises, this view remains on the fringe and "doesn't necessarily always make it out to the public at large." Even if it does, the *human* cost of displacement, gentrification, "reno-victions," and even simple inconveniences related to these projects can be hard to quantify, especially when compared with the "hundreds of millions" of tourists or building dollars promised by bid organizers. These organizers, hopeful politicians, and sport governing bodies can also be purposely ambiguous about specific legacy outputs and the timeline of these outputs—like Coe promising that "much" of the new housing stock in East London would be affordable, without providing a firm percentage or total—to shield themselves from blame for failing to deliver on a pre-event promise.

Positive press and research about event legacies also comes from sport organizations themselves, either directly or indirectly. This research demonstrates some of the legacy benefits of mega-sport events and stadiums—often based around more intangible notions of civic pride—but there are two issues that should be noted. First, much of this research is funded by organizations like the IOC,[90] FIFA,[91] and other large sport organizations like National Olympic Committees.[92] These organizations have a clear vested interest in promoting the positive legacies of their events, as they are vital to their bids for future games and to their own viability as organizations. It's possible that they will still accept proposals and research that paints their organization or mission in a negative light, but unlikely.

Second, even if we take this positive legacy research at face value, it is dwarfed by the negative consequences of these same events. While feelings of civic pride and short-term increases in sport participation (longer-term increases have rarely been proven)[93] are great, they aren't enough to balance out the money shelled out by cities and governments for limited-use and luxury infrastructure that prices longtime residents out and drains state funds that could have been used to deal with much more pressing issues related to homelessness, housing insecurity, and other cost-of-living crises. Kellison explains, "It doesn't take much digging to find the negative impacts that occurred before, during, and after the event," and these impacts often outweigh the real positive impacts that do occur.

Positive legacy research also comes predominantly via surveys and interviews with residents of the area (those who haven't been pushed out) and event organizers. While there's nothing wrong with this on its face, and surveys *are* one of the best options for conducting large-scale research on the subject, this methodology necessarily ignores the most marginalized members of society, who are always hit the hardest by negative event legacies. According to Kellison, "Those who are impacted most by these events in a negative way are also those with the least amount of power and the least amount of voice in a community or in a neighborhood." These people almost never have a voice in the bids and plans for events and are left powerless in the face of sport capital.

This voicelessness mirrors the relationship that most working-class people have to the decisions made about their neighborhoods and the lives they can live. The imperatives of capitalism—profit above all other considerations, stakeholder primacy, exploitation and use *of* (rather than use *for*) people and the environment—don't allow for the real input of those with either no capital and no political power or those who stand (both figuratively and literally) "in the way" of profitmaking. With mega and large sport events focused on elite competition, TV, streaming and sponsorship dollars, and putting on a great show at all costs, the romanticized promised benefits of sport to local communities fall further and further down the promised priority list, if they even remain there at all.

Environmental Devastation and Greenwashing

Elite capitalist sport generally and especially sport mega-events also have devastating environmental impacts. Given the fact too much consumption is killing our planet, this should come as no surprise; anything with the word "mega" in the title (that isn't followed by "sustainable" or "carbon-cutting") is probably going to be pretty harmful for the environment.

There are, of course, the individual examples of environmental waste and broken sustainability promises in specific Games. The Sochi Olympics were "a massive disaster from an environmental point of view,"[94] with tons of new construction and building on already ecologically threatened areas. For example, the Olympic Park was built in Imeretinskaya Bay, the last natural lowland of Southern Russia that was home to numerous specimens of endangered birds and plants. The site was filled with construction waste, as "regulations on construction in environmentally protected areas were eased to convert protected natural sites into building zones."[95]

The Vancouver Games was infamously forced to truck in snow for the Games,[96] and though South Korean organizers promised "the most advanced environmentally friendly strategies" for the Pyeongchang Olympics, "they (then) chopped down 58,000 trees in a sacred 500-year-old forest on Mt. Gariwang to make way for a ski run."[97] For the 2014 Rio World Cup, Arena de Amazônia was built in the heart of the Amazon rainforest (at a cost of $220–300 million) and used for a grand total of four matches. It's since been mostly abandoned, used only for the odd music gig.[98]

But the main environmental issue for mega-events is actually more structural and simpler than this. It isn't even about individual cases of ecological devastation in the building of venues; the biggest environmental cost of worldwide events is the worldwide fan travel needed to economically sustain them. Athlete and equipment travel has a high carbon-emission cost as well, but even this is dwarfed by fan travel.

As these events have grown in size and investment in our age of celebration capitalism, they require more and more tourist dollars and international travel to pay for them. When budgets reach the mid-billions, ticket costs, sponsorship deals, and tourist dollars need to rise with them. This means that Olympics, World Cups, and other mega-events can't sustain themselves off local revenue alone; they require the wealthy of the world to descend onto the city in droves.

Because of this, as sport ecologist Madeleine Orr explained[99]—discussing the Paris 2024 Games, which promised to be the "most sustainable" Olympics ever—"the most sustainable sport event is the one that doesn't happen." While mega-events can and should try to be more environmentally sustainable than their predecessors—through carbon offsetting, fewer new venue and infrastructure construction, reductions in fossil fuel use, and better recycling and composting programs (among other strategies)—by their very nature they will continue to be environmentally damaging. The only real way to rid mega-events of their environmentally destructive character is to make them less mega. This may sound simple, but under contemporary capitalist constraints—where bigger is better, revenue growth is imperative, and organizers justify high event spending by touting the even higher tourist revenue that they will supposedly generate—it will be difficult to convince them that these events must become more local.

So How Do They Justify It?

Justifying the environmental destruction created by many of these same events and by elite capitalist sport is generally accomplished through similar avoidance and deflection strategies mentioned above, but with a special green twist. Aside from breaking promises and sweeping bad news about air pollution and carbon emissions under the rug, sport organizations and governing bodies also participate, on both sides of the equation, in what's known as "greenwashing."

According to Orr, "greenwashing in sport comes in many forms—one is by investment in sport as a distraction from environmental wrongdoing, and another is by sports brands overemphasizing their environmental good works." Sport leagues and organizations act as both the greenwasher and the greenwashee.

As a greenwashee, sport is used by large emitters like fossil fuel guzzling mega-corporations, oil and gas, and automobile and air travel companies to accomplish *their* greenwashing. These companies will make themselves visible sponsors in sport to sanitize and cleanse their own reputations, distracting the public from their disastrous climate impacts. Orr explains, "When Ineos or Gazprom sponsor cycling teams and football events in Europe, they're quietly buying the approval of sports fans and subduing any critiques of their extractive and exploitative business models."

Examples of this kind of greenwashing are everywhere,[100] so I'll give just a few. As of late 2024, Petro-Canada is one of the main sponsors of the Canadian Olympic Committee, which has signed on to the United Nations Sport for Climate Action Framework and touts its sustainability credentials at every turn, including during in the bid for the 2010 Vancouver Olympics and in its current 2030 bid. Similarly, Toyota, Bridgestone, Coca-Cola, and Proctor and Gamble are four of the thirteen official sponsors of the Olympic Games, which claimed "the environment" as the third pillar of the Olympic Charter in the early 2000s. For those keeping score at home, that's Toyota, one of the world's largest automakers and the world's third highest funder of fossil fuel lobbying (behind only Chevron and Exxon Mobil);[101] Bridgestone, the world's biggest tire producer; and Coca-Cola and Proctor and Gamble, two of the largest purveyors of single-use plastics.

In 2021 the Rapid Transition Alliance released their *Sweat Not Oil* report,[102] which revealed over 250 sponsorship deals between oil and gas companies and sports properties. These kinds of partnerships are everywhere, spanning from elite professional sport all the way down to youth sports. Orr recalls from a trip she took through the American oil belt, from Houston to New Orleans: "You notice that there are signs for countless fossil fuel-sponsored art events and sports teams in the area—think high school football fields with fossil fuel logos on the scoreboards and music festivals sponsored by Shell. This area's called 'Cancer Alley' for a reason—extractive industries have devastating health consequences for the people living on the other side of the fence—and everybody knows it. But fossil fuel industries have been buying their silence and acceptance for years by funding their kid's teams."

On the other hand, there's sport as a greenwasher. The sport industry itself is a huge emitter of carbon, whether it's through excessive and inefficiently routed travel, mega-stadiums built outside of cities and requiring car transport, concessions full of single-use plastics, and a variety of other practices. The imperatives of capitalist growth—more ticket sales, more sponsorship, more merchandise, more league expansion to more places—are at odds with emissions-reduction goals. Before the climate crisis worsened and the public (and especially young people) became attuned to this crisis, the high-emitting nature of elite capitalist sport was not considered a problem by those in charge. Like athlete violence against women, rising awareness levels among the public have caused leagues and organizations to feel they need to create a *perception* that they care about the climate and green initiatives, to keep fans interested, engaged, and spending. This is where greenwashing comes in.

Orr explains that sport organizations and leagues are greenwashing when they "engage in a few symbolic initiatives to 'green' their products or events and pass it off as sustainable, without making any large-scale changes to their business models to be less extractive, use less plastics, waste less, reduce travel, and so on." Like NFL football teams cutting a backup player after an arrest but keeping a convicted star player, FIFA might claim efforts to be carbon neutral while at the same time holding the World Cup in Qatar—requiring the building of brand-new stadiums and outdoor air conditioning—and then in Canada, the United States, and Mexico—requiring intercontinental air travel *within* the tournament. FIFA also plans to expand the tournament from 32 to 48 and even possibly 64 teams, which would bring even more games, fan and team air travel, and emissions.

Similarly, organizations might add paper straws and recyclable plastic cups to their stadium concessions, and then fail to offer any vegetarian or vegan options on the menu, and few if any public transportation options to get to that stadium. These decisions are cold, dollars-and-cents calculations, with an artificial green façade. Veggie meals are much less profitable than meat options, and parking income is a huge profit-maker for the venues. For some leagues, like the NFL, parking lots also have dual value as both moneymaker and sponsor-pleaser, as parking lots are sold to partners as great sites for advertisement during tailgating hours. Here we have a greenwashing double whammy. While touting their own green initiatives, sport organizations encourage and structurally coerce (by not providing other viable options) people to drive to games and pay for parking, *and* make money on these fan eyeballs by slapping sponsorships for high-emitting companies like Coca-Cola, Budweiser, and Exxon Mobil around their parking lots.

Greenwashing, in its many forms, is a version of performative capitalism that is well propped up by the PR teams of sport organizations and high-emitting companies. So how do these greenwashing efforts remain successful? Beyond PR teams hell-bent on ensuring that their "We're green!" message gets out, greenwashing is possible because there are few laws or agencies that actually govern what can be called green or sustainable. Organizations like the Forest Stewardship Council and Green Sports Alliance do their best to give seals of approval or produce report cards about the emissions and green initiative of different sport organizations, leagues, and governing bodies, and journalists and scholars work hard to call out greenwashing when they see it,[103] but there isn't much to stop companies from claiming that they're "green" or "sustainable."[104] A 2022 New Climate Institute and Carbon Watch report[105] found that of the 25 net-zero pledges by large companies (think Amazon, Google, Nestle, Walmart) in 2021, only one was deemed as having "reasonable integrity," and "nearly all claims relied on loopholes or tricks to exaggerate the ambition of their claims and climate targets."[106] Orr echoes this claim, saying that "in the absence of governance and standards, anybody can call anything green."

This makes greenwashing an especially powerful tool of blame-avoidance for sport stakeholders, as it blunts consumers' best weapon against performative social justice capitalism. By making it difficult for consumers to know whether organizations and leagues are making real changes to improve their carbon footprint or just dressing up their environmental destruction in a pretty green bow, fans don't even know where to withhold their consumer dollars. This can result in situations where fans either take organizations' greenwashing claims at face value and support them, or believe that all organizations are lying about it, so it doesn't matter which they support. Either way, ownership, stakeholders, and the PR teams in high-emitting, fossil fuel sponsoring, greenwashing organizations are celebrating, and that's not good for us or the planet.

CHAPTER EIGHT

The Way Forward
Reimagining Sport Now and for the Future

So, in the words of Lenin: What is to be done?

For Marxists, the obvious answer is a simple one: we need a revolutionary, socialist change to the way we organize society (including sports), to a society based not around profit and capital accumulation but instead on fulfilling the material and social needs of all. This change to society's mode of production—from capitalism to socialism, with the input of working people, for working people—would have monumental impacts on the rest of the superstructure, including sport.

Revolutionary social change would mean a transformation of sport to an institution that puts universal participation and the safety and well-being of athletes and the wider community at the forefront. Under a social system divorced from win-at-all-costs profit imperatives, sport systems would actually be able to stress health and physical activity, fun, entertainment, and values of teamwork and resilience, without coming at the expense of athlete well-being and the safety of wider society. In my view, this kind of fundamental change to the way we organize society *must* be the end goal. As Nathan Kalman-Lamb explains: "I don't know that there is any idealized form of capitalist sport possible. I think that capitalist sport, fundamentally, instrumentalizes, extracts and exploits. The entire purpose of it is competition, which is the fundamental core capitalist principle. And so it's all about dominating, getting the most that you can out of the body, and winning. It's all commodified in that sense. And so as a model for anything, I think that that's profoundly inhumane, dehumanizing and harmful." While moving away from racial capitalism is the ultimate goal, I don't think our potential solutions can or should end here. Though revolutionary change is necessary, as of right now it's not the only thing we can and should strive for.

There are two competing though not necessarily contradictory dilemmas that face anyone seeking to transform any harmful institution, structure, culture, or behavior: While we may need revolutionary transformation soon, we also need harm reduction *right now*.

This final chapter is devoted to both of these vital needs. I will attempt to sketch out, in broad terms, the policy, regulatory, and institutional changes that are necessary today. Though these changes would undoubtedly receive pushback due to profit-making imperatives within our current sport systems, they could still be implemented *within* the existing capitalist sport structure. But I will also pursue a loftier goal: reimagining what sport could be in its most idealized form.

To reimagine sports holistically, I've called in reinforcements. Over the last year, I've contacted many of the critical sport scholars that I know (and many that I don't) to get their input. While much has been written about the various changes and improvements that can be made to curb incidents of harm within capitalist sport—many contemporary academic journals ask for a section on policy recommendations or "what to do" sections for articles discussing a particular social problem—comparatively less has been written about the ideal way to organize sport, especially outside the confines of capitalism. Beyond this lack of written and recorded scholarly work, I'm also not arrogant or confident enough to assume that I have all the answers, and in a book that pushes for socialism and collective action, I think it's important to practice what I preach. We must reimagine sport collectively.

It might seem strange, but this section on how to improve sport—both within its current capitalist structure and ideally free of these shackles—won't be very complicated. This does not mean that actually implementing any of these changes within the many professional, international, national, and youth sport organizations will be easy; only that the broad solutions proposed here are not new, and they are not complex. In many ways, I think most people already know them. As sport scholar Courtney Szto explained,[1] "An 'ideal' sports system would simply be the one that actually implements the ideas that we have been sold."

When discussing harm reduction in sport, and really in almost any business or institution, there are a few words that often come up: regulation, accountability, oversight, independent review, culture change. Sport is not all that different.

Regulation and Accountability

To ensure that harmful practices aren't allowed to proliferate and harmful people cannot continue to work and control sport organizations and governing bodies, it is imperative that organizations are regulated externally, by some sort of independent, overarching body. This body must be charged with independent oversight over the actions and decisions of the sport organization. It can't have overlapping interests with the organization or people it's regulating, and more than that, it can't even financially benefit from the financial success of the organization or people. This independent regulatory body must also have coercive power over the sport organizations in its purview. These organizations and the people working within them have to be accountable, and this is much easier said than done.

For obvious reasons, it is hard to create and run regulatory bodies that are *this* independent, with this much jurisdiction and power, and that have this level of buy-in from organizations. Under capitalism, it is the organizations that bring in the revenue that enable sport leagues or larger professional sport systems to continue to function, profit, and employ people. Regulatory bodies are then often left toothless (sometimes purposely, sometimes not), only able to make *recommendations* and without the ability to demand action or inaction from the organizations they ostensibly regulate.

Beyond just the difficulty of creating, implementing, and funding such independent regulatory bodies, it is also vital that these bodies do not have *too much* power, and that they can't wield this power unfairly or disproportionately. It is also important that athletes themselves are represented on these bodies, to ensure their voices and experiences are well-accounted for.

None of these ideas are new or innovative, but they are also not easy. To illustrate what's needed and why these ideas are difficult to implement, let's take two examples where regulatory bodies would be needed to curb harmful behavior: physical and emotional violence against athletes (chapters 3 and 4), and violence against women by athletes (chapter 5).

Independent Regulation and Accountability

For all types of physical, emotional, and sexual violence suffered by athletes in the course of their athletic labor, overarching regulation and firm guardrails are a necessary first step for reducing harm. Organizations do whatever it takes to win, and athletes themselves have often internalized this explicit and implicit messaging such that they too will sacrifice almost anything for athletic success. Trusting organizations and athletes to self-regulate has not worked up to this point, and given the primacy of wins and profit over athlete well-being under capitalism, we shouldn't expect it to. Independent bodies must be put in place to review organizational decisions, and at times, to save athletes from their own (highly socially structured) choices.

There has to be a decision-making body that can change policies for hiring and firing coaches and athletic trainers, so that organizations cannot keep the Larry Nassers and Jerry Sanduskys of the world employed. These bodies *must* include current and former athletes, of all levels. Worker control and worker democracy are necessary to ensure accountability among power brokers in sports (and in any industry), and to ensure that the needs and experiences of athletes (workers) are voiced and properly understood. There must also be independently run background checks for all staff, and confidential interviews and frequent check-ins with athletes. Doctors must be able to rule players ineligible and unable to practice or play, regardless of what coaches or athletes think or want.

It is also *vital* that sport doctors are hired and work independently, so that they are not beholden to particular teams or organizations. While individual doctors and the organizations employing them will surely say that they already act independently and in the best interests of athletes, countless athletes have described situations where this has been shown to be untrue (or at the very least questionable), and many elite athletes have begun hiring and even traveling with their own doctors and medical teams. As long as doctors are hired and paid for by sport organizations, their continued employment hinges on that organization's evaluation of their work. This means doctors can be incentivized to push athletes to play through injury (including to the brain), to recommend treatments that help athletes right now but hurt them in the long term, or to prescribe potentially harmful pain medication that can lead to addiction and disease.

Athlete-employed doctors are a step up from those employed by teams, assuming these doctors center athlete short- and long-term health and aren't easily convinced to let players play through potentially debilitating injury and pain. Athlete-employed doctors are not a sustainable and scalable solution, though, as the vast majority of athletes at the youth and even elite levels cannot afford to hire their own medical staff. Athletes must either hire their own doctors collectively through their unions, or leagues should be mandated to provide truly independent medical care. Either way, the sport organizations cannot be the ones who directly pay doctors' salaries, and any way you slice it, building in this kind of independent medical oversight will cost leagues or athletes money that they would likely not want to spend.

In terms of athletes perpetrating violence, we know that sport organizations' and leagues' excusal of talented players' violent behavior impacts the continued violence against women perpetrated by elite athletes (chapter 5). But it is nevertheless difficult to enact league or team policies and practices that balance the need to provide proportionate justice to survivors and deterrence for future athlete perpetrators while also ensuring that athletes are also treated fairly (even when they are accused of violence). While this may understandably strike some people the wrong way—given the way many elite male athletes have escaped repercussions in the past, even in the face of overwhelming evidence—handing complete disciplinary power over to ownership and management is not a solution. We must be cautious about how much power is granted to professional leagues and their organizations to punish players without any sort of legal or investigatory process, especially because some of the same unequal power relations that exist between athletes and alleged victims also exist between ownership and athletes.[2]

Even if there were an independent review body to assess cases of alleged athlete VAW, under capitalism there would still be the tension between ensuring accountability for players' bad behavior while also ensuring that these players are treated fairly as workers. It would also be especially salient in cases of VAW by NBA and NFL players, as well as other sports with large contingents of Black athletes. In a criminal legal system and in societies that remain structurally racist, patriarchal, and unequal, these situations often involve both a group of alleged perpetrators who historically have been mistreated and overly criminalized (Black men) and a group of victims who historically have been ignored and underserved (women victims of men's violence).

Understanding this tension is an important first step. VAW remains an issue in men's elite and professional sport; many of the athletes in these sports are Black men; and Black men are often the targets of unfair and biased treatment at all levels of the criminal justice system. All of these things can be true at the same time, and this combination of truths means that incidents of violence need to be handled deftly. No matter how independent or powerful the regulatory body, this would be a difficult job. If players could be punished for merely being apprehended or questioned by law enforcement, this could unjustly hurt Black athletes, who are more frequently stopped by police. However, requiring that players can't be sanctioned unless they've been *legally convicted* would leave many victims without justice, and would not deter future players from committing similar behavior.

One of the core issues right now is that organizational success is not determined by how much teams genuinely care about any social issue or even about their own employees. The structures of capitalist sport are such that it is purely happenstance if some owners or managements do genuinely care about underserved groups. If anything, the astronomical costs of buying and owning a sports team today makes it less likely that those who do own teams will espouse values that push toward equity for minoritized and underserved groups, given the fact that extreme wealth is nearly always predicated on extreme levels of exploitation somewhere along the profit line. For more evidence, look no further than to the large donations made to the Republican Party and other politically conservative groups by owners in the NBA, which is often heralded as the "progressive" member[3] of men's professional sports leagues in North America.

While again, an independent body to review cases of alleged VAW by athletes would be helpful, there may not be a clear-cut regulatory or policy solution to this issue within elite capitalist sport, especially given that this elite capitalist sport exists within a fundamentally stratified, unjust society. Only in a sport system based around the public good, rather than around profit for individual owners and other sport stakeholders, will we see real accountability for the most talented athletes who commit harm.

Workers' Control: Unionization, Strikes, and Boycotts

Capitalist relations of production and profit imperatives generally act as a hindrance to making positive social change, but the clear primacy of business considerations for sport organizations does point to the power that fans and athletes have in shaping responses to all manner of violence. In terms of explicitly professional sports, organizations' goals of winning and making money are unlikely to change considerably as long as capitalism remains unchallenged. These moneymaking goals will also continue to hinge on consumer interest. The consumer product of sport leagues and teams is based on the value-added provided by the labor of athletes; as I've said before, fans come to the pitch to watch Erling Haaland score goals or Steph Curry knock down threes, not to see Sheikh Mansour or Joe Lacob sitting in the owner's box. Athletes withholding their labor or fans withholding their dollars if teams employ abusive players or coaches, or if ownership groups are engaging in exploitative, destructive, or dangerous business practices, may be the best way to hit ownership and management where it hurts them the most—in their pockets.

On the athlete side, unionization is what makes this kind of collective action possible. Unionization and collective action by labor has historically been the only way for workers to substantially improve their working conditions, and the history of professional sports is no different. The material gains made by minor league baseball players are the clearest recent example of this, as unionization changed the fortunes of thousands of players overnight, bringing the kinds of drastic improvements that could only be accomplished through collective action and collective pressure. However, the work of athlete labor organizing is far from over. As sport scholar Derek Silva explains: "Athletic workers must be given *all* of the protections that exist in other labor environments, including the right to unionize and occupational health and safety protections. This must be a top-to-bottom reformation and *must* include not only professional athletes, but also amateur athletes and youth athletes." Higher-level professional athletes learned the value of unionization a long time ago, as the creation of players associations in North American professional sports leagues throughout the twentieth century helped earn athletes a larger share of revenue. While their current share is still not enough, and worker exploitation can only be truly eradicated with worker control of all enterprises, labor-related gains can only be made when athletes bargain, work, and threaten to withhold their labor *collectively*.

Links between organized labor and sports have existed since the earliest forms of organized sports; many of the first de facto professional sports teams were founded by working men's clubs,[4] reflecting the increased and newfound power of organized labor. From 1921 to 1937, the Socialist Workers Sports International even organized and hosted International Workers' Olympiads, with athletes coming from labor unions, mostly in Europe. During this time, workers formed their own athletic associations, often within their local socialist party apparatuses. Competitions were scheduled between these associations throughout Europe and covered by local working-class and socialist newspapers.[5] In 1931 the Workers' Olympiad in Vienna saw 100,000 athletes participate, with over 250,000 in-person spectators. Eschewing the nationalism of the traditional Olympics, athletes participated under the same red flag, representing the international working class to which they all belonged.[6] Unfortunately, following World War II, capitalists and ruling elites succeeded in even further wrestling material control of sports away from athletic workers and local communities. Ruling-class control over sports and other media, as well as over the historical record, have also largely erased movements like the Workers' Olympiad from our collective memory.

In the last few years, however, we have seen some athletes recognize the structural power they hold and use it for good, even without the backing of any specific labor organizations. This kind of athlete power exists in both professional and unexplicitly "professional" sports, as even national and international sport organizations exist under capitalist frameworks and are responsive to consumer critique and demand.

Before the 2021 Summer Olympics, six members of the US Olympic fencing team expressed concerns about team member Alen Hadzic, who was under investigation following allegations of sexual assault from at least six different women to the US Center for Safe Sport. Safe Sport initially ruled Hadzic ineligible for the Games, but this was overturned after Hadzic appealed. The US Olympic Team decided to bring Hadzic to Tokyo but didn't allow him to sleep in the Olympic Village or train in the same room as any of his women teammates. After these teammates made their concerns known to their team administration and to the public, the US women fencers wore pink facemasks before competition, in solidarity with victims of domestic and sexual violence. Even though they were not able to get Hadzic banned from the Tokyo Games, investigations were restarted following the games and that October he was banned from future competitions.[7] Hadzic was held accountable only because of the constant advocacy and pressure from the women on the US fencing team, not because the organizations and leagues in question unilaterally decided to "do the right thing."

Though not related to violence or harm *within* the sport sphere, the Milwaukee Bucks refused to participate in a playoff game during America's 2020 summer of protest for racial justice, following the police killing of Jacob Blake in Wisconsin. The next day the entire slate of NBA playoff games was postponed, and the Milwaukee Brewers baseball team also refused to play.[8] The Bucks released a statement calling for the "Wisconsin State Legislature to reconvene after months of inaction and take up meaningful measures to address issues of police accountability, brutality and criminal justice reform." Though this was not a matter of standing up against their own organization or league, the team demonstrated the platform athletes have to impact what happens in their leagues, reminiscent of the work of Black athletes like Muhammad Ali and Kareem Abdul Jabbar during the American civil rights movements of the 1960s and 1970s.

In terms of athletes accused of violence, organizations' decision-making about player acquisitions is also—whether management likes it or will admit to it—responsive to fan and media reactions. As one of NBA journalists I interviewed explained: "If a team wants a guy . . . and somebody says, 'look, we're gonna [sic] get destroyed by the media, fans are going to hate us for this signing,' that could [have an] impact. They could say 'you know what, it's not worth it. It's not worth the backlash.' Their whole business is based on fans consuming the product."

For fans, their withholding of support for teams engaging in harmful behavior or inaction may be their best lever for reducing violence and harm in sport. While we might like to think that organizations should "do the right thing" as a matter of principle, it may be up to everyday people to force their hand.

This is a big ask though, especially for people who use sports as a means of escape and to "turn their brains off" for a few hours, or for those who derive vital meaning and community from sports. As discussed in chapters 2 and 7, alienation under capitalism has created a sort of "sports dependency" for many. Asking athletes and fans to be aware of the many harms produced by sports organizations and then act collectively to strike (for athletes) and boycott (for fans) may be an unfair request. The real answer to this issue—and the way to stop organizations from producing harm in their pursuit of profit—is much more widespread structural and cultural change.

Cultural and Structural Change

When my partner and I moved to London in 2021, one of the first things I did was find adult recreational leagues to play basketball and tennis. I was pretty quickly able to join a local tennis league that matched players from similar areas with (hopefully) similar skill levels, and through this league I met someone who played in a few weekly basketball pickup runs. He invited me to one, and from that first Saturday on, I played in that league (and another one that I was invited to through the same network) every week I could, until my partner and I returned to Canada two years later.

For our two years in London, I can't overstate how important these pickup runs were. They were a source of community, friendship, physical activity, and joy. They were something I looked forward to every week, especially in stressful times, when my mental health was teetering or I was feeling lonely. In the spring and summer, I also played pickup basketball at Finsbury Park in North London once or twice a week. After moving to a city where I knew almost no one, pickup basketball—both in my organized leagues and at the park—gave me community, stress relief, and fun.

For each of my weekly, more organized leagues, gym fees were split evenly among all players. Ages ranged from about twenty-five to sixty, and players' countries of origin included France, Belgium, Spain, Italy, Serbia, Croatia, Cyprus, Greece, Turkey, Switzerland, Hong Kong, Canada, the United States, Chile, Brazil, and yes, even the UK.

There are no refs, and players call their own fouls. While sometimes people voice their displeasure with a particular call, it's generally understood that if someone calls a foul, you respect the call. Teams are divided up equally to ensure competitive games, and games were to 13 or 15. Everyone who shows up gets to play, though players' individual time on the court can vary, depending on how successful your team is.

Everyone plays hard—we battle for rebounds and loose balls, get in a defensive stance (or as much of a stance as our old knees can get to), and try to pass, move, cut, and make the right play. There are few things that bring me as much joy as making a nice pass to a cutting teammate for a layup or open shot, and then both of us giving the customary index finger point to each other, universal basketball language for "nice pass" or "nice play."

We all want to win, but we don't *need* to. If a player takes a hard fall or gets leveled by a screen, it's generally understood that we stop the game and make sure they're okay. We still get annoyed at opponents and complain about a bad shot or a missed box-out by a teammate, but it never lasts long. Everyone wants to win and plays seriously between the lines, and then we go for beers afterward. If players are getting too angry or not respecting these unwritten rules, someone will talk to them, and in the most extreme case, they won't be invited back.

I don't bring this up just to wax poetic about pickup basketball, as much as I'd enjoy that.[9] I bring it up because as I continued to play over the last year, and as I began sketching out, making notes, and ultimately writing this book at the same time, I realized that in many ways adult recreational sports are a model for what sports should be.

Of course, pickup basketball and other recreational sports are not always perfect. There are still barriers to entry, especially in a city like London with high gym fees. This can limit participation. Groups that play together are often organized along class-based lines, with many working in similar fields or living in similar areas.

Living under capitalism, competition and dominance are still hardwired into many, such that even in pickup games with absolutely no stakes, some people get angry and lash out. Internalizing sport and masculine values around toughness and playing through injuries, emulating our professional athlete heroes, and perhaps wanting to prove that we're not washed up quite yet, many of us also play through injury and pain, even when we know we shouldn't. I know I do.

But even under capitalism, and even with the harmful value system that it has embedded in us, adult recreational sports provide all the benefits that coaches, sport leaders, and athletes like to talk about, without much of the harm. Joy, teamwork, physical health, community, accountability—it's all there, and it doesn't require state-of-the-art facilities or TV deals. As sport scholar Macintosh Ross explains, "We don't need all this glitz and glamour, we don't need all the money behind it. It doesn't have to be a massive vehicle for capitalism."

There is no reason youth sports can't look like this. Youth sports should be based around participation, socialization, and fun. Grassroots sport must be accessible and inclusive, with athlete enjoyment and well-being the barometers for success. Winning cannot be the only goal. We still need the accountability and regulation described above, but this top-down policy implementation must be met with bottom-up, holistic cultural change. Elite sport will of course look different in some ways, but if we hope to remove so much of the violence and harm from elite sport, it too needs this kind of cultural shift.

This kind of cultural shift in sport can also spill over and filter down to all levels of society, given sport's cultural importance and the ability it has already shown to impact behavior and public discourse. As Canadian sport scholar Cheryl MacDonald explains, "A holistic approach to sport ... [will lead to] an increase in compassion and empathy, which will result in the reduction of harm both in the sporting context and in society more broadly."

Sport must be reimagined as a space for joy, creativity, and play, rather than as a vehicle for pure performance and profit. Burstyn Varda, a writer and activist, wrote this about her hopes back in 1999: "I hope that we can find ways to treat our bodies, our children, and our biosphere with respect and affirmation for our diverse and sensuous natures, and for the cooperative capacities that make us capable of helping, not just dominating, our fellow creatures."[10]

Sport scholar Derek Silva makes a similar point: "The only possible horizon I see to create an 'ideal' sport system is the eradication of a global racial capitalist order that creates the conditions of contemporary sport and thus privileges and necessitates both harm and violence. [We need] the return to 'play' and 'games,' the devaluing of athletic competition as the sole marker of elite sport and the emphasis on the playful, the artistic, the skill, etc. Importantly, this cannot happen in a vacuum—for as long as the capitalist project structures the political economy of global geopolitics, so too will it condition contemporary sport."

Brazilian scholar Eduardo Galeano is famous for his writing on the aesthetic beauty and passion of soccer played by the masses in Brazil, the connections between soccer and social life more broadly, and the loss of this beauty in a cold, commodified, corporatized sports world. When sport is transformed as a vehicle for corporate profit-making, when every dollar is squeezed out of it, every interaction commodified, and even the youngest players measured, recorded, quantified as potential future revenue producers, it not only opens the door to all sorts of harm, but it also removes the very essence of what makes sports enjoyable. Galeano writes in *Soccer in Sun and Shadow*, "To win without magic, without surprise or beauty, isn't that worse than losing?" Fellow Brazilian soccer star Socrates echoes this idea: "Never has the world been so unequal in the opportunities it offers and so equalizing in the habits it imposes: in this end of the century world, whoever doesn't die of hunger dies of boredom.... Soccer is now mass-produced, and it comes out colder than a freezer and as merciless as a meat-grinder. It's a soccer for robots."[11] While ownership and management might love professional sports played by robots, turning athletes into machines who never get injured, do not need to be paid, and who are never at risk of striking, this has no benefit for the rest of us. Sports are not meant as a vehicle for profit or a toy for elites, but as a creative, aesthetic cultural form to be enjoyed by all.

Mass Participation for All

This kind of cultural shift from competition and elite-level dominance to sport for passion, joy, and collective well-being will only truly be accomplished when everyone can benefit from its positive impacts. This means that instead of public funding being used for elite sport, this funding should be used on ensuring participation opportunities for all. Ironically, true mass participation—where every person regardless of their class or socioeconomic status has the opportunity to participate and (if they want to) excel in sports—would also likely result in either similar or improved results in terms of medal- and championship-defined performance, as was seen throughout the Soviet Union and Yugoslavia in the twentieth century. While these nations also engaged in realpolitik through sport—using the dominance of their athletes as a source of national pride and as proof of their ideological superiority (which could also prompt some of the issues of abuse and overtraining discussed throughout this book)—participation in sport (and the arts and sciences) were made available to all youth,[12] and it is clear that this had a strong effect on the quality of sport, arts, and science in socialist-run nations.[13] Some even link Yugoslavian sport-for-all ethos and principles of mass participation to modern Balkan sport success.[14]

Only by guaranteeing mass participation—by making sport freely available and creating the broader social conditions that give people the time and energy to use these sport opportunities—will we truly eradicate inequitable opportunities and outcomes in sports. This includes not just class-based-inequities, but those by race, ability status, and any other identity characteristics. Inclusive sport cultures undoubtedly also require better education for participants and coaches, more accountability for decision makers and management, and more voice for athletes. Unless these barriers to sport participation are removed, sport cultures will continue to exclude minoritized and marginalized groups. Beyond explicit exclusion, if sports remain predominantly spaces for particular class, sex, or racial groups, and don't have the participation and active involvement (including in decision making) of other groups, even members of those groups who do manage to push through participation barriers will not accrue all the benefits that come from inclusive and meaningful sport. It is not enough for each sport to have a few "token" members of minoritized groups.

Participatory, public-funded sport also must not just include children and teenagers, but people of all ages. Research has shown us the benefits of adult and even older-adult sport, and this needs to be fostered.[15] There is no age limit on health and well-being, and if anything, older adults need the positive physical and mental health benefits of sports even more than younger people do.

The Way Forward

This kind of holistic cultural change may seem like a pipe dream, the naïve utopian fantasies of someone divorced from the "real world." I understand the skepticism, because these changes are not really possible under capitalism, and many still believe there is no alternative to this economic system. Admittedly, capitalist media and mythmaking have done a great job of shaping this discourse, to the point that, as Frederic Jameson infamously said, "it's easier to imagine the end of the world than the end of capitalism."[16] While it may be easier to pretend this is the case than it is to imagine better alternatives, I'll respond to this with another saying: "It always seems impossible until it's done."[17]

The fundamental cultural changes I suggest above are only truly possible with fundamental structural change, and with the transition from capitalism to socialism. So, if we want to improve sports (just like if we want to survive the climate crisis or end exploitative labor practices), this is what needs to be done. While some might think that this is an exaggeration, and that the drastic improvements to sport that we need can be made without this sort of wholesale change to our economic systems, I urge you to consider any of the problems identified in this book, as well the potential solutions.

Consider something like mass sport participation, a great way to try to improve issues of equity in sports involvement. Mass participation is reliant on other social conditions being equitable, including people having the necessary time and energy to participate. If participation in sports is made free at the point of access, but capitalist relations of production and the subsequent inequality it produces remains intact, then many will still be functionally excluded from participation, even if there are no clear barriers to sport access itself. If people are too busy laboring to survive, they won't have any time for sports. Similarly, regulation of professional sports would undoubtedly help with athlete injury issues, abusive coaching practices, and off-field violence, but if organizations and teams are fundamentally moneymaking enterprises whose survival depend on profits, then, as we've seen, they will put these profits ahead of human well-being time and time again.

If we want to ensure that countries and corporations don't use sport events as a way to line their pockets and continue polluting the planet, the incentives need to change drastically. It is not enough to slap some penalties onto organizing committees who over-pollute or miss their budget target. Global goals must be reoriented, to a world where states and organizations are run by the workers who make up these populations, working together for collective good. The ownership models of professional sports, especially in North America, are not built for this, and these models are a direct reflection of the capitalist system that underlies them.

As long as our collective North Star remains profit, expansion, and beating the competition, organizations and the people who run them will continue (some by choice, some by structural coercion) to sacrifice the collective well-being of both people and planet to the alter of capital.

It's well past time for us to serve a new master, or really, no master at all. Athletes are so often told to "play for each other," for their teammates, for the team. As long as that team is controlled by the athletes actually doing the work, and decisions are made to promote human flourishing and well-being, I say we heed that advice. Let's reclaim sport, and bring it back to a space for joy, creative expression, and community. We may just fix the rest of the world on the way.

Acknowledgments

In a book that centers collective struggle and the need for a better, kinder socialist future, I would be remiss if I did not acknowledge and thank the many, many people who made this book possible. Nobody does anything in this world alone, and I am sure as heck no exception.

First off, thank you to the people at The University of North Carolina Press and to my editor Lucas Church, who supported me throughout this process and let me take this book where I think it needed to go. Thanks for taking a chance on a first-time author and for giving me room to grow.

To my many academic colleagues and friends, thank you for letting me build atop the incredible work you've done, and for your guidance and support throughout my young academic journey and specifically in the research and writing of this book. Your conversations, read-throughs, and edits have been so instrumental: Eran Shor, Peter McMahan, Derek Silva, Nathan Kalman-Lamb, Cheryl McDonald, Victoria Silverwood, Deana Simonetto, Paul Bleakley, Miltonette Craig, Rima Saini, Shireen Ahmed. To other friends and family who read through chapters, I so appreciate your support (and labor): Pascal, Evan, Ryan, Kevin, Josh, mom and dad, and Cole.

Thank you so much to my parents for your unconditional love and care, and for always supporting my academic and other pursuits. Thanks for pushing me to be curious and to pursue what makes me happy and fulfilled, no matter where that path leads.

Sybil and Brandon, and to Jen, Hannah, Nathaniel, Leona, Danielle, Benji, Elana, Lucas, Noel, Jesse, Brian, and Jonas, thank you for being there to provide a kind word, a sarcastic joke, a Shabbat/holiday dinner, and a meaningful conversation whenever Maddy and I need it most. Delaney and Pascal, thank you for being the coolest and most supportive family I could have hoped to marry into, for always being there with a bed or a couch to sleep on, and for the many meals and laughs we share. Karine, Jordan, and the girls, thank you for being the most wonderful new family I could ever ask for, and for demonstrating every day what it means to live and be in community with those you care about, while working to make the world a better place for all. Patricia and Jan, thank you for being the best in-laws I could have ever hoped for—for the incredible dinners, and for the love and guidance through all of life's celebrations and its challenges.

And lastly and most importantly, thank you to Maddy. Everything that I've done in the last seven years of my life, I owe to you. You are the best partner, friend, coeditor, and now mother to our daughter that I could have ever hoped for. You believe in me when even I don't, and are there to help and support me in whatever way that I need, whenever I need it. I love you.

Notes

Introduction

1. Even when the stadium is named after an investment banking firm. No, Raymond James is not a famous football star or war hero.
2. Big jump here from a stadium named after an investment bank to an insurance company!
3. Derek Silva and Liam Kennedy, "Introduction: Toward a Critical Criminology of Sport," in *Power Played: A Critical Criminology of Sport*, ed. Derek Silva and Liam Kennedy (UBC Press, 2022).
4. Dan Neil, "The fierce war over Pat Tillman," *Los Angeles Times*, September 11, 2009, https://www.latimes.com/archives/la-xpm-2009-sep-11-et-book11-story.html.
5. Dave Zirin, "Why People Don't Even Trust the Super Bowl," *The Nation*, February 13, 2023, www.thenation.com/article/society/super-bowl-rigged-trust/.
6. Alan Blinder, "What the N.F.L. Says, and What It Doesn't, about Injuries," *New York Times*, January 3, 2023, sec. Sports, www.nytimes.com/2023/01/03/sports/football/nfl-injuries-statistics.html.
7. Brian Bushard, "Tennessee Titans Break NFL Record with $1.26 Billion in Public Money for New Stadium," *Forbes*, April 26, 2023, www.forbes.com/sites/brianbushard/2023/04/26/tennessee-titans-break-nfl-record-with-126-billion-in-public-money-for-new-stadium/.
8. "Violence Prevention Alliance Approach," World Health Organization, accessed May 4, 2023, www.who.int/groups/violence-prevention-alliance/approach.
9. "Violence Prevention Alliance Approach," World Health Organization.
10. Maive Jackson Collett, "Deviant Leisure Explores a Radical Criminological Framework to Examine Neo-Liberal Capitalism: Can Deviant Leisure Be Revisioned by Feminism to Include the Emerging 'Other'?," *International Journal of Social Sciences and Educational Studies* 7, no. 3 (2020); Thomas Raymen and Oliver Smith, "Deviant Leisure: A Critical Criminological Perspective for the Twenty-First Century," *Critical Criminology* 27, no. 1 (March 1, 2019): 115–30, https://doi.org/10.1007/s10612-019-09435-x; Paddy Hillyard and Steve Tombs, "Social Harm and Zemiology," in *The Oxford Handbook of Criminology* (Oxford University Press, 2017), 284–305.
11. Collett, "Deviant Leisure," 104.
12. Raymond J. Michalowski, "What Is Crime?," *Critical Criminology* 24, no. 2 (June 1, 2016): 188, https://doi.org/10.1007/s10612-015-9303-6.
13. J. Hargreaves, "Sport, Power and Culture: A Social and Historical Analysis of Popular Sports in Britain," in *Sport, Power and Culture: A Social and Historical Analysis of Popular Sports in Britain* (St. Martin's Press, 1986).
14. Joshua I. Newman, "Sport without Management," *Journal of Sport Management* 28, no. 6 (2014): 605.

15. Zak Cope, *The Wealth of (Some) Nations: Imperialism and the Mechanics of Value Transfer* (Pluto Press London, 2019), www.bib.irb.hr:8443/1072501/download/1072501 .Rubini_-_The_Wealth_of_Some_Nations_Book_Review.pdf.

16. Chen Chen, "Naming the Ghost of Capitalism in Sport Management," *European Sport Management Quarterly* 22, no. 5 (2022): 676, www.tandfonline.com/doi/full/10.1080 /16184742.2022.2046123.

17. Silva and Kennedy, "Introduction," 31–32.

18. Marx, K. (1845/1975). Theses on Feuerbach. Marx and Engels: Collected Works. New York: International.

Chapter One

1. Karl Marx, *Das Kapital: A Critique of Political Economy*, ed. Friedrich Engels (Regnery, 1959), 2.

2. Larry Ceplair, "The Base and Superstructure Debate in the Hollywood Communist Party," *Science & Society* 72, no. 3 (2008): 319–48.

3. This valuation is an approximation of how much the team would be sold for, given its recent revenues, assets, liabilities, and other factors. This valuation is often based on recent team sales, which have increased in price significantly.

4. "Golden State Warriors Revenue 2021," Statista, 2022, www.statista.com/statistics /196716/revenue-of-the-golden-state-warriors-since-2006/.

5. "Epistemology" is a fancy word for theory of knowledge, or how we come to know what we know.

6. Karl Marx, "Preface to a Contribution to the Critique of Political Economy," in *The Marx-Engels Reader*, vol. 2 (1859): 3–6.

7. Vladimir Lenin, "On the Question of Dialectics" (1925), in *Collected Works*, 4th ed. (Progress Publishers, 1976), 38:357–61, www.marxists.org/archive/lenin/works/1915/misc /x02.htm.

8. Mao Zedong, *On Practice: On the Relation between Knowledge and Practice—between Knowing and Doing* (Peking: n.p., 1951).

9. Mao Zedong, *On Practice*.

10. Marx, *Das Kapital*.

11. Mao, *On Practice*, 1.

12. Engels, Friedrich. Engels to Borgius, London, January 25, 1894. In *New International*, no. 3 (1934).

13. Though those who have not tried to understand or read any Marxist literature always accuse Marxists of being exactly this.

14. Engels, Friedrich. Engels to Paul Ernst, June 5, 1890. In *Marx and Engels Correspondence, 1890*, edited by Angel Flores (Critics Group: New York, 1937).

15. Stephen A. Resnick and Richard D. Wolff, "Marxist Epistemology: The Critique of Economic Determinism," *Social Text*, no. 6 (1982): 39.

16. Resnick and Wolff, "Marxist Epistemology," 40.

17. Karl Marx, *Theses on Feuerbach*, 1845.

18. Resnick and Wolff, "Marxist Epistemology," 40–41.

19. Derek Silva and Liam Kennedy, *Power Played: A Critical Criminology of Sport* (UBC Press, 2022), 16.

20. I once heard (I think it was on a podcast, apologies to whoever said it) that all MBAs and all Marxists know pretty much the same things, it's just that one group thinks they're good, and the other wants to change them.

21. Resnick and Wolff, "Marxist Epistemology."

22. Often in the field of sport management, though in sport sociology as well.

23. Chen, "Naming the Ghost," 673.

24. "Democracies" is in quotation marks because capitalist democracies are in truth generally democracies of the powerful only, both in terms of who is eventually elected and whose interests they serve. They also provide for this "democracy" only every few years, when the general public get to decide between several usually handpicked candidates. Elected "representatives" are almost always from the upper strata of society, and those who are not still largely serve capital and big business interests. Include the lack of democracy in decision making in workplaces (especially in countries like Canada and the United States, which have embarrassingly low union rates), and lack of democracy in ownership of the means of production, and the democracies of liberal democratic capitalist states stop looking so democratic.

25. Chen, "Naming the Ghost."

26. Chen, "Naming the Ghost," 675.

27. Cope, *Wealth of (Some) Nations*.

28. Robert McAfee Brown, *Unexpected News: Reading the Bible with Third World Eyes* (Westminster John Knox Press, 1984).

29. Richard S. Gruneau, *Class, Sports and Social Development: A Study in Social Theory and Historical Sociology* (University of Massachusetts Press, 1983), xxiii.

30. Lenin, "On the Question of Dialectics."

31. Karl Marx, "A Contribution to the Critique of Hegel's Philosophy of Right: Introduction" in *Marx and Engels Collected Works*, vol. 3 (London, 1975), 175.

32. Marx, "A Contribution to the Critique."

33. Thorstein Veblen, "Chapter Four: Conspicuous Consumption," in *The Theory of the Leisure Class* (Macmillan,1899), 23–33.

34. Gruneau, "Class, Sports and Social Development."

35. Gruneau, "Class, Sports and Social Development."

36. Gruneau, "Class, Sports and Social Development," 91.

37. Gruneau, "Class, Sports and Social Development."

38. Jennifer A. Hargreaves, "Where's the Virtue? Where's the Grace? A Discussion of the Social Production of Gender Relations in and through Sport," *Theory, Culture & Society* 3, no. 1 (1986): 109–21; Gruneau, "Class, Sports and Social Development."

39. Norbert Elias and Eric Dunning, *Quest for Excitement: Sport and Leisure in the Civilizing Process* (Basil Blackwell, 1986).

40. Grace Gallacher, "The (De) Civilizing Process: An Ultra-Realist Examination of Sport," in Silva and Kennedy, *Power Played*, 106.

41. Edward R. Watkins and Henrietta Roberts, "Reflecting on Rumination: Consequences, Causes, Mechanisms and Treatment of Rumination," *Behaviour Research and Therapy* 127 (2020): 103573.

42. Malcolm MacLean, "Engaging (with) Indigeneity: Decolonization and Indigenous/Indigenizing Sport History," *Journal of Sport History* 46, no. 2 (2019): 189–207.

43. Gallacher, "The (De) Civilizing Process," 111.

44. B. Rigauer, *Sport and Work* (Columbia University Press, 1981), 67–68.

45. Rigauer, *Sport and Work*.

46. Nathan Kalman-Lamb, "Athletic Labor and Social Reproduction," *Journal of Sport and Social Issues* 43, no. 6 (2019): 515–30.

47. Barbara Laslett and Johanna Brenner, "Gender and Social Reproduction: Historical Perspectives," *Annual Review of Sociology* 15 (1989): 383.

48. Kalman-Lamb, "Athletic Labor and Social Reproduction."

49. K. Marx, *Economic and Philosophic Manuscripts of 1844*, ed. Dirk J. Struik, trans. Martin Milligan (International Publishers, 1964), 15.

50. Stephen J. McNamee and Robert K. Miller, *The Meritocracy Myth*, 2nd ed. (Rowman and Littlefield, 2009).

51. You might think this kind of reward system and manner of organizing society is sensible and right, though in that case I don't think we can be friends.

52. Michael Silk and David L. Andrews, *Sport and the Neoliberal Conjuncture: Complicating the Consensus* (Project Muse 4, 2012), 1–19.

53. Jo Littler, "Meritocracy as Plutocracy: The Marketising of 'Equality' under Neoliberalism," *New Formations* 80, no. 80 (2013): 62.

54. Thomas R. Bates, "Gramsci and the Theory of Hegemony," *Journal of the History of Ideas* 36, no. 2 (1975): 352, https://doi.org/10.2307/2708933.

55. Bates, "Gramsci and the Theory of Hegemony."

56. Gruneau, "Class, Sports and Social Development."

57. Hargreaves, "Where's the Virtue?"; Kalman-Lamb, "Athletic Labor and Social Reproduction."

58. Hargreaves, "Where's the Virtue?"; Eric Dunning, *Sport Matters: Sociological Studies of Sport, Violence, and Civilization* (Psychology Press, 1999).

59. Meredith Nash, "'Let's Work on Your Weaknesses': Australian CrossFit Coaching, Masculinity and Neoliberal Framings of 'Health' and 'Fitness,'" *Sport in Society* 21, no. 9 (September 2, 2018): 1432–53, https://doi.org/10.1080/17430437.2017.1390565.

60. R. W. Connell, *Masculinities* (University of California Press, 1995), 77.

61. Colleen English, "Toward Sport Reform: Hegemonic Masculinity and Reconceptualizing Competition," *Journal of the Philosophy of Sport* 44, no. 2 (May 4, 2017): 183–98, https://doi.org/10.1080/00948705.2017.1300538.

Chapter Two

1. "Frequently Asked Questions about CTE," BU Research CTE Center, accessed March 31, 2023, www.bu.edu/cte/about/frequently-asked-questions/.

2. Michael Dong, "Football's CTE Problem Is Real—Divulging the NFL's Dismissal of the Disease and Downplaying of . . . ," Medium (blog), November 5, 2019, https://medium.com/@michaeld830/footballs-cte-problem-is-real-divulging-the-nfl-s-dismissal-of-the-disease-and-downplaying-of-3287f8b21863; Rachel Grashow et al., "Healthspan and Chronic Disease Burden among Young Adult and Middle-Aged Male Former American-Style Profes-

sional Football Players," *British Journal of Sports Medicine* 57, no. 3 (2023): 166–71; Everett J. Lehman et al., "Neurodegenerative Causes of Death among Retired National Football League Players," *Neurology* 79, no. 19 (2012): 1970–74.

3. Boston University CTE Center, "Researchers Find CTE in 92% of Former NFL Players," *The Brink*, February 7, 2023, https://www.bu.edu/articles/2023/bu-finds-cte-in-nearly-92-percent-of-former-nfl-players-studied/.

4. There were diagnoses of football players suffering from cognitive issues, often called either *pugilista* or "punch-drunk" syndrome, in the late nineteenth century and early and mid-twentieth century. These conditions are considered by sport and health historians as early versions of what was later determined to be CTE.

5. And several thousand playing in other leagues around the world—thankfully, American football has not taken the rest of the world by storm quite yet, and hopefully never will.

6. Hana Walker-Brown, *A Delicate Game: Brain Injury, Sport and Sacrifice* (Hodder and Stoughton, 2022), 4.

7. Walker-Brown, *A Delicate Game*, 22.

8. Craig W. Lindsley, "Chronic Traumatic Encephalopathy (CTE): A Brief Historical Overview and Recent Focus on NFL Players," *ACS Chemical Neuroscience* 8, no. 8 (August 16, 2017): 1629, doi.org/10.1021/acschemneuro.7b00291.

9. Walker-Brown, *A Delicate Game*, 146.

10. G. Bellomo et al., "A Systematic Review on the Risk of Neurodegenerative Diseases and Neurocognitive Disorders in Professional and Varsity Athletes," *Neurological Sciences* 43, no. 12 (December 1, 2022): 6667, doi.org/10.1007/s10072-022-06319-x.

11. Grashow et al., "Healthspan and Chronic Disease."

12. Walker-Brown, *A Delicate Game*.

13. Victoria Silverwood, "Looking beyond the Athlete 'Offender': Re-contextualizing Violence and Harm in the NHL," in *Power Played: A Critical Criminology of Sport*, ed. Derek Silva and Liam Kennedy (UBC Press, 2022), 241.

14. Emma R. Russell et al., "Neurodegenerative Disease Risk among Former International Rugby Union Players," *Journal of Neurology, Neurosurgery & Psychiatry* 93 (2022): 1262–68, doi.org/10.1136/jnnp-2022-329675; Alice Theadom et al., "Incidence of Sports-Related Traumatic Brain Injury of All Severities: A Systematic Review," *Neuroepidemiology* 54, no. 2 (2020): 192–99.

15. Abigail C. Bretzin et al., "Association of Sex with Adolescent Soccer Concussion Incidence and Characteristics," *JAMA Network Open* 4, no. 4 (2021): e218191; Neil K. McGroarty, Symone M. Brown, and Mary K. Mulcahey, "Sport-Related Concussion in Female Athletes: A Systematic Review," *Orthopaedic Journal of Sports Medicine* 8, no. 7 (2020): 2325967120932306.

16. Walker-Brown, *A Delicate Game*.

17. Matthew Futterman, "Sledding Athletes Are Taking Their Lives: Did Brain-Rattling Rides and High-Speed Crashes Damage Their Brains?," *New York Times*, July 26, 2020, sec. Sports, www.nytimes.com/2020/07/26/sports/olympics/olympics-bobsled-suicide-brain-injuries.html.

18. B. DeArdo, "NFL Teams Earn $402.3 Million in National Revenue," CBS Sports, accessed September 18, 2024, https://www.cbssports.com/nfl/news/nfl-breaks-the-bank-heres-how-much-each-team-made-in-national-revenue-in-2023/.

19. Josh Sim, "UFC Guides Endeavor to US$1.26bn in Q4 Revenue," SportsPro (blog), March 1, 2023, www.sportspromedia.com/news/endeavor-ufc-wme-agency-q4-2022-finances-revenue-losses/.

20. "The Cooperative Human," *Nature Human Behaviour* 2, no. 7 (July 2018): 427–28, doi.org/10.1038/s41562-018-0389-1; Nichola Raihani, *The Social Instinct: How Cooperation Shaped the World* (St. Martin's Press, 2021).

21. Rebecca Solnit, *A Paradise Built in Hell: The Extraordinary Communities That Arise in Disaster* (Penguin, 2010).

22. Dean Spade, *Mutual Aid: Building Solidarity during This Crisis (and the Next)* (Verso Books, 2020).

23. Peter Singer, *A Darwinian Left: Politics, Evolution and Cooperation* (Yale University Press, 2000).

24. Nathan Kalman-Lamb, *Game Misconduct: Injury, Fandom, and the Business of Sport* (Fernwood, 2018), 142.

25. In an interview done for this book.

26. The diamond industry might actually be an example where this is the case, but this is an exception.

27. George Dohrmann, "Inside the NFL's Tobacco-Style Strategy to Hook Your Kids," *Huffington Post*, 2016, https://highline.huffingtonpost.com/articles/en/nfl-football-moms-kids/.

28. Paul Eliason et al., "No Association Found between Body Checking Experience and Injury or Concussion Rates in Adolescent Ice Hockey Players," *British Journal of Sports Medicine* 56, no. 23 (December 1, 2022): 1337–44, doi.org/10.1136/bjsports-2021-104691; Charles H. Tator, Victoria Blanchet, and Jin Ma, "Persisting Concussion Symptoms from Bodychecking: Unrecognized Toll in Boys' Ice Hockey," *Canadian Journal of Neurological Sciences* (August 22, 2022): 1–9, doi.org/10.1017/cjn.2022.289; Carolyn Emery et al., "Risk of Injury Associated with Bodychecking Experience among Youth Hockey Players," *Canadian Medical Association Journal* 183, no. 11 (2011): 1249–56.

29. Blake Harper, "Is Youth Football Child Abuse? Interview with Dr. Bennett Omalu," Fatherly, November 22, 2022, www.fatherly.com/entertainment/dr-bennet-omalu-youth-football-child-abuse.

30. Dohrmann, " NFL's Tobacco-Style Strategy."

31. Dohrmann, " NFL's Tobacco-Style Strategy"; Patrick Hruby, "How the NFL Brands Itself in American Classrooms," Vice (blog), February 17, 2015, www.vice.com/en/article/8qpjep/how-the-nfl-brands-itself-in-american-classrooms.

32. Michael Messner, "Boyhood, Organized Sports, and the Construction of Masculinities," *Journal of Contemporary Ethnography* 18, no. 4 (1990): 416–44.

33. J. D. Campbell, "'Training for Sport Is Training for War': Sport and the Transformation of the British Army, 1860–1914," *International Journal of the History of Sport* 17, no. 4 (December 1, 2000): 21–58, doi.org/10.1080/09523360008714145.

34. See: every high school football movie speech since the beginning of time.

35. Varda Burstyn, *The Rites of Men: Manhood, Politics, and the Culture of Sport* (University of Toronto Press, 1999), 4.

36. Kristi A. Allain, "'Real Fast and Tough': The Construction of Canadian Hockey Masculinity," *Sociology of Sport Journal* 25, no. 4 (2008): 462–81; Cheryl MacDonald, "'That's

Just What People Think of a Hockey Player, Right?': Manifestations of Masculinity among Major Junior Ice Hockey Players" (master's thesis, Concordia University, 2012), https://spectrum.library.concordia.ca/974057/.

37. Teresa Anne Fowler, Shannon D. M. Moore, and Tim Skuce, "The Penalty That's Never Called: Sexism in Men's Hockey Culture," *Sociology of Sport Journal* 1, no. 4 (2023): 1–11.

38. Michael Atkinson and Kevin Young, *Deviance and Social Control in Sport* (Human Kinetics, 2008).

39. Stephanie A. Stadden, *The Influence of Athletic Identity, Expectation of Toughness, and Attitude toward Pain and Injury on Athletes' Help-Seeking Tendencies* (The University of North Carolina at Greensboro, 2007).

40. Fighting comes with a five-minute penalty, but referees do not immediately stop the fights. It is the only sport that allows fighting in this way, and the only sport where fighting midgame does not immediately result in suspensions, fines, or even more severe punishment for the athletes involved.

41. Tom Cohen, "Three Hockey Enforcers Die Young in Four Months, Raising Questions," CNN, accessed April 2, 2023, http://edition.cnn.com/2011/SPORT/09/01/nhl.enforcers.deaths/index.html.

42. Silverwood, "Looking beyond the Athlete 'Offender.'"

43. Grace C. Plassche et al., "Fighting in Professional Ice Hockey: It's Time for a Change," *Physician and Sportsmedicine* 51, no. 5 (2022):405–13, doi.org/10.1080/00913847.2022.2078170.

44. Duane W. Rockerbie, "Fighting as a Profit Maximizing Strategy in the National Hockey League: More Evidence," *Applied Economics* 48, no. 4 (2016): 292–99, doi.org/10.1080/00036846.2015.1078446.

45. Sonny Sachdeva, "The Misadventures of Matt Rempe: A Timeline of the Rookie's Wild Year," Sportsnet, March 12, 2024, www.sportsnet.ca/nhl/the-adventures-of-matt-rempe-a-timeline-of-the-nhls-newest-fighter/.

46. Daniel Sailofsky and Madeleine Orr, "One Step Forward, Two Tweets Back: Exploring Cultural Backlash and Hockey Masculinity on Twitter," *Sociology of Sport Journal* 38, no. 1 (2020): 1–11.

47. Dennis Coates, Marcel Battré, and Christian Deutscher, "Does Violence in Professional Ice Hockey Pay? Cross Country Evidence from Three Leagues," in *Violence and Aggression in Sporting Contests: Economics, History and Policy*, ed. R. Todd Jewell (Springer, 2012), 47–63, doi.org/10.1007/978-1-4419-6630-8_4.

48. The existence and success of which is evidence enough of the popularity of fighting, still.

49. Nicolas A. Martineau, "Combien gagne réellement un joueur de hockey professionnel?," *Journal de Montréal*, October 2, 2020, www.journaldemontreal.com/2020/10/02/combien-gagne-reellement-un-joueur-de-hockey-professionnel.

50. "The High Cost of Painkiller Abuse in Professional Hockey," W5, 2020, www.youtube.com/watch?v=s_Sb664bCYU.

51. "The High Cost of Painkiller Abuse in Professional Hockey."

52. Katie Liston et al., "On Being 'Head Strong': The Pain Zone and Concussion in Non-Elite Rugby Union," *International Review for the Sociology of Sport* 53, no. 6 (2018): 668–84.

53. Alex Channon and Christopher R. Matthews, "Communicating Consent in Sport: A Typological Model of Athletes' Consent Practices within Combat Sports," *International Review for the Sociology of Sport* 57, no. 6 (September 1, 2022): 899–917, doi.org/10.1177/10126902211043992; Christopher R. Matthews, "'The Fog Soon Clears': Bodily Negotiations, Embodied Understandings, Competent Body Action and 'Brain Injuries' in Boxing," *International Review for the Sociology of Sport* 56, no. 5 (2021): 719–38.

54. Reem AlHashmi and Christopher R. Matthews, "Athletes' Understanding of Concussion—Uncertainty, Certainty and the 'Expert' on the Street," *Qualitative Research in Sport, Exercise and Health* 14, no. 3 (2022): 444–59.

55. Liston et al., "On Being 'Head Strong,'" 15.

56. John Winter, "Why Are NFL Player Careers So Short? (Explained)," Rugby Dome (blog), March 22, 2022, https://rugbydome.com/nfl-career-length/.

57. Dalton Miller, "What Byron Jones' Tweet Means for the Miami Dolphins," Pro Football Network, February 27, 2023, www.profootballnetwork.com/what-byron-jones-tweet-means-for-the-miami-dolphins/.

58. Walker-Brown, *A Delicate Game*.

59. Theadom et al., "Incidence of Sports-Related Traumatic Brain Injury"; Russell et al., "Neurodegenerative Disease Risk."

60. Mary Jane De Souza et al., "2014 Female Athlete Triad Coalition Consensus Statement on Treatment and Return to Play of the Female Athlete Triad: 1st International Conference Held in San Francisco, California, May 2012 and 2nd International Conference Held in Indianapolis, Indiana, May 2013," *British Journal of Sports Medicine* 48, no. 4 (February 1, 2014), doi.org/10.1136/bjsports-2013-093218.

61. Joseph Bylak and Mark R. Hutchinson, "Common Sports Injuries in Young Tennis Players," *Sports Medicine* 26, no. 2 (August 1, 1998): 119–32, doi.org/10.2165/00007256-199826020-00005.

62. Zachary Y. Kerr et al., "Epidemiology of Exertional Heat Illness among US High School Athletes," *American Journal of Preventive Medicine* 44, no. 1 (January 2013): 8–14, doi.org/10.1016/j.amepre.2012.09.058.

63. Emily A. Harrison, "The First Concussion Crisis: Head Injury and Evidence in Early American Football," *American Journal of Public Health* 104, no. 5 (May 2014): 822–33, doi.org/10.2105/AJPH.2013.301840.

64. Aaron Gordon, "Did Football Cause 20 Deaths in 1905? Re-Investigating a Serial Killer," Deadspin, 2014, https://deadspin.com/did-football-cause-20-deaths-in-1905-re-investigating-1506758181.

65. Ingfei Chen, "The Forgotten History of Head Injuries in Sports," *New Yorker*, February 11, 2023, www.newyorker.com/news/annals-of-inquiry/the-forgotten-history-of-head-injuries-in-sports.

66. Not only did the NFL refuse to believe the evidence of Webster's brain trauma at his death, but they also refused to acknowledge the harm the sport had caused him while he was alive. Webster had shown clear signs of brain injury and memory loss, and was evaluated by four separate doctors, who all confirmed that he had a closed-head injury due to multiple concussions. When Webster's lawyer, Bob Fitzsimmons, applied for disability from the NFL, Webster was awarded the lowest possible level: partial disability, and $3,000 a month. This came even after the NFL's own doctor evaluated Webster and found that he

had a closed-head brain injury. Thankfully, Fitzsimmons filed and won an appeal with the US District Court, which reversed the decision of the NFL's pension board, the first time in history this had happened. Even after this ruling, the NFL continued to fight, claiming that Webster, "who had endured probably 25,000 violent collisions during his career and now was living on Pringles and Little Debbie pecan rolls, who was occasionally catatonic, in a fetal position for days," did not qualify for disability.

67. Condé Nast, "Game Brain: Football Players and Concussions," *GQ*, September 15, 2009, www.gq.com/story/nfl-players-brain-dementia-study-memory-concussions.

68. Jeanne Marie Laskas, "Bennet Omalu, Concussions, and the NFL: How One Doctor Changed Football Forever" *GQ*, September 14, 2009, https://www.gq.com/story/nfl-players-brain-dementia-study-memory-concussions.

69. Condé Nast, "Game Brain."

70. Lauren Ezell, "Timeline: The NFL's Concussion Crisis" *FRONTLINE*, October 8, 2013, https://www.pbs.org/wgbh/frontline/article/timeline-the-nfls-concussion-crisis/.

71. Will Hobson, "The Broken Promises of the NFL Concussion Settlement," *Washington Post*, January 31, 2024, www.washingtonpost.com/sports/interactive/2024/nfl-concussion-settlement/.

72. Hobson, "Broken Promises."

73. Hobson, "Broken Promises."

74. Suril B. Sheth et al., "Orthopaedic and Brain Injuries over Last 10 Seasons in the National Football League (NFL): Number and Effect on Missed Playing Time," *BMJ Open Sport & Exercise Medicine* 6, no. 1 (April 1, 2020): e000684, doi.org/10.1136/bmjsem-2019-000684.

75. Sheth et al., "Orthopaedic and Brain Injuries."

76. Blinder, "What the N.F.L. Says, and What It Doesn't, about Injuries"; Walker-Brown, *A Delicate Game*, 183; Judy Battista, "NFL's Prioritization of Player Safety Leads to Promising Injury Data for 2023 Season," NFL.com, February 2, 2024, www.nfl.com/news/nfl-s-prioritization-of-player-safety-leads-to-promising-injury-data-for-2023-season.

77. "SCF: Pay the Price," NHL, 2019, www.facebook.com/watch/?v=371597046810132.

78. When entire blocks of text are in italics, they present general comments I've heard among friends and family, people I've met, message boards, comment sections, and so on. They represent common narratives that I'm trying to dispel or provide context for throughout the book.

79. Kevin Young, "Hidden in Plain Sight: Sports-Related Violence," in Silva and Kennedy, *Power Played*, 65.

80. Rob Maaddi (host), "Episode with Thomas Jones, Miles Sanders, and Dr. Chris Nowinski," *AP Pro Football Podcast*, July 7, 2022, https://podcasts.apple.com/ie/podcast/honor-roll/id1531528440?i=1000569138773.

81. Friedrich A. Hayek, *The Constitution of Liberty* (University of Chicago Press, 1960), 11–12.

82. Sébastien Rioux, Genevieve LeBaron, and Peter J. Verovšek, "Capitalism and Unfree Labor: A Review of Marxist Perspectives on Modern Slavery," *Review of International Political Economy* 27, no. 3 (May 3, 2020): 709–31, doi.org/10.1080/09692290.2019.1650094.

83. Jill A. Fisher, "Expanding the Frame of 'Voluntariness' in Informed Consent: Structural Coercion and the Power of Social and Economic Context," *Kennedy Institute of Ethics Journal* 23, no. 4 (December 2013): 355–79, doi.org/10.1353/ken.2013.0018.

84. Paul E. Farmer et al., "Structural Violence and Clinical Medicine," *PLoS Medicine* 3, no. 10 (2006): 1686.

85. Nathan Kalman-Lamb, Derek Silva, and Johanna Mellis, "Race, Money and Exploitation: Why College Sport Is Still the 'New Plantation,'" *The Guardian*, September 7, 2021, sec. Sport, www.theguardian.com/sport/2021/sep/07/race-money-and-exploitation-why-college-sport-is-still-the-new-plantation.

86. And increasingly in other Western countries like Canada and the United Kingdom.

87. Jon Wertheim, "Hotter Temperatures Are Leading to More Football Deaths," *Sports Illustrated*, October 7, 2022, www.si.com/high-school/2022/10/07/football-climate-change-daily-cover.

88. Mike Murphy, "A Former NHL Agitator Is Fighting the League over the Dangers of Head Trauma in Hockey," SBNation.com, December 21, 2018, www.sbnation.com/nhl/2018/12/21/18092086/dan-carcillo-nhl-concussions-cte-interview.

Chapter Three

1. Victor Mather, "Former USA Gymnastics Doctor Faces New Sexual Assault Charges," *New York Times*, February 22, 2017, sec. Sports, www.nytimes.com/2017/02/22/sports/olympics/usa-gymnastics-doctor-larry-nassar-sexual-assault-charges.html.

2. Hadley Freeman, "How Was Larry Nassar Able to Abuse So Many Gymnasts for So Long?," *The Guardian*, January 26, 2018, sec. Sport, www.theguardian.com/sport/2018/jan/26/larry-nassar-abuse-gymnasts-scandal-culture.

3. Des Bieler, "Here Are the Larry Nassar Comments That Drew Gasps in the Courtroom," *Washington Post*, November 27, 2021, www.washingtonpost.com/news/early-lead/wp/2018/01/24/here-are-the-larrry-nassar-comments-that-drew-gasps-in-the-courtroom/.

4. Mather, "Former USA Gymnastics Doctor."

5. Mather, "Former USA Gymnastics Doctor."

6. Sylvie Parent and Kristine Fortier, "Comprehensive Overview of the Problem of Violence against Athletes in Sport," *Journal of Sport and Social Issues* 42, no. 4 (2018): 228.

7. Joe Boylan, "Penn State Football Scandal: Now We Know What Joe Paterno Knew," Bleacher Report, July 13, 2012, bleacherreport.com/articles/1256931-penn-state-football-scandal-now-we-know-what-joe-paterno-knew.

8. Jay Cohen, "Chicago's NHL Team and Kyle Beach Settle Lawsuit," CBC, December 15, 2021.

9. "Theo Fleury Details Sexual Abuse by Hockey Coach," *CTV News*, October 9, 2009.

10. Aishwarya Kumar, "Tennis Player's Former Coach Charged with Rape," ESPN, September 2, 2022, www.espn.co.uk/tennis/story/_/id/34504568/fiona-ferro-former-coach-charged-rape-sexual-assault.

11. Gordon Darroch, "Senior Tennis Coach under Investigation over Sexual Assault Claims," DutchNews.Nl (blog), June 15, 2022, www.dutchnews.nl/news/2022/06/senior-tennis-coach-under-investigation-over-sexual-assault-claims/.

12. Ed Aarons, Romain Molina, and Alex Cizmic, "'I've Seen Hell': The Allegations Rocking Women's Football in Sierra Leone," *The Guardian*, March 26, 2023, https://www

.theguardian.com/football/2023/mar/26/ive-seen-hell-the-allegations-rocking-womens-football-in-sierra-leone.

13. Ariane Lacoursière and Simon-Olivier Lorange, "Sévices dans la LHJMQ: Le rêve brisé de Carl Latulippe," *La Presse*, April 3, 2023, sec. Hockey, www.lapresse.ca/sports/hockey/2023-04-03/sevices-dans-la-lhjmq/le-reve-brise-de-carl-latulippe.php.

14. Margo Mountjoy et al., "Safeguarding the Child Athlete in Sport: A Review, a Framework and Recommendations for the IOC Youth Athlete Development Model," *British Journal of Sports Medicine* 49, no. 13 (2015): 883–86.

15. "USOC Designates USA Gymnastics National Team Training Center at Karolyi Ranch as Newest US Olympic Training Site," USA Gymnastics, accessed April 4, 2023, https://usagym.org/pages/post.html?PostID=6979.

16. Atkinson and Young, *Deviance and Social Control in Sport*.

17. Erving Goffman, *Asylums: Essays on the Social Situation of Mental Patients and Other Inmates*, (Garden City, NY: Anchor Books, 1961).

18. J. East, "The Causes of Violence in Sport: Who Is to Blame," in *Sport, Children's Rights and Violence Prevention: A Sourcebook on Global Issues and Local Programmes* (Brunel University Press, 2012), 18–24.

19. Robert Hughes and Jay Coakley, "Positive Deviance among Athletes: The Implications of Overconformity to the Sport Ethic," *Sociology of Sport Journal* 8, no. 4 (December 1, 1991): 307–25, doi.org/10.1123/ssj.8.4.307.

20. "Athletes Speak Out on the Toxic Culture of Abuse in Canadian Gymnastics," W5 Investigation, 2022, www.youtube.com/watch?v=_BpTacY_UHY.

21. "Athletes Speak Out."

22. Ryley P. Mancine et al., "Prevalence of Disordered Eating in Athletes Categorized by Emphasis on Leanness and Activity Type—A Systematic Review," *Journal of Eating Disorders* 8, no. 1 (December 2020): 1–9, doi.org/10.1186/s40337-020-00323-2.

23. Laura D. DiPasquale and Trent A. Petrie, "Prevalence of Disordered Eating: A Comparison of Male and Female Collegiate Athletes and Nonathletes," *Journal of Clinical Sport Psychology* 7, no. 3 (September 1, 2013): 186–97, doi.org/10.1123/jcsp.7.3.186.

24. Alanis Thames and Jonathan Abrams, "Female College Athletes Say Pressure to Cut Body Fat Is Toxic," *New York Times*, November 10, 2022, sec. Sports, www.nytimes.com/2022/11/10/sports/college-athletes-body-fat-women.html; Yannis Karrer et al., "Disordered Eating and Eating Disorders in Male Elite Athletes: A Scoping Review," *BMJ Open Sport & Exercise Medicine* 6, no. 1 (October 1, 2020): e000801, doi.org/10.1136/bmjsem-2020-000801; Mancine et al., "Prevalence of Disordered Eating in Athletes."

25. Thames and Abrams, "Female College Athletes Say Pressure to Cut Body Fat Is Toxic."

26. "Athletes Speak Out."

27. "Athletes Speak Out."

28. "Athletes Speak Out."

29. Parent and Fortier, "Comprehensive Overview of the Problem of Violence against Athletes in Sport"; Jeannine Ohlert et al., "Sexual Violence in Organized Sport in Germany," *German Journal of Exercise and Sport Research* 48, no. 1 (2018): 59–68.

30. Robert M. Malina, "Early Sport Specialization: Roots, Effectiveness, Risks," *Current Sports Medicine Reports* 9, no. 6 (2010): 364–71; Jon L. Oliver and Rhodri S. Lloyd, "Physical

Training as a Potential Form of Abuse," in *Safeguarding, Child Protection and Abuse in Sport*, ed. Melanie Lang and Mike Hartill (Routledge, 2014), 183–91.

31. Joel S. Brenner and Council on Sports Medicine and Fitness, "Sports Specialization and Intensive Training in Young Athletes," *Pediatrics* 138, no. 3 (September 1, 2016): e20162148, doi.org/10.1542/peds.2016-2148.

32. Charlotte L. Wilinsky and Allyssa McCabe, "A Review of Emotional and Sexual Abuse of Elite Child Athletes by Their Coaches," *Sports Coaching Review* 10, no. 1 (2021): 84–109.

33. "Athletes Speak Out."

34. "Athletes Speak Out."

35. Froukje Smits, Frank Jacobs, and Annelies Knoppers, "'Everything Revolves around Gymnastics': Athletes and Parents Make Sense of Elite Youth Sport," *Sport in Society* 20, no. 1 (2017): 66–83.

36. The "masculinity in crisis" narrative has been around for about 150 years—seriously, you can find newspaper archives from the 1800s (at least that I've seen from Canada and the United States) with writers saying that masculinity is in crisis and boys need to be whipped into shape.

37. Jeffrey L. Sauvé et al., "What Supports and What Thwarts Olympic Athlete Well-Being? Coach and Organizational Perspectives," *Journal of Applied Sport Psychology* 35, no. 6 (2023): 983–1004, doi.org/10.1080/10413200.2023.2166156.

38. Juliet Macur, "Gymnasts Worldwide Push Back on Their Sport's Culture of Abuse," *New York Times*, August 3, 2020, sec. Sports, www.nytimes.com/2020/08/03/sports/olympics/gymnastics-abuse-athlete-a.html.

39. Judith L. Komaki and Yetsa A. Tuakli-Wosornu, "Using Carrots Not Sticks to Cultivate a Culture of Safeguarding in Sport," *Frontiers in Sports and Active Living* 3 (2021): 625410; Jennifer Freeman et al., "MTSS Coaching: Bridging Knowing to Doing," *Theory into Practice* 56, no. 1 (January 2, 2017): 29–37, doi.org/10.1080/00405841.2016.1241946; Hsing-Chieh Huang et al., "A Study on the Perceived Positive Coaching Leadership, Sports Enthusiasm, and Happiness of Boxing Athletes," *Sustainability* 13, no. 13 (January 2021): 7199, doi.org/10.3390/su13137199.

40. Komaki and Tuakli-Wosornu, "Using Carrots Not Sticks."

41. Ed Aarons, Romain Molina, and Alex Cizmic, "'I've Seen Hell': The Allegations Rocking Women's Football in Sierra Leone," *The Observer*, March 26, 2023, sec. Football, www.theguardian.com/football/2023/mar/26/ive-seen-hell-the-allegations-rocking-womens-football-in-sierra-leone.

42. Curtis Fogel and Andrea Quinlan, "Sexual Assault in the Locker Room: Sexually Violent Hazing in Canadian Sport," *Journal of Sexual Aggression* 27, no. 3 (2021): 353–72.

43. Martin D. Schwartz, "Masculinities, Sport, and Violence against Women: The Contribution of Male Peer Support Theory," *Violence against Women* 27, no. 5 (2021): 688–707.

44. "Athletes Speak Out."

45. Though some do, and the numbers have been rising every year.

46. This story has a somewhat happy ending, at least. After a new coach was brought in, two of the six players who quit returned. After a strong first year with their new coach, and a good recruiting class, the team followed up that first season with a storybook second sea-

son, winning the provincial league championship and going all the way to the national finals, led by their two returning stars.

47. Silva and Kennedy, *Power Played*.

48. Rick Westhead, "Boynton: Investigators Probing Alleged Abuse of Former Blackhawks Players Ask, 'Who Knew?,'" TSN, July 29, 2021, www.tsn.ca/boynton-investigators-probing-alleged-abuse-of-former-blackhawks-players-ask-who-knew-1.1674971; Silva and Kennedy, *Power Played*.

49. As we saw with the 2023 SAG-AFTA strikes, where thousands of writers and actors who make up the majority of Hollywood talent struck for better working conditions, pay, and protection from AI and predatory TV and movie studios.

50. Jenkins, Daisy M. "Pro Athletes, Big Winners and Losers When the Career Clock Goes to Zero." *HuffPost*, June 17, 2014, https://www.huffpost.com/entry/pro-athletes-big-winners-and-losers-when-the-career-clock-goes-to-zero_b_5501234.

51. Devah Pager, *Marked: Race, Crime, and Finding Work in an Era of Mass Incarceration* (University of Chicago Press, 2008); Devah Pager, "The Mark of a Criminal Record," *American Journal of Sociology* 108, no. 5 (2003): 937–75; David Jacobs and Jason T. Carmichael, "The Politics of Punishment across Time and Space: A Pooled Time-Series Analysis of Imprisonment Rates," *Social Forces* 80, no. 1 (2001): 61–89; Mike Vuolo, Sarah Lageson, and Christopher Uggen, "Criminal Record Questions in the Era of 'Ban the Box,'" *Criminology & Public Policy* 16, no. 1 (2017): 139–65; Derek Van Rheenen, "Exploitation in College Sports: Race, Revenue, and Educational Reward," *International Review for the Sociology of Sport* 48, no. 5 (October 1, 2013): 550–71, doi.org/10.1177/1012690212450218; Christopher Rogers, "DON'T TOUCH MY HAIR: How Hegemony Operates through Dress Codes to Reproduce Whiteness in Schools," *Du Bois Review: Social Science Research on Race* 19, no. 1 (2022): 175–91, doi.org/10.1017/S1742058X22000017; Wade C. Jacobsen, "School Punishment and Interpersonal Exclusion: Rejection, Withdrawal, and Separation from Friends," *Criminology* 58, no. 1 (2020): 35–69, doi.org/10.1111/1745-9125.12227; Brian P. Soebbing, Pamela Wicker, and Nicholas M. Watanabe, "NFL Player Career Earnings and Off-Field Behavior," *Review of Black Political Economy* 50, no. 1 (2022): 81–96, doi.org/10.1177/00346446221076868.

52. Kristin Nicole Dukes and Sarah E. Gaither, "Black Racial Stereotypes and Victim Blaming: Implications for Media Coverage and Criminal Proceedings in Cases of Police Violence against Racial and Ethnic Minorities," *Journal of Social Issues* 73, no. 4 (2017): 789–807; Moya Bailey and Trudy, "On Misogynoir: Citation, Erasure, and Plagiarism," *Feminist Media Studies* 18, no. 4 (2018): 762–68; Danielle C. Slakoff and Pauline K. Brennan, "The Differential Representation of Latina and Black Female Victims in Front-Page News Stories: A Qualitative Document Analysis," *Feminist Criminology* 14, no. 4 (October 1, 2019): 488–516, doi.org/10.1177/1557085117747031.

53. Dukes and Gaither, "Black Racial Stereotypes"; Rebecca M. Hayes and Kate Luther, "#Notallmen: Media and Crime Victimization," in *#Crime: Social Media, Crime, and the Criminal Legal System*, ed. Rebecca M. Hayes and Kate Luther (Springer International, 2018), 123–51, doi.org/10.1007/978-3-319-89444-7_4; Linda Adeniji, "The Unrapeable Black Woman: How the Lack of Legal Protection through the Centuries Promoted the Tradition of Unreported Sexual Assaults" (December 12, 2015), SSRN 2702861.

54. Salim Valji, "Akim Aliu's Account of Racism Pushes Hockey to Search Its Soul," *New York Times*, May 23, 2020, sec. Sports, www.nytimes.com/2020/05/23/sports/hockey/akim-aliu-nhl-racism.html.

55. Melissa Block, "Olympic Runner Caster Semenya Wants to Compete, Not Defend Her Womanhood," NPR, July 28, 2021, sec. Live Updates: The Tokyo Olympics, www.npr.org/sections/tokyo-olympics-live-updates/2021/07/28/1021503989/women-runners-testosterone-olympics; Eddie Pells, "Track Bans Transgender Athletes, Tightens Rules for Semenya," ABC News, March 23, 2023, https://abcnews.go.com/Sports/wireStory/track-bans-transgender-athletes-tightens-rules-semenya-98079298.

56. Ravi Ubha and Gianluca Mezzofiore, "Mario Balotelli Suffers Racist Abuse as Incidents Continue in Serie A," CNN, November 8, 2019, https://edition.cnn.com/2019/11/04/football/balotelli-racist-chants-football-serie-a-intl-spt/index.html; Becky Sullivan, "Three Black Soccer Players Are Facing Racist Abuse after England's Euro 2020 Defeat," NPR, July 12, 2021, sec. Sports, www.npr.org/2021/07/12/1015239599/prince-william-and-boris-johnson-denounce-the-racist-abuse-of-englands-soccer-te; Glynn A. Hill, "Three French Players Face Racist Online Abuse after World Cup Loss," *Washington Post*, December 21, 2022, www.washingtonpost.com/sports/2022/12/20/french-players-racism-world-cup/.

57. Peter Sunjic, "'I Chose the Wrong Slave Today'—Chris Boucher Reveals a Disgusting Message He Got from a Fan after Losing a Parlay," Basketball Network, April 1, 2023, www.basketballnetwork.net/off-the-court/chris-boucher-reveals-salty-message-he-got-from-a-fan-after-losing-a-parlay.

58. Courtney Szto, *Changing on the Fly: Hockey through the Voices of South Asian Canadians* (Rutgers University Press, 2020).

59. Richard Norman et al., "'Building Back Better': Seeking an Equitable Return to Sport for Development in the Wake of COVID-19," *Sociology of Sport Journal* 40, no. 2 (2023): 197–212.

60. Szto, *Changing on the Fly*.

61. Aarti Ratna, "'Who Are Ya?' The National Identities and Belongings of British Asian Football Fans," *Patterns of Prejudice* 48, no. 3 (2014): 286–308; Sine Agergaard and Verena Lenneis, "Everyday Bordering. Theoretical Perspectives on National 'Others' in Sport and Leisure Time Physical Activity," *Sport in Society* 24, no. 11 (2021): 1971–86, doi.org/10.1080/17430437.2021.1904904.

62. Norman et al., "'Building Back Better'"; Yomee Lee, "From Forever Foreigners to Model Minority: Asian American Men in Sports," *Physical Culture and Sport. Studies and Research* 72, no. 1 (2016): 23–32.

63. Kalman-Lamb, Silva, and Mellis, "Race, Money and Exploitation."

64. Eric Anderson and Mark McCormack, "Inclusive Masculinity Theory: Overview, Reflection and Refinement," *Journal of Gender Studies* 27, no. 5 (2018): 547–61.

65. Joe Hernandez, "Why There Are Few Openly Gay Athletes in Men's Professional Sports," NPR, July 21, 2021, sec. Sports, www.npr.org/2021/07/21/1018404859/openly-gay-athletes-in-mens-pro-sports-few.

66. Richard O. De Visser and Elizabeth J. McDonnell, "'Man Points': Masculine Capital and Young Men's Health," *Health Psychology* 32, no. 1 (2013): 5; Richard O. De Visser, Jonathan A. Smith, and Elizabeth J. McDonnell, "'That's Not Masculine': Masculine Capital and Health-Related Behaviour," *Journal of Health Psychology* 14, no. 7 (2009): 1047–58.

67. Robb Willer et al., "Overdoing Gender: A Test of the Masculine Overcompensation Thesis," *American Journal of Sociology* 118, no. 4 (January 2013): 980–1022, doi.org/10.1086/668417.

68. Jessica G. Finkeldey, "Adolescent Male Sports Participation and Violence in Emerging Adulthood: Examining Variation by Gender-Typed Behavior," *Deviant Behavior* 40, no. 11 (2019): 1391–1408, doi.org/10.1080/01639625.2018.1512259.

69. Jennifer L. Knight and Traci A. Giuliano, "Blood, Sweat, and Jeers: The Impact of the Media's Heterosexist Portrayals on Perceptions of Male and Female Athletes," *Journal of Sport Behavior* 26, no. 3 (2003).

70. Katie Barnes, "Who Gets to Be the Face of the WNBA? Jonquel Jones Is Ready for Her Close-Up," ESPN.com, June 22, 2022, www.espn.co.uk/wnba/story/_/id/34109460/jonquel-jones-untold-story-wnba-reigning-mvp.

71. Daniel Sailofsky, "The privilege to do it all? Exploring the contradictions of name, image and likeness (NIL) rights for women athletes and women's sports," *International Review for the Sociology of Sport* (2024): 10126902241268278.

72. Burstyn, *The Rites of Men*.

73. Daniel Sailofsky, "More Talent, More Leeway: Do Violence against Women Arrests Really Hurt NFL Player Careers?," *Violence against Women* 29, no. 6–7 (2022), doi.org/10.1177/10778012221092477.

74. Joon Sung Lee and Dae Hee Kwak, "Can Winning Take Care of Everything? A Longitudinal Assessment of Post-Transgression Actions on Repairing Trust in an Athlete Endorser," *Sport Management Review* 20, no. 3 (2017): 261–72; Coral Rae, Andrew C. Billings, and Kenon A. Brown, "Exploring Social and Economic Capital within Sport-Related Transgressions," in *Evolution of the Modern Sports Fan: Communicative Approaches*, ed. Andrew C. Billings and Kenon A. Brown (Lexington Books, 2017), 147; Kenon A. Brown, Breann Murphy, and Lindsey C. Maxwell, "Tried in the Court of Public Opinion: Effects of Involvement in Criminal Transgressions on Athlete Image," *Communication & Sport* 6, no. 3 (2018): 283–307, doi.org/10.1177/2167479517697426.

75. A judicial inquiry, or public inquiry, is an investigation done to understand an issue, social problem, or event. According to the Government of Canada' website, a judicial inquiry is called by the governing party's Cabinet to investigate and understand the roots of problems deemed to be of "national importance." These inquiries can subpoena witnesses but cannot convict defendants. The recommendations from judicial inquiries are also not binding. The National Inquiry into Missing and Murdered Indigenous Women and Girls is another example of a Canadian judicial inquiry.

76. "Open Letter to Prime Minister Trudeau," Scholars Against Abuse, April 3, 2023, www.scholarsagainstabuse.com.

77. Victoria Roberts, Victor Sojo, and Felix Grant, "Organisational Factors and Non-Accidental Violence in Sport: A Systematic Review," *Sport Management Review* 23, no. 1 (2020): 11; Robert H. Frank and Philip J. Cook, "Winner-Take-All Markets," *Studies in Microeconomics* 1, no. 2 (2013): 131–54, doi.org/10.1177/2321022213501254.

78. Gretchen Kerr, Bruce Kidd, and Peter Donnelly, "One Step Forward, Two Steps Back: The Struggle for Child Protection in Canadian Sport," *Social Sciences* 9, no. 5 (May 2020): 68, doi.org/10.3390/socsci9050068.

79. Sauvé et al., "What Supports and What Thwarts Olympic Athlete Well-Being?," 4.

80. Karl Marx, "The Eighteenth Brumaire of Louis Napoleon," *Die Revolution*, 1852.

81. Lauren McKeon, "The Harder They Fall: Inside Canada's Gymnastics Abuse Scandal," *Maclean's*, February 2023.

82. Komaki and Tuakli-Wosornu, "Using Carrots Not Sticks."

83. Kristoffer Henriksen et al., "Consensus Statement on Improving the Mental Health of High Performance Athletes," *International Journal of Sport and Exercise Psychology* 18, no. 5 (2020): 553–60, doi.org/10.1080/1612197X.2019.1570473; Cindy Chang et al., "Mental Health Issues and Psychological Factors in Athletes: Detection, Management, Effect on Performance and Prevention: American Medical Society for Sports Medicine Position Statement—Executive Summary," *British Journal of Sports Medicine* 54, no. 4 (2020): 216–20; Claudia L. Reardon et al., "Mental Health in Elite Athletes: International Olympic Committee Consensus Statement (2019)," *British Journal of Sports Medicine* 53, no. 11 (2019): 667–99, doi.org/10.1136/bjsports-2019-100715.

84. Sauvé et al., "What Supports and What Thwarts Olympic Athlete Well-Being?," 1.

85. I'm not getting into the endless debate about China's communist/capitalist classification here, sorry (or you're welcome).

86. If our political landscape continues in this direction, we can expect austerity and cuts to public services in the coming years in any of these countries, and these cuts will undoubtedly hit the arts, culture, and community sport sectors, as they always have.

Chapter Four

1. Gordon A. Bloom and Michael D. Smith, "Hockey Violence: A Test of Cultural Spillover Theory," *Sociology of Sport Journal* 13, no. 1 (1996): 65–77.

2. Chen Chen, "Naming the Ghost of Capitalism in Sport Management."

3. I've written this whole book about this, and I study and teach about it for a living, but if you show me a highlight package of from the 2019 Toronto Raptors title run, I also momentarily lose myself and may literally start crying.

4. Steve Henson, "What Happened with Kobe Bryant's Sexual Assault Case," *Los Angeles Times*, January 27, 2020, www.latimes.com/sports/story/2020-01-26/what-happened-kobe-bryant-sexual-assault-case.

5. Paul Harris, "Basketball Star's Rape Trial Turns Spotlight on Accuser," *The Guardian*, July 24, 2004, sec. World News, www.theguardian.com/world/2004/jul/25/usa.paulharris.

6. Forbes, "Kobe Bryant," Forbes, 2020, www.forbes.com/nft-profile/kobe-bryant/.

7. Aaron Reiss, "Timeline of Deshaun Watson Sexual Assault Lawsuits," *The Athletic*, 2022, theathletic.com/2496073/2022/06/27/deshaun-watson-sexual-assault/.

8. Reiss, "Timeline."

9. Jenny Vrentas, "How the Texans and a Spa Enabled Deshaun Watson's Troubling Behavior," *New York Times*, June 7, 2022, sec. Sports, www.nytimes.com/2022/06/07/sports/football/deshaun-watson.html.

10. Vrentas, "How the Texans and a Spa Enabled Deshaun Watson's Troubling Behavior."

11. Jacob Stern and David Yaffe-Bellany, "Why Has the World Gone Easy on Cristiano Ronaldo?," *New Republic*, January 2, 2019, https://newrepublic.com/article/152828/world-gone-easy-cristiano-ronaldo.

12. Andy Rose, "Rape Case against Soccer Star Cristiano Ronaldo Dismissed due to 'misconduct' by Plaintiff's Attorney," CNN, June 11, 2022, www.cnn.com/2022/06/11/sport/cristiano-ronaldo-rape-case-dismissed/index.html.

13. Stern and Yaffe-Bellany, "Why Has the World Gone Easy on Cristiano Ronaldo?"

14. Mayne, Joshua. "Alexander Zverev Reaches Roland-Garros Final Amid Domestic Abuse Allegations." *The Sporting News Australia*. Accessed September 20, 2024, https://www.sportingnews.com/au/tennis/news/alexander-zverev-domestic-violence-allegations-explained/195628d6011f8776c481a9ef.

15. Mike Freeman, "NFL Insiders: Jameis Winston Needs a Handler, No Matter What Bucs Say," Bleacher Report, 2015, https://bleacherreport.com/articles/2450036-nfl-team-officials-jameis-winston-needs-a-handler-no-matter-what-bucs-say.

16. Amana F. Carvalho et al., "Internalized Sexual Minority Stressors and Same-Sex Intimate Partner Violence," *Journal of Family Violence* 26, no. 7 (2011): 501–9, doi.org/10.1007/s10896-011-9384-2.

17. Todd W. Crosset, "Athletes, Sexual Assault, and Universities' Failure to Address Rape-Prone Subcultures on Campus," in *The Crisis of Campus Sexual Violence*, ed. Sara Carrigan Wooten and Roland Mitchell (Routledge, 2015), 74–91; Todd W. Crosset, Jeffrey R. Benedict, and Mark A. McDonald, "Male Student-Athletes Reported for Sexual Assault: A Survey of Campus Police Departments and Judicial Affairs Offices," *Journal of Sport and Social Issues* 19, no. 2 (1995): 126–40; Wanda Leal, Marc Gertz, and Alex R Piquero, "The National Felon League? A Comparison of NFL Arrests to General Population Arrests," *Journal of Criminal Justice* 43, no. 5 (2015): 397–403; Kathleen E Miller et al., "Athletic Involvement and Adolescent Delinquency," *Journal of Youth and Adolescence* 36, no. 5 (2007): 711; Derek A. Kreager, "Unnecessary Roughness? School Sports, Peer Networks, and Male Adolescent Violence," *American Sociological Review* 72, no. 5 (2007): 705–24; Belinda-Rose Young et al., "Sexual Coercion Practices among Undergraduate Male Recreational Athletes, Intercollegiate Athletes, and Non-Athletes," *Violence against Women* 23, no. 7 (2017): 795–812; Neal B. Kimble et al., "Revealing an Empirical Understanding of Aggression and Violent Behavior in Athletics," *Aggression and Violent Behavior* 15, no. 6 (2010): 446–62.

18. This is actually the case for almost any social problem—even during the most intense moral panics about "crime waves," *most* of the people in any society or any group are not committing the criminal or deviant act in question. This does not mean that structural or cultural factors that affect an entire society or an entire group do not impact the likelihood of someone committing that act. For example, the lack of legal and social consequences for most acts of white-collar crime undoubtedly makes this behavior more common, even though *most* people still don't actually engage in it.

19. Wanda Leal, Marc Gertz, and Alex R Piquero, "Are NFL Arrestees Violent Specialists or High Frequency Offenders or Both?," *Deviant Behavior* 37, no. 4 (2016): 456–70.

20. Eric Anderson, "'I Used to Think Women Were Weak': Orthodox Masculinity, Gender Segregation, and Sport," in *Sociological Forum* 23 (2008), 257–80; Burstyn, *The Rites of Men*; Cheryl Cooky and Michael A. Messner, *No Slam Dunk: Gender, Sport and the Unevenness of Social Change* (Rutgers University Press, 2018), http://muse.jhu.edu/book/59134.

21. Kreager, "Unnecessary Roughness?"; Rosemary Ricciardelli, Kimberley A. Clow, and Philip White, "Investigating Hegemonic Masculinity: Portrayals of Masculinity in Men's

Lifestyle Magazines," *Sex Roles* 63, no. 1–2 (2010): 64–78; James Messerschmidt and Raewyn Connell, "Hegemonic Masculinity: Rethinking the Concept," *Gender & Society* 19, no. 6 (2005), https://journals-sagepub-com.proxy3.library.mcgill.ca/doi/10.1177/0891243205278639.

22. Eric Anderson, *21st Century Jocks: Sporting Men and Contemporary Heterosexuality* (Palgrave Macmillan, 2014), doi.org/10.1057/9781137379641; Cooky and Messner, *No Slam Dunk*.

23. John C. Navarro and Richard Tewksbury, "National Comparisons of Rape Myth Acceptance Predictors between Nonathletes and Athletes from Multi-Institutional Settings," *Sexual Abuse* 31, no. 5 (2019): 543–59; Elizabeth Ann Gage, "Gender Attitudes and Sexual Behaviors: Comparing Center and Marginal Athletes and Nonathletes in a Collegiate Setting," *Violence against Women* 14, no. 9 (2008): 1014–32; Kathleen E. Miller, "Sport-Related Identities and the 'Toxic Jock,'" *Journal of Sport Behavior* 32, no. 1 (2009): 69.

24. Anderson, *21st Century Jocks*; Eric Anderson, *Inclusive Masculinity: The Changing Nature of Masculinities* (Routledge, 2010), doi.org/10.4324/9780203871485.

25. Kreager, "Unnecessary Roughness?," 706.

26. Robert Ambrose, "The NFL Makes It Rain: Through Strict Enforcement of Its Conduct Policy, the NFL Protects Its Integrity, Wealth, and Popularity," *William Mitchell Law Review* 34 (2007): 1069; Maleaha L Brown, "When Pros Become Cons: Ending the NFL's History of Domestic Violence Leniency," *Family Law Quarterly* 50, no. 1 (2016): 193–212; Janine Young Kim and Matthew J. Parlow, "Off-Court Misbehavior: Sports Leagues and Private Punishment," *Journal of Criminal Law and Criminology* 99, no. 3 (2009): 573–98.

27. Alison McCann, "The NFL's Uneven History of Punishing Domestic Violence," FiveThirtyEight (2014), https://fivethirtyeight.com/features/nfl-domestic-violence-policy-suspensions/.

28. Michael Palmer, Quinlan Duhan, and Brian P. Soebbing, "College Deviance and the Effects on NFL Amateur Draft Selection: Analyzing the Personal Conduct Policy," *Journal of Sports Analytics* 1, no. 2 (2015): 121–32.

29. Don Van Natta Jr. and Kevin Valkenburg, "Rice Case: Purposeful Misdirection by Team, Scant Investigation by NFL," ESPN, September 19, 2014, www.espn.com/espn/otl/story/_/id/11551518/how-ray-rice-scandal-unfolded-baltimore-ravens-roger-goodell-nfl.

30. Jenny Vrentas, "N.F.L. Players Pay a Small Price When Accused of Violence against Women," *New York Times*, July 13, 2022, sec. Sports, www.nytimes.com/2022/07/13/sports/football/nfl-players-pay-a-small-price-when-accused-of-violence-against-women.html.

31. Alyssa Lott, "Illegal Contact: Tackling Domestic Violence in the NFL," *Widener Law Review* 25 (2019): 135.

32. Daniel Sailofsky and Eran Shor, "'It Will Ruin His Career': Does Violence against Women Really Damage the Careers of NBA Players?," *Journal of Interpersonal Violence* 37, no. 1–2 (2022): 239–57.

33. Sailofsky, "More Talent, More Leeway."

34. Age would have an impact only if the crime or act of violence happened at a young enough age where a team could determine that the player should not be held responsible. Age does impact how long players' careers last following an arrest, but likely because younger players are generally more "valuable" for organizations because they are often on cheaper contracts, and/or have more potential to improve as players.

35. Kim Becker, "Chad Wheeler and the Seattle Seahawks Issue Official Statements regarding Domestic Violence Allegations," Sports Illustrated, USC Trojans News, 2021, www.si.com/college/usc/football/seahawks-issue-official-statement-regarding-chad-wheeler; Mike Freeman, "Opinion: Chad Wheeler Case Shows That NFL Teams, Like Society, Still Don't Care about Domestic Violence," USA Today, January 2021, www.usatoday.com/story/sports/columnist/mike-freeman/2021/01/28/chad-wheeler-case-nfl-teams-dont-care-domestic-violence/4292496001/; Tesfatsion Master, "Vikings Notes: Jefferson Released after Arrest," *Star Tribune*, 2013, www.startribune.com/vikings-notes-jefferson-released-after-arrest/233400981/.

36. Sailofsky, "More Talent, More Leeway"; Sailofsky and Shor, "'It Will Ruin His Career.'"

37. Tadd Haislop, "Tyreek Hill's Timeline of Trouble: From a Domestic Violence Arrest in College to Child Abuse Investigation with Chiefs," Sporting News, 2020, www.sportingnews.com/us/nfl/news/tyreek-hill-domestic-violence-child-abuse-investigation/neqfn40200lt16ik2142ay772.

38. Haislop, "Tyreek Hill's Timeline of Trouble."

39. Alec Nathan, "Kendrick Nunn Charged with Domestic Battery: Latest Details and Comments," Bleacher Report, March 17, 2016, https://bleacherreport.com/articles/2625652-kendrick-nunn-charged-with-domestic-battery-latest-details-and-comments.

40. The NBA's development league, directly under the NBA.

41. Nunn is no longer in the NBA and plays in the Euroleague, but this is due strictly to performance. He was given every chance to succeed in the NBA following his collegiate career.

42. Monique Douty, "Revisiting Ben Roethlisberger's Sexual Assault Allegations in the #MeToo Era," Sportscasting | Pure Sports (blog), July 23, 2020, www.sportscasting.com/revisiting-ben-roethlisbergers-sexual-assault-allegations-in-the-metoo-era/.

43. Spotrac.Com, 2020, www.spotrac.com/.

44. Ken Belson, "Kareem Hunt Is Cut by the Chiefs after a Video Showed Him Attacking a Woman," *New York Times*, December 1, 2018, sec. Sports, www.nytimes.com/2018/11/30/sports/kareem-hunt-chiefs-video.html.

45. Sejung Marina Choi and Nora J Rifon, "Who Is the Celebrity in Advertising? Understanding Dimensions of Celebrity Images," *Journal of Popular Culture* 40, no. 2 (2007): 304–24.

46. Kim and Parlow, "Off-Court Misbehavior."

47. Michael M O'Hear, "Blue-Collar Crimes/White-Collar Criminals: Sentencing Elite Athletes Who Commit Violent Crimes," *Marquette Sports Law Review* 12 (2001): 427; Kimberly M Trebon, "There Is No I in Team: The Commission of Group Sexual Assault by Collegiate and Professional Athletes," *DePaul Journal of Sports Law and Contemporary Problems* 4, no. 1 (2007): 65; Jacklin R. Wallgren, "An Examination of Criminal Arrests and Convictions of Football Student-Athletes at Atlantic Coast Conference Institutions as Reported by the Media" (PhD thesis, The University of North Carolina at Chapel Hill, 2009).

48. Torben Iversen and David Soskice, *Democracy and Prosperity: Reinventing Capitalism through a Turbulent Century* (Princeton University Press, 2020); Harold Demsetz, *From Economic Man to Economic System: Essays on Human Behavior and the Institutions of Capitalism* (Cambridge University Press, 2011).

49. There must be video, or else the police just engage in outright denial.

50. The full expression is "One bad apple can spoil the bunch" and is therefore the exact opposite of how we colloquially use the term, but I digress.

51. M. Candace Christensen, Emmett Gill, and Alfred Pérez, "The Ray Rice Domestic Violence Case: Constructing Black Masculinity through Newspaper Reports," *Journal of Sport and Social Issues* 40, no. 5 (2016): 363–86, doi.org/10.1177/0193723516655576; Dana E. Mastro, Erin Blecha, and Anita Atwell Seate, "Characterizations of Criminal Athletes: A Systematic Examination of Sports News Depictions of Race and Crime," *Journal of Broadcasting & Electronic Media* 55, no. 4 (2011): 526–42.

52. Mastro, Blecha, and Atwell Seate, "Characterizations of Criminal Athletes," 539.

53. Kobena Mercer, *Welcome to the Jungle: New Positions in Black Cultural Studies* (Routledge, 2013), 178.

54. Christensen, Gill, and Pérez, "Ray Rice Domestic Violence Case."

55. Adam Rugg, "Civilizing the Child: Violence, Masculinity, and Race in Media Narratives of James Harrison," *Communication & Sport* 7, no. 1 (2019): 46–63, doi.org/10.1177/2167479517745299.

56. Rugg, "Civilizing the Child," 46.

57. At least for now—even during the time when I've been writing this book—there has already been some backsliding on the small gains in public discourse, support, and legislative changes regarding the unequal treatment of Black people in the criminal legal system.

58. Jeffrey H. Reiman and Paul Leighton, *The Rich Get Richer and the Poor Get Prison: Ideology, Class, and Criminal Justice* (Routledge, 2015).

59. Mark Lanier, *Essential Criminology* (Routledge, 2018); Reiman and Leighton, *The Rich Get Richer*; Jonathan H. Turner, "Why Are Elegant Theories Under-Utilized by Sociologists?," ed. Donald Black, *Contemporary Sociology* 31, no. 6 (2002): 664–68, doi.org/10.2307/3089916.

60. Reiss, "Deshaun Watson Sexual Assault Lawsuits."

61. Yes, that Robert Mueller, of Donald Trump impeachment investigation fame.

62. Robert Mueller, "Report to the National Football League of an Independent Investigation into the Ray Rice Incident," Static, January 8, 2015, https://www.nfl.com/news/robert-mueller-releases-report-on-rice-investigation-0ap3000000455483.

63. Jeanna Thomas, *No, NFL Viewership Wasn't Down because of Anthem Protests*, SBNation.com, July 27, 2017, www.sbnation.com/2017/7/27/16050800/nfl-viewership-national-anthem-protests-jd-power-survey-2017.

64. Todd Crosset, "Male Athletes' Violence against Women: A Critical Assessment of the Athletic Affiliation, Violence against Women Debate," *Quest* 51, no. 3 (1999): 244–57; Carrie A Moser, "Penalties, Fouls, and Errors: Professional Athletes and Violence against Women," *Sports Lawyers Journal* 11 (2004): 69.

65. William Beaver, "College Athletes and Sexual Assault," *Society* 56, no. 6 (2019): 620–24.

66. Billy Hawkins, *The New Plantation: Black Athletes, College Sports, and Predominantly White NCAA Institutions* (Palgrave Macmillan, 2013).

67. Eric L. Nelson, "If You Want to Convict a Domestic Violence Batterer, List Multiple Charges in the Police Report," *SAGE Open* 4, no. 1 (January 1, 2014), doi.org/10.1177/2158244013517246.

68. Daniel Sailofsky, "Masculinity, Cancel Culture and Woke Capitalism: Exploring Twitter Response to Brendan Leipsic's Leaked Conversation," *International Review for the Sociology of Sport* 57, no. 5 (2021): 734–57, doi.org/10.1177/10126902211039768.

69. Freeman, "Opinion."

70. Freeman, "Opinion."

Chapter Five

1. It's hard to get clear numbers for exactly how much each sport produced, but it is clear that these two sports are the highest grossing. The NCAA men's basketball tournament alone generated $1 billion in 2022.

2. Andrew Zimbalist, "Analysis: Who Is Winning in the High-Revenue World of College Sports?," PBS NewsHour, March 18, 2023, www.pbs.org/newshour/economy/analysis-who-is-winning-in-the-high-revenue-world-of-college-sports.

3. From Nathan Kalman-Lamb and Derek Silva, "'Play'Ing College Football: Campus Athletic Worker Experiences of Exploitation," *Critical Sociology* 50, no. 4–5 (2023), doi.org/10.1177/08969205231208036, "Campus athletic worker" is a term coined by critical sport scholars to properly recognize the labor position of elite varsity athletes in universities, as an alternative to the nefarious sham-amateur title of "student athletes."

4. Van Rheenen, "Exploitation in College Sports."

5. Cedric J. Robinson, *Black Marxism: The Making of the Black Radical Tradition*, 3rd ed., rev. (The University of North Carolina Press Books, 2000).

6. Liam Kennedy and Derek Silva, "'Discipline That Hurts': Punitive Logics and Governance in Sport," *Punishment & Society* 22, no. 5 (December 1, 2020): 658–80, doi.org/10.1177/1462474520925159.

7. Michael Ralph and Maya Singhal, "Racial Capitalism," *Theory and Society* 48, no. 6 (2019): 851–81.

8. Robinson, *Black Marxism*, 2.

9. Jodi Melamed, "Racial Capitalism," *Critical Ethnic Studies* 1, no. 1 (2015): 77, doi.org/10.5749/jcritethnstud.1.1.0076.

10. Melamed, "Racial Capitalism," 77.

11. Robinson, *Black Marxism*, 2.

12. Melamed, "Racial Capitalism," 78.

13. Bero Rigauer, "Sport and Work," in *Sport and Work* (Columbia University Press, 1981), 68.

14. Hawkins, *The New Plantation*; Johanna Mellis, Nathan Kalman-Lamb, and Derek Silva, "Race, Money and Exploitation: Why College Sport Is Still the 'New Plantation,'" *The Guardian*, September 7, 2021, www.theguardian.com/sport/2021/sep/07/race-money-and-exploitation-why-college-sport-is-still-the-new-plantation.

15. Stanton Wheeler, "Rethinking Amateurism and the NCAA." *Stan. L. & Pol'y Rev.* 15 (2004): 213.

16. Rigauer, "Sport and Work"; Eric Dunning, *Sport Matters*; Hawkins, *The New Plantation*.

17. Dunning, *Sport Matters*.

18. National Collegiate Athletic Assn. v. Alston, 141 S. Ct. 2141 (Supreme Court 2021).

19. At the time of this writing, there are many questions that are still yet to be determined about this plan. These include: Which athletes will get paid, and how much? Will athletes in women's sports and athletes in men's sports both benefit, and how will the money be divided up? What about schools that are not in the Power Five?

20. Billy Witz and Mark Shimabukuro, "Big Money. College Athletes and the N.C.A.A.: A Timeline," *New York Times*, May 29, 2024, sec. US, www.nytimes.com/2024/05/29/us/ncaa-college-athletes-pay-history.html; Becky Sullivan, "What We Know and What We Don't about a Historic Settlement to Pay College Athletes," NPR, May 24, 2024, www.npr.org/2024/05/24/nx-s1-4978680/house-ncaa-settlement-pay-college-athletes.

21. "Ohio State Athletics Reports Rebound in Revenue in 2022," Ohio State News, January 26, 2023, https://news.osu.edu/ohio-state-athletics-reports-rebound-in-revenue-in-2022/.

22. "NCAA Demographics Database," NCAA.org, accessed April 18, 2023, www.ncaa.org/sports/2018/12/13/ncaa-demographics-database.aspx.

23. With even higher proportions if we look only at the Power Five conferences.

24. "NCAA Demographics Database."

25. For a more thorough overview of exploitation and harm in college football, please read Nathan Kalman-Lamb and Derek Silva, *The End of College Football: On the Human Cost of an All-American Game* (Houghton Mifflin Harcourt, 2014).

26. Steve Berkowitz and Tom Schad, "5 Surprising Findings from College Football Coaches Salaries Report," *USA Today*, 2021, www.usatoday.com/story/sports/ncaaf/2020/10/14/college-football-coaches-salaries-five-surprising-findings-data/5900066002/.

27. "Who Gets Paid More, Your College Coach or Your Governor?," ESPN.com, accessed April 19, 2023, www.espn.com/espn/feature/story/_/id/22454170/highest-paid-state-employees-include-ncaa-coaches-nick-saban-john-calipari-dabo-swinney-bill-self-bob-huggins.

28. Kevin Trahan, "All the Stupid Shit Dabo Swinney Has Said, Ranked," Vice (blog), January 1, 2017, www.vice.com/en/article/yp87gy/all-the-stupid-shit-dabo-swinney-has-said-ranked.

29. Dennis Dodd, "As NCAA Zeroes In on College Football Staff Sizes, Survey Shows Inconsistencies," CBSSports.com, May 15, 2017, www.cbssports.com/college-football/news/as-ncaa-zeroes-in-on-college-football-staff-sizes-survey-shows-inconsistencies/.

30. Tom Schad, "Highest-Paid College Football Assistant Coaches: Breaking Down Top 10," *USA Today*, 2022, https://eu.usatoday.com/story/sports/ncaaf/2021/12/09/highest-paid-college-football-assistant-coaches/8889193002/.

31. Division I football is further subdivided into FBS and FCS schools, with FBS accounting for 129 universities, including all of the highest ranked and most prestigious football programs. FCS contains 124 schools, most of which are smaller and play in their own year-end playoff apart from FBS schools.

32. This isn't a hypothetical example. In the most American partnership in history, the weapons producer Lockheed Martin is the title sponsor for a college football postseason bowl game.

33. Isaac Trotter, "Transfer Portal Notebook: Tom Izzo blasts new rules, Matthew Cleveland bombshell, UNC's sneaky-big addition," 247Sports, April 12, 2023, 247sports.com

/LongFormArticle/Transfer-Portal-Notebook-Tom-Izzo-blasts-new-rules-Matthew-Cleveland-bombshell-UNCs-sneaky-big-addition-208206808/.

34. Andrew McGregor, "The Anti-Intellectual Coach: The Cultural Politics of College Football Coaching from the New Left to the Present," *Journal of Sport and Social Issues*, May 16, 2022, 01937235221098915, doi.org/10.1177/01937235221098915.

35. Though with very little concrete action taken on these issues, and a predictable backsliding from whatever small changes did happen in some cities and states.

36. Jake New, "Outrage over a Coach's Comments," Inside Higher Ed, September 15, 2016, www.insidehighered.com/news/2016/09/16/clemson-coach-faces-criticism-over-comments-about-athlete-protests.

37. McGregor, "The Anti-Intellectual Coach," 14.

38. McGregor, "The Anti-Intellectual Coach," 13–14.

39. Erin Hatton, *Coerced: Work under Threat of Punishment* (University of California Press, 2020).

40. Hatton, *Coerced*.

41. Hatton, *Coerced*.

42. Fisher, "Expanding the Frame of 'Voluntariness' in Informed Consent."

43. In an interview for this book.

44. Theresa Runstedtler, "More than Just Play: Unmasking Black Child Labor in the Athletic Industrial Complex," *Journal of Sport and Social Issues* 42, no. 3 (2018): 152–69, doi.org/10.1177/0193723518758458.

45. George Dohrmann, *Play Their Hearts Out: A Coach, His Star Recruit, and the Youth Basketball Machine* (Ballantine Books, 2012), 90.

46. Luke Kane, "Deion Sanders Prefers QBs from Dual-Parent Households, Single Mama Homes for Defensive Linemen When Recruiting." *Mediaite*, February 24, 2023. https://www.mediaite.com/sports/deion-sanders-prefers-qbs-from-dual-parent-households-single-mama-homes-for-defensive-linemen-when-recruiting/.

47. David J. Leonard and C. Richard King, "Introduction: Celebrities, Commodities and Criminals: African American Athletes and the Racial Politics of Culture," in *Commodified and Criminalized: New Racism and African Americans in Contemporary Sports*, ed. David L. Andrews et al. (Rowman and Littlefield, 2010), 9.

48. Van Rheenen, "Exploitation in College Sports."

49. Van Rheenen, "Exploitation in College Sports," 560.

50. Hawkins, *The New Plantation*, 71.

51. Van Rheenen, "Exploitation in College Sports," 562.

52. Rigauer, "Sport and Work."

53. Derek Van Rheenen, "Exploitation in the American Academy: College Athletes and Self-Perceptions of Value," *International Journal of Sport & Society* 2, no. 4 (2011): 19.

54. Shaun Harper, "Black Male Student-Athletes and Racial Inequities in NCAA Division I College Sports," USC Race and Equity Center (2018), https://race.usc.edu/wp-content/uploads/2020/08/Pub-2-Harper-Sports-Report.pdf.

55. In an interview for this book.

56. Statistics Canada, The Daily, "Tuition Fees for Degree Programs, 2021/2022," September 8, 2021, www150.statcan.gc.ca/n1/daily-quotidien/210908/dq210908a-eng.htm.

57. Kalman-Lamb, Silva, and Mellis, "Race, Money and Exploitation."

58. Sara Ganim and Devon Sayers, "UNC Athletics Report Finds 18 Years of Academic Fraud," CNN, October 23, 2014, https://edition.cnn.com/2014/10/22/us/unc-report-academic-fraud/index.html.

59. Shaun R. Harper, Collin D. Williams, and Horatio W. Blackman, *Black Male Student-Athletes and Racial Inequities in NCAA Division I College Sports* (University of Pennsylvania, Center for the Study of Race and Equity in Education, 2013).

60. Think *Grapes of Wrath*.

61. Victoria L. Jackson, "Op-Ed: Take It from a Former Division I Athlete: College Sports Are Like Jim Crow," *Los Angeles Times*, January 11, 2018, www.latimes.com/opinion/op-ed/la-oe-jackson-college-sports-20180111-story.html.

62. Burstyn, *The Rites of Men*, 141.

63. Daniel Taylor, "'13 Years Down the Drain. Just like That'—The Premier League's Forgotten Kids," *The Athletic*, April 12, 2020, https://theathletic.com/1721538/2020/04/12/premier-league-manchester-united-city-academy-released/?source=twitterads&ad_id=37335173&twclid=2-4trbgq2gfbc4f0o16zonlivkb.

64. Tim Gill, "In the WWE, Wrestlers Say Labor Abuses Are Everywhere," *Jacobin*, October 13, 2022, https://jacobin.com/2022/10/wwe-vince-mcmahon-wrestling-unions-health.

65. James Caldwell, "Forbes Publishes Top 10 List of WWE Wrestler Pay, Including Percentage Compared to Rest of the Roster & Total WWE Revenue," Pro Wrestling Torch (blog), March 31, 2016, www.pwtorch.com/site/2016/03/31/forbes-publishes-top-10-list-wwe-wrestler-pay-including-percentage-compared-rest-roster-total-wwe-revenue/.

66. K. M. Corteen, "A Critical Criminology of Professional Wrestling and Sports Entertainment," *Popular Culture Studies Journal: Special Edition-Professional Wrestling* 6, no. 1 (2018): 138–54.

67. Corteen, "A Critical Criminology," 149.

68. Hillyard and Tombs, "Social Harm and Zemiology."

69. Karen Corteen, "Critical Criminology and State Power," in *A Companion to Criminal Justice, Mental Health and Risk*, ed. Paul Taylor, Karen Corteen, and Sharon Morley (Policy Press, 2014).

70. Michalowski, "What Is Crime?," 188.

71. Friedrich Engels, *The Condition of the Working Class in England* (Oxford University Press, 1845), 126–27.

72. Corteen, "A Critical Criminology of Professional Wrestling and Sports Entertainment," 148.

73. Jon Swartz, "High Death Rate Lingers behind Fun Facade of Pro Wrestling," *USA Today*, 2004, 2C.

74. ABC News, "Benoit's Brain Showed Severe Damage from Multiple Concussions, Doctor and Dad Say," ABC News, January 8, 2009, https://abcnews.go.com/GMA/story?id=3560015.

75. Gill, "In the WWE, Wrestlers Say Labor Abuses Are Everywhere."

76. Gill, "In the WWE, Wrestlers Say Labor Abuses Are Everywhere."

77. Corteen, "A Critical Criminology of Professional Wrestling and Sports Entertainment."

78. Dan O'Sullivan, "Money in the Bank," in *The Best American Sports Writing, 2015*, ed. Wright Thompson (Houghton Mifflin Harcourt, 2015).

79. Corteen, "A Critical Criminology of Professional Wrestling and Sports Entertainment," 143.

80. Gill, "In the WWE, Wrestlers Say Labor Abuses Are Everywhere."

81. Marc Normandin, "Here's Why Minor League Baseball Players Haven't Unionized," SBNation.com, June 5, 2018, www.sbnation.com/mlb/2018/6/5/17251534/mlb-draft-minor-league-baseball-union-phpa.

82. Normandin, "Here's Why Minor League Baseball Players Haven't Unionized."

83. Michael Baumann, "The Disgrace of Minor League Baseball," The Ringer, April 20, 2018, www.theringer.com/mlb/2018/4/20/17259846/minor-league-baseball-anti-labor-ronald-acuna-scott-kingery.

84. Stephen Shimshi, "Major League Baseball and the Exploitation of Latin American Children: Confronting Baseball's Greatest Sin," *Family Court Review* 60, no. 4 (2022): 904, doi.org/10.1111/fcre.12682.

85. Diana L. Spagnuolo, "Swinging for the Fence: A Call for Institutional Reform as Dominican Boys Risk Their Futures for a Chance in Major League Baseball," *University of Pennsylvania Journal of International Law* 24 (2003): 263; Shimshi, "Major League Baseball."

86. Emily B. Ottenson, "The Social Cost of Baseball: Addressing the Effects of Major League Baseball Recruitment in Latin America and the Caribbean," *Washington University Global Studies Law Review* 13 (2014): 767.

87. Juan Herrera, "Latin American Baseball Players Face Hurdles in Their Quest to Reach the Big League," Latino Reporter (blog), July 20, 2018, https://latinoreporter.org/2018/latin-american-baseball-players-face-hurdles-in-their-quest-to-reach-the-big-league/.

88. Shimshi, "Major League Baseball."

89. Normandin, "Here's Why Minor League Baseball Players Haven't Unionized."

90. Kelly Candaele and Peter Dreier, "How Minor League Ballplayers Won a Union," *The Nation*, March 6, 2023, www.thenation.com/article/society/minor-league-baseball-union-bill-fletcher/.

91. Jeff Passan, "Sources: Minor Leaguers, MLB Reach Deal on CBA," ESPN.com, March 30, 2023, www.espn.com/mlb/story/_/id/35998626/minor-leaguers-mlb-reach-tentative-deal-historic-1st-cba.

92. Karl Marx and Friedrich Engels, "Address of the Central Committee to the Communist League by Marx and Engels," 1850, www.marxists.org/archive/marx/works/1847/communist-league/1850-ad1.htm.

93. Candaele and Dreier, "How Minor League Ballplayers Won a Union."

94. Candaele and Dreier, "How Minor League Ballplayers Won a Union."

95. Candaele and Dreier, "How Minor League Ballplayers Won a Union."

96. Candaele and Dreier, "How Minor League Ballplayers Won a Union."

97. I'm looking at you, fossil fuel executives and financial analysts.

98. David J. Leonard, *Playing While White: Privilege and Power on and off the Field*, (Seattle: University of Washington Press, 2017), 37–38.

99. Karl Marx, *Das Kapital: A Critique of Political Economy*, ed. Friedrich Engels (Regnery, 1959), 48.

100. Normandin, "Here's Why Minor League Baseball Players Haven't Unionized."

101. Nathan Kalman-Lamb and Derek Silva, "'Play'Ing College Football: Campus Athletic Worker Experiences of Exploitation," *Critical Sociology* 50, no. 4–5 (2023), doi.org/10.1177/08969205231208036.

102. Matthew G. Hawzen et al., "Cruel Optimism in Sport Management: Fans, Affective Labor, and the Political Economy of Internships in the Sport Industry," *Journal of Sport and Social Issues* 42, no. 3 (June 2018): 184–204, doi.org/10.1177/0193723518758457.

103. Lauren Berlant, *Cruel Optimism* (Duke University Press, 2011), 1, doi.org/10.1515/9780822394716.

104. Hawzen et al., "Cruel Optimism in Sport Management."

105. Marx, *Das Kapital: A Critique of Political Economy*.

106. Hawzen et al., "Cruel Optimism in Sport Management," 195.

107. Hawzen et al., "Cruel Optimism in Sport Management."

108. Ben Solomen, "Duke's Basketball Managers Strive to Be (What Else?) Elite," *New York Times*, March 22, 2018, https://www.nytimes.com/2018/03/22/sports/ncaabasketball/duke-managers.html.

Chapter Six

1. Kevin Young, *Sport, Violence and Society*, 1st ed. (Routledge, 2012), 42.

2. Jerry M. Lewis, *Sports Fan Violence in North America* (Rowman and Littlefield, 2007).

3. Lewis, *Sports Fan Violence*; Kevin Young, *Sport, Violence and Society*, 2nd ed. (Routledge, 2019); Lynn Marie Jamieson and Thomas J. Orr, *Sport and Violence: A Critical Examination of Sport* (Routledge, 2009).

4. Jens Omli and Nicole M. LaVoi, "Emotional Experiences of Youth Sport Parents I: Anger," *Journal of Applied Sport Psychology* 24, no. 1 (2012): 10–25.

5. Daniel L. Wann et al., "Sport Team Identification and Willingness to Consider Anonymous Acts of Hostile Aggression," *Aggressive Behavior: Official Journal of the International Society for Research on Aggression* 29, no. 5 (2003): 406–13.

6. Peter E. Marsh, *Aggro: Illusion of Violence* (J. M. Dent, 1978).

7. Eric Dunning et al., *Fighting Fans: Football Hooliganism as a World Phenomenon* (University College Dublin Press, 2002).

8. Ian Taylor, "Putting the Boot into a Working-Class Sport: British Soccer after Bradford and Brussels," *Sociology of Sport Journal* 4, no. 2 (June 1, 1987): 171–91, doi.org/10.1123/ssj.4.2.171.

9. Peter E. Marsh, *Aggro: Illusion of Violence* (J. M. Dent, 1978).

10. Bill Gilbert and Lisa Twyman, "Violence: Out of Hand in the Stands," *Sports Illustrated* 58, no. 4 (1983): 71.

11. Scott A. Melzer, "Gender, Work, and Intimate Violence: Men's Occupational Violence Spillover and Compensatory Violence," *Journal of Marriage and Family* 64, no. 4 (2002): 820–32, doi.org/10.1111/j.1741-3737.2002.00820.x; Susan J. Lambert, "Processes Linking Work and Family: A Critical Review and Research Agenda," *Human Relations* 43, no. 3 (1990): 239–57.

12. Robert L. Peralta and Lori A. Tuttle, "Male Perpetrators of Heterosexual-Partner-Violence: The Role of Threats to Masculinity," *Journal of Men's Studies* 21, no. 3 (2013): 255–76.

13. Young, *Sport, Violence and Society*, 2nd ed., 115.

14. I know math is more complicated than this, but you get what I mean.

15. In Taylor's case, his work was clearly not trying to villainize working-class people but instead was meant to highlight the structural conditions of capitalism and their role in alienating working-class people, but the effect of linking spectator violence solely with working-class people in the media and cultural mainstream had this broader effect.

16. Young, *Sport, Violence and Society*, 2nd ed., 119.

17. Young, *Sport, Violence and Society*, 2nd ed., 131; Nyla R. Branscombe and Daniel L. Wann, "Role of Identification with a Group, Arousal, Categorization Processes, and Self-Esteem in Sports Spectator Aggression," *Human Relations* 45, no. 10 (1992): 1013–33; Daniel L. Wann et al., *Sport Fans: The Psychology and Social Impact of Spectators* (Routledge, 2001).

18. Branscombe and Wann, "Role of Identification with a Group," 1017.

19. Ramón Spaaij, "Sports Crowd Violence: An Interdisciplinary Synthesis," *Aggression and Violent Behavior* 19, no. 2 (March 1, 2014): 146–55, doi.org/10.1016/j.avb.2014.02.002.

20. Russell E. Ward Jr, "Fan Violence: Social Problem or Moral Panic?," *Aggression and Violent Behavior* 7, no. 5 (2002): 2.

21. Gamal Abdel-Shehid, *Who da man?: Black masculinities and sporting cultures*, (Canadian Scholars' Press, 2005); Nathan Kalman-Lamb, "Imagined communities of fandom: sport, spectatorship, meaning and alienation in late capitalism," *Sport in Society* 24, no. 6 (2021): 922–936. For a modern, non-sport example, take what is happening in America right now, with regards to the constant deluge of anti-China reporting as the United States begins its next iteration of the Cold War.

22. Obviously not everything is predetermined in a concert or performance—the set list might be different, the quality of a particular performance or event can be drastically different from show to show, a politician may say something crazy—but this is quite different from the final result of a sporting event being unknown when it starts.

23. Young, *Sport, Violence and Society*, 2nd ed., 132.

24. Kalman-Lamb, "Imagined Communities of Fandom."

25. Merim Bilalić, Bartosz Gula, and Nemanja Vaci, "Home Advantage Mediated (HAM) by Referee Bias and Team Performance during Covid," *Scientific Reports* 11, no. 1 (November 3, 2021): 21558, doi.org/10.1038/s41598-021-00784-8.

26. Kevin Young has written extensively on the topics of spectator violence and hooliganism. See Young, *Sport, Violence and Society*, 1st ed. (2012), 2nd ed. (2019); Young, "'The Killing Field': Themes in Mass Media Responses to the Heysel Stadium Riot," *International Review for the Sociology of Sport* 21, no. 2–3 (June 1, 1986): 253–66, doi.org/10.1177/101269028602100213; Young, "Hidden in Plain Sight: Sports-Related Violence"; Michael Atkinson and Kevin Young, "Shadowed by the Corpse of War: Sport Spectacles and the Spirit of Terrorism," *International Review for the Sociology of Sport* 47, no. 3 (2012): 286–306.

27. Young, *Sport, Violence and Society*, 1st ed., 66.

28. Spaaij, "Sports Crowd Violence," 150.

29. Spaaij, "Sports Crowd Violence," 153.

30. To "mark," for my European football (soccer) fans/readers.

31. An increasingly common occurrence in our new sport gambling-scape.

32. I have a very vivid memory of being floored while reading about this phenomenon, and then actually speaking to someone (a vehement sports hater) at a party about this

around the same time. I think it hit me so hard because I realized that for so long I had been guilty of this, as I still am now, though to a lesser extent. When I was seventeen, I could tell you every member of the New York Giants team and of Team Canada's Olympic men's hockey team, and not a thing about Montreal or Quebec politics.

33. Hargreaves, "Sport, Power and Culture."

34. Jules Boykoff, "Toward a theory of sportswashing: Mega-events, soft power, and political conflict," *Sociology of sport journal* 39, no. 4 (2022): 342–51; Paul Hoch, *Rip Off the Big Game: The Exploitation of Sports by the Power Elite* (Doubleday, 1972); M. Weed, "Are sport mega-events an opiate for the middle classes?" *Journal of Sport & Tourism*, 21 (4) (2017), 243–44.

35. Which arose because of the resistance and demands of organized labor, not because of any "altruism" from the bosses. Don't let big business propaganda get the best of you!

36. Hargreaves, "Sport, Power and Culture."

37. Marx, *Economic and Philosophic Manuscripts of 1844*, 15.

38. Kalman-Lamb, "Athletic Labor and Social Reproduction."

39. Kalman-Lamb, "Athletic Labor and Social Reproduction."

40. Nathan Kalman-Lamb, *Game Misconduct: Injury, Fandom, and the Business of Sport* (Fernwood, 2018); Benedict Anderson, *Imagined Communities: Reflections on the Origin and Spread of Nationalism* (Verso, 1991).

41. Jay Coakley, *Sports in Society: Issues and Controversies*. 6th ed. (New York: McGraw Hill, 1998), 204.

42. In Canada, "minor hockey" refers to amateur, unpaid, nonprofessional playing levels. Most minor hockey league players are under the age of eighteen, and most spectators at minor hockey games are friends or relatives of players, with parents as the most frequent spectators.

43. Nicholas L. Holt et al., "Parental Involvement in Competitive Youth Sport Settings," *Psychology of Sport and Exercise* 9, no. 5 (2008): 663–85; Jens Omli and Diane M. Wiese-Bjornstal, "Kids Speak: Preferred Parental Behavior at Youth Sport Events," *Research Quarterly for Exercise and Sport* 82, no. 4 (2011): 702–11.

44. Daniel Sailofsky and Curtis Fogel, "Rage at the Rink: Parental Aggression in Quebec Minor Hockey," *Journal of Emerging Sport Studies* 9 (2023), https://journals.library.brocku.ca/index.php/jess/article/view/4398.

45. Sailofsky and Fogel, "Rage at the Rink."

46. Brian Fowler et al., "Ice Hockey Officiating Retention: A Qualitative Understanding of Junior Ice Hockey Officials' Motivations in Canada," *Managing Sport and Leisure* 24 (January 13, 2019): 3, doi.org/10.1080/23750472.2019.1565944.

47. Brittany L. Jacobs et al., "Exploring Referee Abuse through the Lens of the Collegiate Rugby Coach," *Sport Management Review* 23, no. 1 (February 1, 2020): 39–51, doi.org/10.1016/j.smr.2019.03.004; Tom Webb et al., "An Analysis of Soccer Referee Experiences in France and the Netherlands: Abuse, Conflict, and Level of Support," *Sport Management Review* 23, no. 1 (2020): 52–65.

48. Annette Lareau, *Unequal Childhoods: Class, Race, and Family Life* (University of California Press, 2011).

49. Sean Gregory, "How Kids' Sports Became a $15 Billion Industry," *Time*, August 24, 2017, https://time.com/4913687/how-kids-sports-became-15-billion-industry/.

50. In many ways we've seen something similar happen with private tutors, test prep, and other efforts from parents trying to ensure that their children get into the best universities. Perhaps it's always been common for wealthier families to pay for private instruction in high school or just to pay (sorry, "donate to") top universities to make sure their children get in, but these processes are now happening earlier and earlier. As school disparities continue to widen in places like the United States and the United Kingdom, it is not uncommon to hear about parents and children stressing about getting into the right middle school or high school, with the understanding that this could impact the rest of their school and career trajectory.

51. Gregory, "How Kids' Sports Became a $15 Billion Industry."

52. Richard Blundell, Jonathan Cribb, Sandra McNally, Ross Warwick, and Xiaowei Xu, "Inequalities in education, skills, and incomes in the UK: The implications of the COVID-19 pandemic," *Institute for Fiscal Studies* (2021): 1–42; Roseanne L. Flores, "The rising gap between rich and poor: A look at the persistence of educational disparities in the United States and why we should worry." *Cogent Social Sciences* 3, no. 1 (2017): 1323698.

53. Audrey Addi-Raccah and Oshra Dana, "Private tutoring intensity in schools: a comparison between high and low socio-economic schools." *International Studies in Sociology of Education* 25, no. 3 (2015): 183–203; M. C. Pascoe, S. E. Hetrick, and A. G. Parker, "The impact of stress on students in secondary school and higher education." *International journal of adolescence and youth*, 25 (1) (2020): 104–12.

54. Roy Cooper and Andy Beshear, "Republicans Want to Loot Public Schools for Private Vouchers," *USA Today*, February 26, 2024, https://www.usatoday.com/story/opinion/2024/02/26/republicans-cut-public-schools-for-private-kentucky-north-carolina/72670677007/.

55. Gregory, "How Kids' Sports Became a $15 Billion Industry."

56. "Amateur Athletic Union (AAU)," accessed April 27, 2023, https://aausports.org/page.php?page_id=99844.

57. Shaun Assael, "Fancy Hotels, Pricey Dinners, $1.5M AAU Payout," ESPN.com, November 19, 2015, www.espn.co.uk/espn/otl/story/_/id/14172814/as-aau-grows-questions-how-spends-money-adheres-mission.

58. I consider myself part of this group, as a former collegiate basketball coach and a current old-school curmudgeon, at least when we're talking about basketball and the best ways to play.

59. "The Circuit to the NBA: A Complete Breakdown of AAU Alumni in the NBA," Circuit Scouting, June 10, 2021, www.circuitscouting.com/news_article/show/1168970-the-circuit-to-the-nba-a-complete-breakdown-of-aau-alumni-in-the-nba.

60. "Football Camps USA—College Football Recruiting Camps," Football Camps USA, accessed April 27, 2023, www.footballcampsusa.com/.

61. Nathan Kalman-Lamb and Ian Kennedy, "How a Toronto Hockey League Turns Kids' Joy into an $8.8m Cash Cow," *The Guardian*, March 10, 2023, sec. Sport, www.theguardian.com/sport/2023/mar/10/greater-toronto-hockey-league-income-fees.

62. Which, for all intents and purposes, are mandatory for those hoping to play the sport professionally.

63. Scott N. Brooks, Stacey Flores, and Anthony J. Weems, "On the Frontlines: Black Boys and Injury in Basketball," in *The Palgrave Handbook of Sport, Politics and Harm*,

ed. Stephen Wagg and Allyson M. Pollock (Springer International, 2021), 365–84, doi.org/10.1007/978-3-030-72826-7_18.

64. Baxter Holmes, "Under the Knife: Exposing America's Youth Basketball Crisis," ESPN.com, July 12, 2019, www.espn.co.uk/nba/story/_/id/27148543/under-knife-exposing-america-youth-basketball-crisis.

65. This tendency to treat young Black children and teenagers as adults is reminiscent of the way police and media often talk about (and act on) young Black boys and teenagers accused of crime or misbehavior. Kids like Trayvon Martin (who was seventeen at the time of his murder by two white "neighborhood watch" men) are framed as "dangerous men," while the Brock Turners and Brett Kavanaughs are described as "promising young boys and men" who have '"made a mistake." Kimberly Lane et al., "The Framing of Race: Trayvon Martin and the Black Lives Matter Movement," *Journal of Black Studies* 51, no. 8 (November 1, 2020): 790–812, doi.org/10.1177/0021934720946802; JoAnne Sweeny, "'Brock Turner Is Not a Rapist': The Danger of Rape Myths in Character Letters in Sexual Assault Cases," *UMKC Law Review* 89 (2020): 121.

66. Runstedtler, "More Than Just Play," 155.

67. Runstedtler, "More than Just Play," 155.

68. Jason Jordan, "A Mixtape Changed His Life at 14. Now He's Picking Up the Pieces," *Sports Illustrated*, March 3, 2022, www.si.com/college/2022/03/03/seventh-woods-viral-video-unc-morgan-state.

69. Maybe I spend too much time on social media, but that's neither here nor there.

70. Parent and Fortier, "Comprehensive Overview of the Problem of Violence against Athletes in Sport"; Brenner and Council on Sports Medicine and Fitness, "Sports Specialization and Intensive Training in Young Athletes"; Karrer et al., "Disordered Eating and Eating Disorders in Male Elite Athletes"; Thames and Abrams, "Female College Athletes Say Pressure to Cut Body Fat Is Toxic."

71. Spaaij, "Sports Crowd Violence," 149; Atkinson and Young, *Deviance and Social Control in Sport*.

72. Agoes Basoeki and Niniek Karmini, "125 Die as Tear Gas Triggers Crush at Indonesia Soccer Match," AP NEWS, October 2, 2022, https://apnews.com/article/sports-soccer-police-indonesia-java-c31edecf524ddbb1d3a4b276c581d0b0.

73. Richard Craig, "Malice in the Palace: The Incident," *Spectrum: A Journal on Black Men* 4, no. 2 (2016): 21–41.

74. Young, "The Killing Field."

75. Ian King, "As Bad As Things Got: Millwall, 13th March 1985," Two Hundred Per Cent (blog), March 7, 2021, https://twohundredpercent.net/bad-things-millwall/.

76. King, "As Bad As Things Got."

77. Young, "The Killing Field," 262.

78. Young, "The Killing Field," 262–63.

79. Andrew Misell, "Good Sports?—Alcohol Advertising and Sponsorship in Sport," Alcohol Change UK, June 2021, https://alcoholchange.org.uk/blog/2021/good-sports.

80. Misell, "Good Sports?"

81. Christina Gough, "Spending on Game Day Alcohol among Sports Fans in the US 2021," Statista, May 19, 2022, www.statista.com/statistics/1224226/sport-fans-game-day-expenditure/.

82. If the complete 180 of sport institutions going from punishing sports gambling to plastering it on every advertisement possible doesn't show you that deviance and crime is a social construction, nothing will.

83. Kalman-Lamb, "Athletic Labor and Social Reproduction."

Chapter Seven

1. Farmer et al., "Structural Violence and Clinical Medicine," 1686.

2. Maurice Roche, *Megaevents and Modernity: Olympics and Expos in the Growth of Global Culture* (Routledge, 2002); John Horne, "Sports Mega-Events—Three Sites of Contemporary Political Contestation," *Sport in Society* 20, no. 3 (2017): 329.

3. Dave Zirin, *Brazil's Dance with the Devil: The World Cup, the Olympics, and the Struggle for Democracy* (Haymarket Books, 2016), 212.

4. The host city and country population are usually the most impacted, but we must also keep in mind the many migrant laborers who build much of the mega-event infrastructure needed.

5. Whether we need to completely reimagine the mega-event structure will come later, in the section on environmental damage.

6. This last claim is especially egregious—obviously governments could just invest in their cities and in their people *without* these kinds of events.

7. Jules Boykoff, "Toward a Theory of Sportswashing: Mega-Events, Soft Power, and Political Conflict," *Sociology of Sport Journal* 39, no. 4 (2022): 1–10, doi.org/10.1123/ssj.2022-0095.

8. It's also important to note that which countries we'd consider "authoritarian" versus "democratic" is in itself a more complicated question than how it is often presented. For example, the United States is often presented as a great democracy, even though citizens (and only citizens—undocumented people, incarcerated people, and many people with past felonies cannot vote) generally vote only once every four years to pick between two candidates, both of whom represent capitalist parties who would, in most worldwide contexts, be considered far-right and center-right options. Many Americans also don't vote, because of either apathy, voter suppression, or the fact that states are often so solidly in favor of one party that their vote is ultimately meaningless. The vast majority of Americans also have no democratic say in their workplaces—union membership is currently sitting at a paltry 11.3 percent—and little say in their local governments. This is not to say that the United States is alone in this kind of lack of representation and democratic say, but instead to point out that our democratic-authoritarian binaries are not as simple as they are presented.

9. Boykoff, "Toward a Theory of Sportswashing."

10. Werner Bonefeld, "Democracy and Dictatorship: Means and Ends of the State," *Critique* 34, no. 3 (2006): 237–52, doi:10.1080/03017600600994661; R. Luxemburg, *Reform or Revolution* (London: Bookmarks, 1899/1989): 47.

11. Joseph S. Nye, "Public Diplomacy and Soft Power," *Annals of the American Academy of Political and Social Science* 616 (2008): 94–109.

12. Janice Bially Mattern, "Why soft power isn't so soft: representational force and the sociolinguistic construction of attraction in world politics," *Millennium* 33, no. 3 (2005): 583–612. This quote is from page 586.

13. IOC, "Olympic Games—Summer, Winter Olympics, YOG & Paralympics," Olympics.com, accessed May 23, 2023, https://olympics.com/en/olympic-games.

14. Vancouver Organizing Committee for the 2010 Olympic and Paralympic Winter Games, "Vancouver 2010 Sustainability Report," 2010, https://digital.la84.org/digital/collection/p17103coll8/id/45479/.

15. Clayton Thomas-Müller, "We Need to Start Calling out Corporate 'Redwashing,'" CBC, March 20, 2017, www.cbc.ca/news/opinion/corporate-redwashing-1.4030443.

16. Though other research has shown dwindling public support within Russia for the Sochi Olympics. Anna Alekseyeva, "Sochi 2014 and the Rhetoric of a New Russia: Image Construction through Mega-Events," *East European Politics* 30, no. 2 (April 3, 2014): 158–74, doi.org/10.1080/21599165.2013.877710.

17. Fan Hong and Yuting Zhong, "China and the Olympic Games," in *The Routledge Handbook of Sport in Asia* (Routledge, 2020).

18. Dogan Gursoy et al., "Temporal Change in Resident Perceptions of a Mega-Event: The Beijing 2008 Olympic Games," *Tourism Geographies* 13, no. 2 (2011): 299–324.

19. Adrian E. Bauman et al., "An Evidence-Based Assessment of the Impact of the Olympic Games on Population Levels of Physical Activity," *Lancet* 398, no. 10298 (2021): 456–64; Simona Azzali, "The Legacies of Sochi 2014 Winter Olympics: An Evaluation of the Adler Olympic Park," *Urban Research & Practice* 10, no. 3 (July 3, 2017): 329–49, doi.org/10.1080/17535069.2016.1216586; Alan Tomlinson, "Olympic Legacies: Recurrent Rhetoric and Harsh Realities," *Contemporary Social Science* 9, no. 2 (April 3, 2014): 137–58, doi.org/10.1080/21582041.2014.912792.

20. Zirin, *Brazil's Dance with the Devil*.

21. Jules Boykoff, "Celebration Capitalism, Sports Mega-Events, and the Tokyo 2020 Olympics," *Journal of Sport and Gender Studies* 19 (2021): 50–66, doi.org/10.18967/sptgender.19.0_50.

22. Jules Boykoff, "What Is the Real Price of the London Olympics?," *The Guardian*, April 4, 2012, sec. Opinion, www.theguardian.com/commentisfree/2012/apr/04/price-of-london-olympics.

23. No, this is not a typo. The Qatar World Cup cost 15 times the previous World Cup in Russia in 2018, due mainly to the sheer number of new mega-stadiums and immense hospitality infrastructure that needed to be built for such a tiny country to host such a huge event.

24. Zirin, *Brazil's Dance with the Devil*, 187.

25. Zirin, *Brazil's Dance with the Devil*, 152.

26. Horne, "Sports Mega-Events," 333.

27. Amy Goodman, Dave Zirin, and Juan Gonzalez, "'A Neo-Liberal Trojan Horse': Dave Zirin on Brazil's Mass Protests against World Cup Displacement," Democracy Now!, accessed May 23, 2023, http://www.democracynow.org/2014/6/19/a_neo_liberal_trojan_horse_dave.

28. Zirin, *Brazil's Dance with the Devil*, 53–54.

29. Zirin, *Brazil's Dance with the Devil*, 179.

30. Zirin, *Brazil's Dance with the Devil*, 179.

31. David Poort, "Brazil World Cup," July 3, 2014, *Al Jazeera*, www.aljazeera.com/sports/2014/7/3/blatter-where-are-brazils-protesters.

32. Zirin, *Brazil's Dance with the Devil*.

33. Pat Hartman, "Vancouver Olympics Aftermath Studied," House the Homeless, February 17, 2011, https://housethehomeless.org/vancouver-olympics-aftermath-studied/.

34. Oliver Harvey, "Homeless and Away," *The Sun*, April 19, 2010.

35. Zirin, *Brazil's Dance with the Devil*, 157.

36. If this name rings a bell, it may be because he is most famous for his statement "The Games must go on" following the murder of eleven Israeli athletes during the 1972 Munich Olympics, or for steadfastly holding to the idea that the apartheid state of Rhodesia should not be excluded from the Games. He was also nicknamed "Slavery Avery" for his antisemitism and anti-Black racism.

37. Mary Beadnell, "Sydney's Homeless to Be Removed for Olympics," World Socialist Web Site, February 3, 2000, www.wsws.org/en/articles/2000/02/olymp-f03.html.

38. Helen Jefferson Lenskyj, *Olympic Industry Resistance: Challenging Olympic Power and Propaganda* (SUNY Press, 2008).

39. Zirin, *Brazil's Dance with the Devil*.

40. Adam Talbot, "There Will Be Gentrification: A Pattern of Displacement at the Olympics," RioOnWatch (blog), February 1, 2016, https://rioonwatch.org/?p=25651.

41. Although media framing and some politicians may present a different picture, most unhoused people have jobs and work.

42. The Khafala system tied workers to their employers, giving the workers no leverage or ability to change jobs or even leave the country. Under this system, workers were functionally indentured servants—employers could withhold pay, work, or even their passports.

43. Pete Pattisson, Niamh McIntyre, and Imran Mukhtar, "Revealed: 6,500 Migrant Workers Have Died in Qatar since World Cup Awarded," *The Guardian*, February 23, 2021, sec. Global Development, www.theguardian.com/global-development/2021/feb/23/revealed-migrant-worker-deaths-qatar-fifa-world-cup-2022.

44. Host governments like to pretend that everyone in the city or country is on board with the mega-event, but striking workers and activists are as much a part of the World Cup and Olympics as competition and Coca-Cola are.

45. The rest of this section on favelas comes from Zirin, *Brazil's Dance with the Devil*, chap. 7, "Target Favelas."

46. Zirin, *Brazil's Dance with the Devil*.

47. In a reverse relationship, compared to most cities, in Rio the poor live on the mountains and the rich in the valley, and have for generations.

48. Just more evidence that organized, collective resistance *can* work.

49. Turns out that building a sliding center in a country with no history of or interest in niche winter sliding sports isn't super sustainable. Who'd have thought?

50. Dave Zirin and Jules Boykoff, "The Gritty Reality of the Winter Games," *Los Angeles Times*, February 8, 2018, sec. Main News, part A, Opinion Desk.

51. Zirin, *Brazil's Dance with the Devil*, 38.

52. Zirin, *Brazil's Dance with the Devil*, 47.

53. Martin Müller, "After Sochi 2014: Costs and Impacts of Russia's Olympic Games," *Eurasian Geography and Economics* 55, no. 6 (2014): 628–55.

54. Zirin, *Brazil's Dance with the Devil*, 187.

55. Azzali, "The Legacies of Sochi 2014 Winter Olympics."
56. Azzali, "The Legacies of Sochi 2014 Winter Olympics," 341.
57. Azzali, "The Legacies of Sochi 2014 Winter Olympics."
58. Zirin, *Brazil's Dance with the Devil*, 27.
59. Jules Boykoff and Dave Zirin, "Will L.A. Rerun Tokyo's Olympics Mistakes?," *Los Angeles Times*, July 24, 2019, sec. Main News, part A, Opinion Desk.
60. Bent Flyvbjerg, Allison Stewart, and Alexander Budzier, "The Oxford Olympics Study 2016: Cost and Cost Overrun at the Games," SSRN Scholarly Paper (Rochester, NY, July 1, 2016), doi.org/10.2139/ssrn.2804554.
61. Zirin, *Brazil's Dance with the Devil*, 14.
62. Anne-Marie Broudehoux, "Mega-Events, Urban Image Construction, and the Politics of Exclusion," in *Mega-Events and Globalization*, ed. Richard S. Gruneau and John Horne (Routledge, 2015).
63. Vida Bajc, "Surveillance and Security of the Olympic Games: Globalization of Inequalities through Sport," in Silva and Kennedy, *Power Played*, 261.
64. Bajc, "Surveillance and Security of the Olympic Games," 263.
65. Sandra Laville, "Olympics Welcome Does Not Extend to All in London as Police Flex Muscles," *The Guardian*, May 4, 2012, sec. UK news, www.theguardian.com/uk/2012/may/04/olympics-welcome-london-police.
66. Jacqueline Kennelly, "Policing the Young and the Poor in Olympic Neighbourhoods: The Security Legacy in Stratford, London (2012)," in Silva and Kennedy, *Power Played*, 308.
67. Boykoff and Zirin, "Will L.A. Rerun Tokyo's Olympics Mistakes?"
68. Canadian Press, "1,000 Security Cameras Watching Vancouver, Whistler," CTV News, February 1, 2010, https://bc.ctvnews.ca/1-000-security-cameras-watching-vancouver-whistler-1.479563.
69. Boykoff and Zirin, "Will L.A. Rerun Tokyo's Olympics Mistakes?"
70. "Japan: UN Special Rapporteur Expresses Concern over the Government's Conspiracy Bill," Human Rights Now, (blog), June 1, 2017, https://hrn.or.jp/eng/news/2017/06/01/japan-conspiracy-bill/.
71. Holger Preuss, "The Conceptualisation and Measurement of Mega Sport Event Legacies," *Journal of Sport & Tourism* 12, no. 3–4 (2007): 211.
72. Jack Todd, "The 40-Year Hangover: How the 1976 Olympics Nearly Broke Montreal," *The Guardian*, July 6, 2016, sec. Cities, www.theguardian.com/cities/2016/jul/06/40-year-hangover-1976-olympic-games-broke-montreal-canada.
73. Judith Mair et al., "Social Impacts of Mega-Events: A Systematic Narrative Review and Research Agenda," *Journal of Sustainable Tourism* 31, no. 2 (2021): 1–22, doi.org/10.1080/09669582.2020.1870989; Madeleine Orr and Nigel Jarvis, "Blinded by Gold: Toronto Sports Community Ignores Negative Legacies of 2015 Pan Am Games," *Event Management* 22, no. 3 (2018): 367–78; Tomlinson, "Olympic Legacies."
74. Orr and Jarvis, "Blinded by Gold."
75. Maryse Zeidler, "10 Years Later, Indigenous Tourism Still Reaps the Benefits of the 2010 Olympics," CBC, February 22, 2020, www.cbc.ca/news/canada/british-columbia/vancouver-olympics-indigenous-tourism-1.5471686.
76. Oliver Wainwright, "'A Massive Betrayal': How London's Olympic Legacy Was Sold Out," *The Guardian*, June 30, 2022, sec. UK News, www.theguardian.com/uk-news/2022

/jun/30/a-massive-betrayal-how-londons-olympic-legacy-was-sold-out; Müller, "After Sochi 2014."

77. Madeleine Orr and Yuhei Inoue, "Practitioner Perspectives of Legacy: Insights from the 2015 Pan Am Games," *Qualitative Research in Sport, Exercise and Health* 12, no. 5 (2020): 717–29, doi.org/10.1080/2159676X.2019.1673468.

78. Wainwright, "'A Massive Betrayal.'"

79. Caroline Taïx, "London Still Awaits Olympic's Promised 'Affordable' Housing," Barron's, March 24, 2024, www.barrons.com/news/london-still-awaits-olympic-s-promised-affordable-housing-62afdfa4.

80. The UK's version of public housing.

81. Wainwright, "'A Massive Betrayal.'"

82. Bauman et al., "An Evidence-Based Assessment of the Impact of the Olympic Games."

83. Bruce Douglas, "Brazil Officials Evict Families from Homes Ahead of 2016 Olympic Games," *The Guardian*, October 28, 2015, sec. World News, www.theguardian.com/world/2015/oct/28/brazil-officials-evicting-families-2016-olympic-games.

84. Michael McDougall and MacIntosh Ross, "The Olympics Is a Disaster for People Who Live in Host Cities," *Washington Post*, July 29, 2021, www.washingtonpost.com/outlook/2021/07/29/olympics-is-disaster-people-who-live-host-cities/.

85. E. M. Swift, "The Road to Rio Is Paved with Broken Promises," WBUR, May 26, 2016, www.wbur.org/cognoscenti/2016/05/26/international-olympic-committee-legacy-sochi-e-m-swift-olympics; Müller, "After Sochi 2014."

86. NOlympics LA, 2022, https://nolympicsla.com/.

87. Recreation Calgary, "Potential Bid for the 2026 Olympic and Paralympic Winter Games," www.calgary.ca/content/www/en/home/csps/recreation/calgary-2026-olympic-bid/olympics-bid-2026.html; Shannon Sims, "How Bostonians Defeated the Olympics," Bloomberg.Com, June 5, 2017, https://www.bloomberg.com/news/articles/2017-06-05/how-boston-citizens-defeated-the-city-s-olympic-bid; Susie An, "Anti-Chicago Olympics Group Is Relieved," WBEZ Chicago, October 2, 2009, www.wbez.org/stories/anti-chicago-olympics-group-is-relieved/8d660df2-4af2-48a1-a973-ac74bcca2efb.

88. London needs a lot of things, but more luxury condos is not one of them.

89. Wainwright, "'A Massive Betrayal.'"

90. IOC, "The Olympic Studies Centre," International Olympic Committee, 2022, https://olympics.com/ioc/olympic-studies-centre/research-grant-programmes.

91. FIFA, "FIFA Research Scholarship," CIES, 2022, www.cies.ch/en/research/fifa-research-scholarship/.

92. UK Sport, "How UK Sport Funding Works," 2022, www.uksport.gov.uk/our-work/investing-in-sport/how-uk-sport-funding-works; Sushma Malhotra, "10 Olympian-Led Projects Receive the 2021 OLY Canada Legacy Grant in Recognition of Community Impact," Sport Information Resource Centre, December 20, 2021, https://sirc.ca/news/10-olympian-led-projects-receive-the-2021-oly-canada-legacy-grant-in-recognition-of-community-impact/.

93. Hoyoon Jung, "Short-Lived Fantasy or Long-Term Legacy? 2018 Pyeongchang Winter Olympics and Nation-Building in South Korea, https://journal.olimpianos.com.br/journal/index.php/Olimpianos/article/view/113; Gulijiazi Yeerkenbieke, Chunci Chen,

and Guizhen He, "Public perceived effects of 2022 Winter Olympics on host city sustainability," *Sustainability* 13, no. 7 (2021): 3787.

94. Azzali, "The Legacies of Sochi 2014 Winter Olympics," 339; Müller, "After Sochi 2014."

95. Azzali, "The Legacies of Sochi 2014 Winter Olympics," 339.

96. Suzanne Goldenberg, "Canada's Mild Climate Leaves Winter Olympics Short of Snow," *The Guardian*, February 10, 2010, sec. Sport, www.theguardian.com/sport/2010/feb/10/vancouver-lacks-snow.

97. Zirin and Boykoff, "The Gritty Reality of the Winter Games."

98. Gene Kim and Clancy Morgan, "Brazil Spent an Estimated $300 Million on a World Cup Stadium That Now Sits Nearly Abandoned," Business Insider, July 8, 2019, www.businessinsider.com/300-million-world-cup-stadium-is-nearly-abandoned-2018-6.

99. In an interview for this book.

100. For a more in-depth exploration of greenwashing in sports, see Toby Miller, *Greenwashing Sport* (Routledge, Taylor and Francis, 2018).

101. InfluenceMap, "Corporate Climate Policy Footprint," November 2021, influencemap.org/report/The-Carbon-Policy-Footprint-Report-2021-670f36863e7859e1ad7848ec601dda97.

102. Emilie Tricario and Andrew Simms, "Sweat Not Oil: Why Sports Should Drop Advertising and Sponsorship from High-Carbon Polluters," Rapid Transition Alliance, March 2021, www.rapidtransition.org/resources/sweat-not-oil-why-sports-should-drop-advertising-and-sponsorship-from-high-carbon-polluters/.

103. Natasha Brison, "Spotting 'Greenwashing' in Sports," Global Sport Matters, April 19, 2022, https://globalsportmatters.com/business/2022/04/19/sports-greenwashing-how-to-spot-it-faq/; Boykoff, "Celebration Capitalism"; Matthew Taylor, "Major Climate Polluters Accused of Greenwashing with Sports Sponsorship," *The Guardian*, March 22, 2021, sec. Environment, www.theguardian.com/environment/2021/mar/22/major-climate-polluters-accused-of-greenwashing-with-sports-sponsorship.

104. Elissa Zill, "No Such Thing as 'Carbon Neutral'—Can Laws and ISO Standards Tame the Wild West of Green Claims?," ECOS (blog), June 7, 2022, https://ecostandard.org/news_events/no-such-thing-as-carbon-neutral-can-laws-and-iso-standards-tame-the-wild-west-of-green-claims/.

105. Thomas Day et al., "Corporate Climate Responsibility Monitor 2022—Assessing the Transparency and Integrity of Companies' Emission Reduction and Net-Zero Targets," New Climate Institute and Carbon Market Watch, 2022, https://carbonmarketwatch.org/publications/regulating-corporate-green-claims/.

106. Zill, "No Such Thing as 'Carbon Neutral.'"

Chapter Eight

1. In an email exchange for this book.

2. Hawkins, *The New Plantation*; Mellis, Kalman-Lamb, and Silva, "Race, Money and Exploitation."

3. John Gonzalez, "The Political Donations of NBA Owners Are Not So Progressive," The Ringer, September 24, 2020, www.theringer.com/nba/2020/9/24/21453818/nba-owners-political-donations-trump-gop.

4. Robert F. Wheeler, "Organized Sport and Organized Labour: The Workers' Sports Movement," *Journal of Contemporary History* 13, no. 2 (1978): 191–210.

5. Wheeler, "Organized Sport and Organized Labour."

6. Nathaniel Flakin, "For a Workers' Olympics!," Left Voice (blog), July 22, 2021, www.leftvoice.org/for-a-workers-olympics/.

7. Brianna Sacks, "USA Fencing Is Blocking a Top Athlete from a Competition after Sexual Assault Accusations. It Took Eight Years and Widespread Outcry," BuzzFeed News, October 22, 2021, ww.buzzfeednews.com/article/briannasacks/usa-fencing-hadzic-competition-safesport.

8. Nick Greene, "The Milwaukee Bucks Players' Strike Instantly Seems Like It Was Inevitable," *Slate*, August 26, 2020, https://slate.com/culture/2020/08/milwaukee-bucks-boycott-nba-playoffs-jacob-blake.html.

9. If you did enjoy this though, just give me a call—I could talk for hours about the scouting reports (not written, just in my head, I have limits) I've developed for every player I've ever played with in pickup hoops.

10. Burstyn, *The Rites of Men*, 276.

11. Zirin, *Brazil's Dance with the Devil*, 127.

12. Reet Howell, "The USSR: Sport and Politics Intertwined," *Comparative Education* 11, no. 2 (1975): 137–45; Evelyn Mertin, "Participation Is Not Enough. The Soviet Union in the Olympic Movement," *Cahiers de l'INSEP* 46, no. 1 (2010): 225–33, doi.org/10.3406/insep.2010.1131.

13. Evelyn Mertin, "Participation Is Not Enough."

14. Carmen A. Horvat and Carolynne Mason, "Country Profile of Slovenia: Sport Policy System in a Small State," *International Journal of Sport Policy and Politics* 14, no. 4 (2022): 743–57, https://doi.org/10.1080/19406940.2022.2137555.

15. Kristi A. Allain, "Winter of Our Contentment: Examining Risk, Pleasure, and Emplacement in Later-Life Physical Activity," *Journal of Aging Studies* 55 (2020): 100895.

16. Fredric Jameson, "Future City," *New Left Review*, no. 21 (June 1, 2003): 65–79.

17. This quote is often attributed to Nelson Mandela, but like with a lot of simple but famous quotes, we're not actually sure Mandela said it. There's no record of him saying it, and the Nelson Mandela Foundation's quote database comes up empty as well. We do know, however, that Pliny the Elder, a Roman philosopher, wrote in *Naturalis Historia*: "How many things, too, are looked upon as quite impossible, until they have been actually effected?"

Index

AAU (Amateur Athletic Union), 113, 145–48
Abdul Jabbar, Kareem, 191
acts of commission, 7, 122
acts of omission, 6
alcohol, 4, 88, 122, 135, 152–53
Ali, Muhammad, 191
alienation, 4, 31–32, 35, 135, 138–41, 152–53, 192
Allain, Kristi, 47
Al Thani, Tamim Bin Hamad, 159
amateurism, 107
American dream, 116, 126
Andrie, George, 37–38
Arsenal, 152, 159
athletic industrial complex (AIC), 147
Atlanta, GA, 164–65, 176
Australia, 31, 165; Sydney, 165

Bajc, Vida, 173
Barcelona, 137, 159
baseball, 23, 42, 105, 120–21, 124–27, 129, 144, 146, 189, 191
basketball, 42, 46, 52, 57, 75, 96, 113, 144–48; college basketball 70, 105–7, 109–11, 116–20, 126, 132–33; pickup basketball 5, 192–93; professional basketball, 20, 75, 86, 93
Beltman, Gerrit, 68
Berkeley, George, 21
BHL (British Hockey League), 50
Bin Salman, Mohammed, 159
blogger, 45, 147
Boateng, Jerome, 86
Borland, Chris, 51
Boston, MA, 37, 39, 176
boxing, 3, 39, 41–42, 44–47, 52–53, 57, 77, 86

Boykoff, Jules, 156, 161, 163, 178
Brazil, 154–55, 160, 164, 166, 168–69, 171–72, 192, 194; Rio de Janeiro, 155, 160, 164–67, 169, 175–76, 180
Bridgestone, 181
Britain, 139, 173
Brohm, Jean-Marie, 28–31, 34, 46
Broschius, Garett, 125, 128
Broudehoux, Anne-Marie, 172
Brubaker, David, 66–68, 71, 78
Brundage, Avery, 165
Bryant, Kobe, 83
Budweiser, 152, 183
Burstyn, Varda, 46, 120, 194
buscones, 126

Calgary, 176
campus athletic workers, 105–11, 113, 117
Canada, 1, 7–9, 31, 47, 67, 70, 73, 76–78, 117, 157–58, 171, 182, 192
capitalism, 3–4, 6–11, 14–16, 18–20, 23, 26–28, 31–34, 36, 40–44, 46, 52, 60–62, 78–79, 81, 83, 91, 96–98, 101, 104–7, 110, 114, 120–21, 128–30, 134, 139–41, 147–49, 152–54, 156, 161–62, 179–80, 183–86, 188–89, 192–93, 196
CCTV, 173
celebration capitalism, 161
Chen, Chen, 10, 27–28
Chevron, 181
Chicago, 71, 82, 131, 176
China, 79, 157, 160
coaches, 2–3, 7, 10, 19, 35, 38, 41–42, 44, 46, 51–52, 60–61, 64–74, 76–78, 95–96, 109–15, 141–47, 149–50, 186–87; abuse by, 3–4, 6, 44–45, 63–69, 71, 73–79, 88, 97, 122, 133, 137, 141, 143, 195; glorification of, 3, 31, 33
Coakley, Jay, 66, 137, 141

commodification, 42, 73, 116–17, 122, 135, 140, 145–148, 173, 184, 194
commodity fetishism, 41–42, 130, 140
commodity spectacle, 42–43, 105, 130, 140–41, 161, 173
concussions, 3, 37, 40, 44, 48, 51–54, 56, 61, 126
consent, 33–34, 45, 58–61
consultants, 147
Consumption, 1, 29, 88, 153, 179
COVID-19, 1, 3, 56, 62, 129
crime, 6, 11–12, 87, 91–92, 94, 99, 101–3, 121–22, 139, 166–67, 174
criminal legal system, 9, 100–102
cruel optimism, 131–33
chronic traumatic encephalopathy (CTE), 3, 37–40, 47, 52, 54–56, 59, 109
culture, 8–9, 36, 67, 81, 87–88, 103, 133, 135, 140, 148, 154, 158, 167, 169, 184–185; cancel, 81, 85, 103, 112; gymnastics, 66; hockey, 47, 50–51, 57; 'hustle,' 42; Indigenous, 31; masculine, 71, 103, 150; media and, 15; sport, 3, 8, 25, 30, 35, 46, 58, 62, 69–71, 73, 78, 88, 99, 123, 137, 142–43, 150, 195; warrior; working class, 4

dehumanization, 42, 73, 91, 97, 116, 122
dementia, 3, 37–39, 50, 55
dialectics, 21–25, 30, 35, 128
dialectical materialism, 21–22, 24, 35
disaster capitalism, 161
displacement, 4, 6, 155, 160, 162–66, 168, 173, 178; Dubin Inquiry, 77
Duke Blue Devils, 137
Dunning, Eric, 30, 107

East Germany, 79
ECHL (East Coast Hockey League), 49
Elias, Norbert, 30
Emirates, 159
Engels, Friedrich, 15, 21, 24, 122
English Premier League, 4–5
environmental harm, 7, 30
Etihad, 159

exploitation, 8, 17–18, 20, 25, 119–21, 130, 133, 161, 179, 188, 190; of college athletes, 88, 105–7, 109, 111, 113–14, 116–19; in minor league baseball, 120; racial, 73, 105–7, 111, 116–19; in wrestling, 121
Exxon Mobil, 181, 183
EYBL (Elite Youth Basketball League), 146

fandom, 4, 45, 82, 130, 139, 141, 151–53; extreme, 4, 51, 73, 140, 143, 149–52, 154, 163, 166, 188, 193; overidentification in, 4, 135
Favela, 166–68
FIFA, 155, 164, 166, 169, 171–72, 178, 182
flamenco, 169
Fluminese club, 169
football, 3–5, 7, 9, 37–40, 42, 44–47, 50–53, 56–61, 64–66, 84–86, 93–94, 99, 144, 146, 182; College football, 101–3, 105–7, 109–11, 114–20, 123, 126, 129, 131; Fantasy football, 37, 44–45; football (soccer), 85–86, 134–36, 151–52, 156, 159, 163–64, 169–71, 181
Forest Stewardship Council, 183

Galeano, Eduardo, 194
gambling, 2, 41, 44, 73, 153; betting, 1
gentrification, 4, 155, 168, 178
Goffman, Erving, 66
Goodell, Roger, 90
Google, 70, 183
Gramsci, Antonio, 33–34
Greece, 157, 166, 169, 173, 192; Athens, 171, 173
Green Sports Alliance, 183
greenwashing, 155, 160, 179, 181–83
Griner, Brittney, 86
Gruneau, Richard, 28–30, 34
Guttman, Allen, 30

Hargreaves, Alan, 30, 34–35
Hawkins, Billy, 116
healthism, 35
Hegel, Georg Wilhelm Friedrich, 21–22
hegemony, 8, 31, 33–35, 45, 75, 139, 157
Hernandez, Aaron, 38

Hill, Tyreek, 3, 93–94, 97
historical materialism, 21, 24, 26
hockey, 3, 7, 9, 31, 39–40, 42, 45–51, 57, 64, 71–74, 86, 102–3, 141–44, 146, 149–50
Horne, John, 162
hospitality, 162, 164, 170
Houston, TX, 84, 182
human rights, 174
Hume, David, 21
Hunt, Kareem, 66, 68, 94

idealism, 21
ideology, 7, 9, 12, 28, 35, 106
incentives, 8, 79, 197
Indigenous people, 158
inequality, 25, 27–28, 33, 79, 100, 106, 112, 139, 161, 171
institutions, 9, 13–15, 34, 98, 105, 184–85; cultural, 13–14; predominantly white (PWI), 105, 108–9, 116–17, 119; religious, 34; sport, 9, 28, 30, 64, 69, 150, 152; total, 69
IOC (International Olympic Committee), 165, 178
Israel, 173

Jackson, Victoria, 120
Jackson, Vincent, 38–39
Japan, 171; Tokyo, 63, 165, 174–75, 191
Jones, Byron, 51
Jones, Cassidy, 67
Jones, Jonquel, 75
Jones, Thomas, 59

Kaepernick, Colin, 2, 92
Kalman-Lamb, Nathan, 32, 43, 114–15, 117–18, 140, 161, 184
Kant, Immanuel, 21
Kellison, Tim, 176–79
Kennelly, Jacqueline, 173
Kesler, Ryan, 50–51

labor, 7, 13–20, 24, 28, 30, 32, 35, 41–43, 52, 58–60, 72–73, 76, 105–17, 119–25, 131–33, 139–40, 147, 171, 186, 189–90, 196; Labor conditions, 27, 127, 139; Labor solidarity, 129, 189–90; Migrant labor, 162; Social reproductive labor, 31–32, 35, 41, 138, 140–41
Lashin, Vladimir, 67, 71, 78
legacy, 174–79
Lenin, Vladimir, 22, 28, 184
liberation, 12, 30, 108
liberty, 59–60, 69, 163, 172–73; negative, 59–60; positive, 59
LNAH (Ligue Nord-Americain de Hockey), 49
lobbying, 129, 156–57, 162, 181
Long, Terry, 38–39, 54
Los Angeles, CA, 83, 94, 119, 171, 176
Luck, Andrew, 51

MacDonald, Cheryl, 47
Maclean, Malcolm, 31
management, 2–3, 10, 35, 52, 61–62, 72, 74–76, 78, 81–82, 90–92, 95–98, 129–32, 188–89, 191, 195; of college sports, 106, 109, 111, 113, 120; glorification, 3; NFL, 41; NHL, 49, 71–72; sport management (university academic department), 27; weight, 68
Manchester City, 159
Manchester United, 86, 134, 152, 159
Maracanã Stadium, 164, 169
Marx, Karl, 11, 13–16, 21–24, 26, 29, 32, 34, 42, 77, 128, 140
Marxism, 7, 12–17, 20–31, 33, 35–36, 59–60, 106, 122, 130, 135, 140–41, 184
Marxist economics, 15; base, 13, 15, 21, 25, 33–34, 36, 79, 96; commodity, 14–18, 32, 41–43, 60, 105–6, 116, 130, 140–41, 161, 168–69, 173; constant capital, 18, 41; enclosure, 16; feudalist mode of production, 13; forces of production, 13; foundation, 13–14, 36; instruments of labor, 13–14; labor power, 16, 18, 20; labor theory of value, 15–16; means of production, 13–16, 23–24, 26, 106; mode of production, 9, 13–15, 24, 26, 33, 79, 184; profit, 6, 15–20, 24–26, 32, 35–36, 41, 47, 50, 52, 78–79, 82, 91–92, 95–96, 98, 102,

Marxist economics (cont.)
107–8, 121–23, 128–29, 147, 152, 155, 161–63, 168–69, 171, 174, 176, 179, 183–86, 188–89, 192, 194–95, 197; imperatives of profit, 25, 36; profit imperative, 20, 26, 35, 47, 52, 98, 128, 184, 189; raw materials, 13, 15; relations of production, 13–14, 25, 31, 34–35, 46, 75, 112, 130, 189, 196; socially necessary labor time, 17; superstructure, 13–15, 33–34, 36, 106, 184; supply and demand, 17, 51; surplus value, 17–19, 25, 96, 108, 131; variable capital, 18

Marxist epistemology, 13, 20–21, 24–26

masculinity, 2, 35, 46–47, 57, 68, 72, 74–75, 88, 99, 112, 135–36; hegemonic, 35, 74, 88, 112; inclusive, 68, 74, 88, 142, 194–96

mass participation, 195–96

McDonald's, 160

McMahon, Vince, 123–24, 126

mega-events, 155–183

meritocracy, 3, 31–33, 61, 116

#MeToo movement, 78, 81, 84, 89, 92

Mexico City, 165

MiLB (Minor League Basketball), 125–26, 128–29

militarism, 2

minor league, 103, 105, 120, 124–25, 127–29, 131, 142–43, 189

MLB (Major League Baseball), 125–29, 152

MMA (Mixed Martial Arts), 3, 39, 42, 57

Montreal, 169, 175–76

Mueller, Robert, 100

Nassar, Larry, 63–65, 71

national chauvinism, 139

NBA, 5, 18–19, 73, 82–83, 89–94, 96–97, 102, 113, 132–34, 145, 147–48, 151–52, 188–89, 191

NCAA, 53, 70, 105, 107–8, 110, 114–16, 118, 120, 147

neoliberalism, 8, 9, 33–34; 35, 46, 61, 98, 101, 161–63

Nestle, 183

New Orleans, LA, 182

NFL, 2–5, 37–41, 44–45, 47, 51–56, 58–59, 81–82, 84–87, 89–97, 99–101, 103, 113, 115, 132, 152, 178, 182–83, 188

NHL, 3, 41, 47–52, 56–58, 61, 71, 86, 103, 152

NIL (name, image, and likeness), 107–8, 113, 127

NOlympics, 176–77

North Carolina Tar Heels, 137

Nowinski, Chris, 44–45

Nunn, Kendrick, 93–94

Nye, Joseph, 157

OHL (Ontario Hockey League), 49

Olympics, 4–5, 63, 77–78, 155–60, 162–65, 167–71, 173–77, 179–81, 190

Omalu, Bennett, 38–40, 45, 53–54, 56, 58

Orr, Madeleine, 180–83

overcompensation, 74–75

over-policing, 4, 82

owners, 3, 15–16, 26, 29, 34–35, 52, 62, 73, 96–97, 105, 119, 121–25, 129–31, 151, 160, 183, 188–89, 195–97; of enslaved people, 111; MLB, 127–29; NBA, 19; NFL, 41, 92

ownership, 129, 188–89

Own the Podium, 77

pandemic, 1

Paré, Matt, 128

patriotism, 139

personal responsibility, 8, 35, 61, 98

Petro-Canada, 181

pickup basketball, 5, 192–93

police, 34, 85–87, 92–93, 98–99, 151, 162, 164–65, 167, 172–74, 188; campus police, 86, 103; police brutality, 2, 99, 112, 164, 191

political economy, 9, 13, 21, 194

Proctor and Gamble, 181

Putin, Vladimir, 162, 169–70

Pyeongchang, South Korea, 169, 180

Qatar, 157–62, 164, 166, 182

Qatar Airways, 159

Qatari royal family, 159

QMJHL (Quebec Major Junior Hockey League), 49, 65
Quincy, Kyle, 52

racial capitalism, 105–7, 110, 114, 184
Rapid Transition Alliance, 181
Real Madrid, 137
regulations, 118, 151, 166, 180, 185–86, 194, 197
resistance, 30, 36, 168
Rice, Ray, 81, 89–92, 99–100
Rigauer, Bero, 31, 106–7
Robinson, Cedric, 106
Rocca Hunt, Melanie, 66, 68
Roethlisberger, Ben, 94, 97
Ronaldo, Cristiano, 85, 120
Ross, Macintosh, 44–45, 77, 193
Roy, Patrick, 86
rugby, 3, 39, 42, 46, 51–52, 57, 152
ruling class, 9, 29, 33, 139, 152
Runstedtler, Theresa, 147
Russia, 102, 157, 159, 164, 166, 169–70, 179; Krashaya Polyana, 176; Sochi, 157–59, 162, 169–70, 176, 179

Salt Lake City, UT, 160, 177
Samaranch, Juan Antonio, 165
Saudi Arabia, 159
scouts, 19, 49, 76, 92, 97, 113–14, 126, 145, 147
Seau, Junior, 38
securitization, 155, 172
security, 4, 111, 116, 125, 155, 162–63, 167, 172–74
Seoul, 77, 164
sexual assault, 6, 72, 83–84, 94, 190
Shell, 16, 182
Silva, Derek, 25, 114–15, 189, 194
social change, 26, 29, 184, 189
social harm, 6, 112, 130
socialism, 9–10, 23, 24, 26, 79, 184–85, 190, 195, 196
social reproduction, 31–32, 35, 41, 138, 140–41
social structure, 9, 60, 106, 137, 147; structural scaffolding, 9, 141
Solo, Hope, 86

South Africa, 159, 163–64, 171; Cape Town, 165; Johannesburg, 165
Soviet Union, 79, 195
Spadafora, Abby, 67, 69
spectator violence, 4, 136; crowd violence, 135–53
SPHL (Southern Professional Hockey League), 49
sportswashing, 154–61
SSB (Adidas 3 Stripes Select Basketball), 146
states of exception, 154, 161
status coercion, 61, 113–14, 133
structural coercion, 50, 60–61, 74, 113, 114, 116, 129, 197; student-athletes, 107, 114–15, 117, 120
Super Bowl, 1–5, 176–77
surveillance, 154, 172–74
Sutherland, Edwin, 12
Szto, Courtney, 73, 185

Tillman, Pat, 2
tourism, 170, 175
Toyota, 181
Tutu, Desmond, 28

UAA (Under Armour Association), 146
unions and unionization, 41, 79, 110, 124–25, 127–29, 187, 189, 195
United Kingdom, 108, 145, 157, 171; London, 173, 175–76, 178, 192–93
United Nations, 181
United Nations Sport for Climate Action Framework, 181
University of North Carolina, 119
USAG (United States Gymnastics), 63–65, 76

Vancouver, 77, 158–60, 162, 165, 171, 173, 175, 180–81
Veblen, Thorsten, 29
Vila Autodromo, 168
violence, 4, 7, 30, 39–41, 43, 45, 47, 49, 51, 53, 55, 57, 59, 61, 73, 83, 86–88, 90, 98, 107–153, 188; deprivation, 6; emotional, 3–4, 6–7, 16, 32, 65–67, 71, 74, 76, 78–79,

violence (cont.)
  136, 139–40, 142, 149, 186; environmental, 4, 7, 30, 137–38, 154–55, 177, 179–81, 183; physical, 5–7, 12, 17, 20–21, 32–35, 37, 40–41, 43, 46–47, 52, 57, 61, 66–67, 69, 71–72, 74, 78, 88, 116, 123–24, 134, 139, 141–43, 145–48, 157, 163, 168, 175, 184, 186, 192–93, 196; political, 7, 9, 13, 15, 21, 25, 27, 33–34, 60, 80, 131, 136–37, 139, 156, 163, 179, 194; psychological, 3, 6, 8–9, 65–68, 78–79, 135–37; structural, 6, 8–9, 30, 52, 60–61, 69, 72, 74, 76, 78–80, 87, 98, 105, 114, 116, 124, 128–29, 133–34, 137–38, 141, 154, 180, 190, 192, 196–97; against women, 88–97, 100, 182, 186–89

wages, 7, 14, 16–20, 29–30, 32, 116–19, 123–24, 127, 129, 131, 139–40
Walker-Brown, Hana, 38
Walmart, 183
war, 2–3, 29–30, 34, 37, 46, 58, 139, 151, 190
Watson, Deshaun, 84–85, 94
Webster, Mike, 38–39, 53–54
Westhead, Rick, 50

white-collar crime, 121
WHL (Western Hockey League), 49
Win-at-all-costs, 11, 58, 61, 69, 77–79, 82, 87–88, 143–44, 153, 184
WNBA (Women's National Basketball Association), 75, 86, 145
working class, 10, 29, 122, 139, 169, 190
working conditions, 3, 30, 65, 72, 125–28, 131–32, 139, 166, 189; unfair, 73, 115, 128, 130, 188, 192; unsafe, 3, 62
World Championship, 5, 176
World Cup, 4, 26, 86, 155–66, 168–74, 176–77, 180, 182
World Health Organization, 5
wrestling, 120–24, 190
WWE, 121–24

Young, Kevin, 58, 134, 136–37

Zedong, Mao, 22
zemiology, 6, 121, 122
Zirin, Dave, 154–55, 162–63, 166, 169, 171
Zverev, Alexander, 86